Specialist dictionaries

Dictionary of Accounting	0 7136 8286 8
Dictionary of Agriculture	0 7136 7778 3
Dictionary of Banking and Finance	0 7136 7739 2
Dictionary of Business	0 7136 7918 2
Dictionary of Computing	0 7475 6622 4
Dictionary of Economics	0 7136 8203 5
Dictionary of Environment and Ecology	0 7475 7201 1
Dictionary of Food Science and Nutrition	0 7136 7784 8
Dictionary of Human Resources and Personnel Management	0 7136 8142 X
Dictionary of Information and Library Management	0 7136 7591 8
Dictionary of Leisure, Travel and Tourism	0 7136 8545 X
Dictionary of Marketing	0 7475 6621 6
Dictionary of Media Studies	0 7136 7593 4
Dictionary of Medical Terms	0 7136 7603 5
Dictionary of Nursing	0 7136 8287 6
Dictionary of Politics and Government	0 7475 7220 8
Dictionary of Publishing and Printing	0 7136 7589 6
Dictionary of Science and Technology	0 7136 8651 0

Easier English™ titles

Easier English Basic Dictionary	0 7475 6644 5
Easier English Basic Synonyms	0 7475 6979 7
Easier English Dictionary: Handy Pocket Edition	0 7475 6625 9
Easier English Intermediate Dictionary	0 7475 6989 4
Easier English Student Dictionary	0 7475 6624 0

Check Your English Vocabulary workbooks

Academic English	0 7136 8285 X
Business and Administration	0 7136 7916 6
Computers and Information Technology	0 7136 7917 4
Human Resources	0 7475 6997 5
Law	0 7136 7592 6
Living in the UK	0 7136 7914 X
Medicine	0 7136 7590 X
FCE +	1 408 10455 5
IELTS	0 7136 7604 3
Phrasal Verbs and Idioms	0 7136 7805 4
TOEFL®	0 7136 8414 3
TOEIC	0 7136 7508 X

Visit our website for full details of all our books: **www.acblack.com**

Dictionary of
Sport and
Exercise Science

A & C Black • London

www.acblack.com

First published in Great Britain in 2006
Reprinted 2008

A & C Black Publishers Ltd
36 Soho Square, London W1D 3QY

© A & C Black Publishers Ltd 2006

A CIP record for this book is available from the British Library

ISBN-10: 0 7136 7785 6
ISBN-13: 978 0 7136 7785 0

Text Production and Proofreading
Heather Bateman, Katy McAdam, Howard Sargeant

This book is produced using paper that is made from wood grown in managed,
sustainable forests. It is natural, renewable and recyclable. The logging and
manufacturing processes conform to the environmental regulations of the country
of origin.

Text typeset by A & C Black
Printed in Spain by Graphycems

Preface

This dictionary provides a basic vocabulary of terms used in sport and exercise science. With a wide coverage of terms from anatomy, medicine, psychology, physiology and sports nutrition, it is an ideal reference for students of sports and exercise sciences, as well as those with a general interest in health and fitness.

Each headword is explained in clear, straightforward English. There are also supplements including anatomical figures, measurement conversions and a list of key industry contacts for athletes and sports scientists.

Thanks are due to Morc Coulson, Programme Leader at University Sport Sunderland, for his help and advice during the production of the text.

A

A *noun* a human blood type of the ABO system, containing the A antigen. Someone with this type of blood can donate to people of the same group or of the AB group, and can receive blood from people with this type or with type O.

AB *noun* a human blood type of the ABO system, containing the A and B antigens. Someone with this type of blood can donate to people of the same group and receive blood from people with this type or with type O, A or B.

A-band *noun* a visible dark band in striated muscle

ABC *abbreviation* airway, breathing, circulation

abdomen *noun* a space inside the body that contains the stomach, intestines, liver and other vital organs

abdominal crunch *noun* same as **crunch**

abdominal fat *noun* fat that is deposited mainly on the abdominal area, thought to indicate a higher risk of heart disease

abdominal muscles *plural noun* same as **abdominals**

abdominal rigidity *noun* extreme tightness of the abdominal muscles caused by injury or insufficient warm-up

abdominal roller *noun* a piece of gym equipment that works the abdominal muscles

abdominals *plural noun* the muscles found in the abdomen, particularly the internal and external obliques

abdominal training *noun* a workout that concentrates on the abdominal muscles, especially with the aim of developing a six-pack

abducens nerve *noun* the sixth cranial nerve, which controls the muscle which makes the eyeball turn outwards. Also called **abducent nerve**

abducent *adjective* used for describing a muscle that brings parts of the body away from each other or moves them away from the central line of the body or a limb. Compare **adducent**

abducent nerve *noun* same as **abducens nerve**

abduct *verb* to pull a leg or arm in a direction that is away from the centre line of the body, or to pull a toe or finger away from the central line of a leg or arm. Compare **adduct**

abduction *noun* movement of a limb away from the body

abductor *noun* a muscle that pulls the body or a limb away from a midpoint or midline

ability *noun* **1.** a natural tendency to do something successfully or well **2.** a high degree of intelligence or competence **3.** a particular gift for doing something well

ability-to-skill transfer *noun* the fact that an ability someone develops in learning one new skill can be extended to learn other skills

ablation *noun* the removal of diseased or unwanted tissue from the body by surgical or other means

able *adjective* **1.** physically or mentally equipped to do something **2.** having the necessary resources or talent to do something

able-bodied *adjective* healthy and physically strong

ableism *noun* discrimination in favour of those who are not physically or mentally disabled

Ablokov test *noun* a test of an athlete's ability to jump from a squat position

ABO system *noun* a system of classifying blood types. ◊ **blood type**

abrasion *noun* a minor injury in the form of a graze to the skin

abs *plural noun* the abdominal muscles, or exercises done to firm them (*informal*)

abscess *noun* a painful swollen area where pus forms (NOTE: The formation of an abscess is often accompanied by a high temperature. The plural is **abscesses**.)

abseil *verb* to descend a steep slope or vertical face using a rope that is secured at the top and passed through a series of coils or a harness around the body

absolute dose *noun* the amount of an ingested drug that is absorbed into the body

absolute load *noun* the amount of resistance against a movement

absolute refractory period *noun* the brief time during which a stimulated muscle fibre is not affected by any further stimulation

absolute strength *noun* the maximum weight that a person can lift

absorption *noun* the process of taking into the body substances such as proteins or fats that have been digested from food and enter the bloodstream from the stomach and intestines

abstain *verb* to choose not to do something

abstemious *adjective* tending not to eat or drink very much

abstracting *noun* the skill of being able to assess a situation in a team game and draw on previous experience to decide a course of action

abuse *noun* the harmful use of drugs or alcohol ■ *verb* to use something in an improper, illegal or harmful way

academic sports psychology *noun* sports psychology that is theoretical and research-based

açaí *noun* a berry with very high concentrations of essential fatty acids and anthocyanins, considered a superfood

acapnia *noun* a medical condition marked by a deficiency of carbon dioxide in the blood and tissues

accelerate *verb* to increase in speed. Opposite **decelerate**

acceleration *noun* **1.** the act of accelerating **2.** the rate of change of velocity. Opposite **deceleration** **3.** an outward force caused by a change in direction without a change in speed

acceleration sprinting *noun* a training exercise in which the athlete begins by jogging and gradually accelerates to a sprint

accelerative force *noun* the force exerted on a body when it travels at an increasing speed, which can lead to injuries such as whiplash

accelerometer *noun* an instrument or device for measuring acceleration, especially one in which a sensor converts acceleration into an electrical signal

access *noun* the easy availability of public sports facilities

accessible *adjective* suitable or adapted for people with disabilities

accessory nerve *noun* the eleventh cranial nerve which supplies the muscles in the neck and shoulders

acclimatisation *noun* the act of gradually getting your body used to something, e.g. heat or altitude

accommodating resistance *noun* the ability to exert maximum force on the muscles at all stages of a movement, usually achieved using specially adapted machines

accommodation principle *noun* the idea that someone attempting to learn a particular sport or skill should first develop general fitness and strength

accomplished *adjective* having considerable talent and skill

accomplishment *noun* something achieved, usually something impressive or aimed for

accredit *verb* to officially recognise a person or organisation as having met a standard or criterion

accredited *adjective* officially recognised as having met a standard or criterion

accuracy *noun* **1.** the state of being correct **2.** the state of being on target

accurate *adjective* **1.** correct **2.** on target

ace *noun* **1.** (*in tennis*) a serve that an opponent cannot reach **2.** (*in golf*) a hole in one **3.** someone who is outstandingly good at a sport (*informal*)

acebutolol *noun* a drug that reduces the heart rate and the force of heart muscle contraction

acetabulum *noun* the part of the pelvic bone, shaped like a cup, into which the head of the femur fits to form the hip joint. Also called **cotyloid cavity** (NOTE: The plural is **acetabula**.)

acetic acid *noun* an acid used in weak dilutions to cool the skin and prevent excessive sweating

acetoacetate *noun* a ketone substance secreted by the liver which indicates a failure of metabolism

acetylcholine *noun* a substance that is released from the ends of some nerve fibres to transmit impulses to other nerve cells or to muscles

acetylcholinesterase *noun* an enzyme, present in blood and some nerve endings, that aids the breakdown of acetylcholine and suppresses its stimulatory effect on nerves

acetyl coenzyme A *noun* a coenzyme produced during the metabolism of carbohydrates, fatty acids and amino acids. Abbreviation **acetyl CoA**

achieved performance velocity *noun* velocity attained in competition, which depends on the athlete's level of training, mental preparation and numerous other factors

achievement *noun* the successful completion of something demanding

achievement age *noun* the age at which a child should be able to perform a specific task successfully

achievement goal *noun* a personal goal that an athlete sets for himself or herself

achievement motivation *noun* the drive to attain a particular personal goal

achievement orientation *noun* the fact of being driven to achieve something either by a desire for success or by a fear of failure

achievement situation *noun* a competitive situation in which a goal can be achieved

achievement sport *noun* a sport in which the aim is to achieve some independent goal that does not purely depending on beating an opponent, e.g. archery

Achilles tendinitis *noun* pain and inflammation of the Achilles tendon usually caused by overexertion

Achilles tendinopathy *noun* pain in the Achilles tendon caused by injury or over-stretching

Achilles tendon *noun* a tendon at the back of the ankle that connects the calf muscles to the heel and acts to pull up the heel when the calf muscle is contracted

acid *noun* a chemical substance that is able to dissolve metals

acidaminuria *noun* an excessive excretion of amino acids in urine

acid food *noun* any food that leaves an acid residue after being metabolised. Compare **basic food**

acidity *noun* the level of acid in a liquid. Also called **acidosis 2**

acidogenic *adjective* producing acids, or promoting the production of acids

acidosis *noun* **1.** a medical condition in which there are more acid waste products than usual in the blood because of a lack of alkali **2.** same as **acidity**

acid reflux *noun* same as **gastric reflux**

ACL *abbreviation* anterior cruciate ligament

acne *noun* an inflammation of the sebaceous glands during puberty which makes blackheads appear on the skin, which often then become infected and produce red raised spots

acoustic nerve *noun* the eighth cranial nerve which governs hearing and balance

acquired ageing *noun* ageing that occurs as a result of an unhealthy lifestyle

acquired motivation *noun* the motivation to achieve some personal goal that is not the result of a basic physiological need

acquisition *noun* the development of a new skill, practice or way of doing things

acrobat *noun* someone who performs gymnastic feats as entertainment

acrodermatitis enteropathica *noun* zinc deficiency

acromion *noun* the pointed top of the scapula, which forms the tip of the shoulder

ACSA *abbreviation* anatomical cross-sectional area

actin *noun* a protein that, with myosin, forms the contractile tissue of muscle

action *noun* **1.** the way somebody or something moves or works, or the movement itself **2.** energetic activity

action point *noun* the point at which a stretched muscle is fully extended and tense, but not painful

action potential *noun* a temporary change in electrical potential that occurs between the inside and the outside of a nerve or muscle fibre when a nerve impulse is sent

activation *noun* the process of getting into an alert state of readiness for action

activator *noun* any compound that stimulates enzymes

active *adjective* **1.** lively and energetic **2.** having an effect on a patient. Compare **dormant 3.** having a medicinal effect

active force *noun* a force that creates movement and is entirely a result of muscle activity. Compare **impact force**

active recovery *noun* rehabilitation from an injury in which gentle exercise is taken to maintain flexibility

active rest *noun* rest for a sports injury in which light exercises are performed, which maintains flexibility without causing more strain

active stretch *noun* a muscle stretch that requires an opposing muscle to contract, as in the relationship between a biceps and triceps

active transport *noun* a transfer of substances across a cell membrane for which energy is required

activity *noun* **1.** something that someone does **2.** the characteristic behaviour of a chemical

activity fragmentation *noun* an approach to learning a new skill that breaks the process down into fragments that are relatively easy to learn

activity level *noun* a measurement of the number and function of enzymes in the digestive tract

actomyosin *noun* a complex of actin and myosin formed in muscle cells during contraction

acupressure *noun* a form of alternative therapy similar to acupuncture that uses manual pressure instead of needles

acupuncture *noun* a medical treatment in which fine needles are inserted through the skin into nerve centres in order to correct imbalances in the body's energy and so relieve pain or treat a disorder

acute *adjective* used for describing pain that is sharp and intense

acute injury *noun* an injury that has happened recently, usually requiring immediate treatment

acute toxicity *noun* a concentration of a toxic substance that is high enough to make people seriously ill

acute trauma certificate *noun* a qualification held by a healthcare professional who is trained to provide immediate care for sports injuries

adaptable *adjective* **1.** able to adjust easily to a new environment or different conditions **2.** capable of being modified to suit different conditions or a different purpose

adaptation *noun* the process by which a sense organ becomes less sensitive to a stimulus after repeated contact

adaptive training *noun* physical training that increases in difficulty as the athlete increases in strength or skill

adaptive work *noun* work done to acclimatise oneself to unfamiliar conditions, e.g. high temperatures or high altitudes

adaptogen *noun* a set of active ingredients in homeopathic remedies

addict *noun* a person who is addicted to a harmful drug

addicted *adjective* physically or psychologically dependent on a harmful substance

addiction *noun* physical or psychological dependence on a harmful substance

Addison's disease *noun* a hormonal disorder in which the adrenal glands do not secrete enough cortisol, causing fatigue, weakness and weight loss

additive *noun* a chemical substance that is added to something, e.g. a chemical added to food to improve its appearance, smell or taste, or to prevent it from going bad

adducent *adjective* referring to a muscle which brings parts of the body together or moves them towards the central line of the body or a limb. Compare **abducent**

adduct *verb* to pull a leg or arm towards the central line of the body, or to pull a toe or finger towards the central line of a leg or arm. Opposite **abduct**

adduction *noun* movement of a limb towards the body. Opposite **abduction**

adductor *noun* a muscle that pulls a leg or arm towards the central line of the body or a toe or finger towards the axis of a leg or arm

adductor magnus *noun* the large muscle of the inner thigh

adenosine *noun* a compound, consisting of the base adenine and the sugar ribose, found in DNA, RNA and energy-carrying molecules such as adenosine triphosphate

adenosine diphosphate *noun* a chemical compound nucleotide involved in energy transfer reactions in living cells. Abbreviation **ADP**

adenosine triphosphate *noun* a chemical that occurs in all cells, but mainly in muscle, where it forms the energy reserve. Abbreviation **ATP**

adenylate kinase *noun* an enzyme involved in the formation of ATP

ADH *abbreviation* antidiuretic hormone

adherence *noun* the act of sticking to a routine or programme

adhesion *noun* a knot of muscle fibres stuck together

adhesive capsulitis *noun* a condition in which the two parts of the shoulder joint adhere together, restricting movement

adipectomy *noun* a surgical operation to remove subcutaneous fat

adipocyte *noun* a cell that synthesises and stores fat

adiponectin *noun* a hormone that affects energy homeostasis

adipose *adjective* fatty

adipose tissue *noun* tissue in which the cells contain fat

adipsia *noun* the absence of thirst

ad libitum *adjective* used for referring to food intake that is not controlled by a strict nutritional plan

adolescent growth spurt *noun* a period during the teenage years in which the skeleton grows rapidly, sometimes causing lack of coordination and weakness in the limbs

ADP *abbreviation* adenosine diphosphate

adrenal cortex *noun* the firm outside layer of an adrenal gland, which secretes a series of hormones affecting the metabolism of carbohydrates and water

adrenal exhaustion *noun* a condition in which the adrenal glands are constantly overworked and lose their ability to regulate hormone levels in the body

adrenal glands *plural noun* two endocrine glands at the top of the kidneys which secrete cortisone, adrenaline and other hormones

adrenaline *noun* a hormone secreted by the medulla of the adrenal glands that has an effect similar to the stimulation of the sympathetic nervous system. Also called **epinephrine**

adrenergic *noun* a substance that has a similar effect in the body to adrenaline

adrenoceptor *noun* part of the autonomic nervous system that produces a bodily response when stimulated by agonist substances

adrenocortical *adjective* relating to the cortex of the adrenal glands

adrenolytic *adjective* acting against the secretion of adrenaline

adrenoreceptor *noun* same as **adrenoceptor**

advantage *noun* (*in tennis*) the point scored after deuce, after which the next point scored wins the game

adventure sport *noun* a sport involving strenuous physical activity with an element of risk, e.g. bungee jumping

aerate *verb* same as **oxygenate**

aerobar *noun* a piece of equipment used for keeping the arms parallel during exercise

aerobic activity *noun* same as **aerobic exercise**

aerobic capacity *noun* same as **VO2Max**

aerobic exercise *noun* exercise such as walking, jogging, cycling and swimming that increases respiration and heart rates

aerobic fitness *noun* the ability to complete longer activities such as running, swimming or climbing that involve aerobic metabolism

aerobic glycolysis *noun* the breakdown of muscle glucose in the presence of oxygen to provide energy

aerobicise *verb* to perform aerobic exercises

aerobic metabolism *noun* the breakdown of carbon and fats into energy using oxygen

aerobic power *noun* same as **VO2Max**

aerobic respiration *noun* the process in which oxygen that is breathed in is used to conserve energy as ATP

aerobics *noun* an active exercise programme done to music, often in a class

aerobic threshold *noun* the heart rate during an exercise at which a training effect will be achieved, usually described as being halfway between the resting heart rate and the maximum heart rate

aerobic training *noun* training that increases the body's capacity for aerobic exercise

aerodynamic *adjective* **1.** used for referring to the way in which objects are affected when they move through the air **2.** used for describing a smooth rounded shape that moves through the air easily

aerodynamics *noun* the science of dynamics and the interaction of moving objects with the atmosphere

aerofoil *noun* a part of an aircraft's or other vehicle's surface that acts on the air to provide lift or control

aerogastria *noun* a medical condition in which the stomach is distended by gas

Aertex a trade name for an open-weave fabric used in sportswear

aetiology *noun* the causes of a disease

affective *adjective* relating to emotional responses

affective sport involvement *noun* an emotional response to a sport that you are not playing, as occurs, e.g., when you are supporting a team

afferent *adjective* conducting liquid or electrical impulses towards the inside. Opposite **efferent**

afferent nerve *noun* same as **sensory nerve**

affiliated *adjective* in a close relationship with others

affiliation *noun* the process of bringing a person or group into a close relationship with another, usually larger group

affiliation incentive *noun* the desire to be part of a team and to feel accepted

afflux *noun* a flow inwards or towards a point, e.g. of blood towards a body organ

Afro-Asian Games *plural noun* a multi-sport event open to all African and Asian nations, first held in India in 2003

aftershock *noun* a delayed psychological or physical reaction to a serious event or trauma

against *preposition* in competition with in a sporting endeavour

ageism *noun* discrimination or prejudice against people of specific ages, especially in employment

agency *noun* the act of carrying out an action in a purposeful and voluntary way

agent *noun* somebody who officially represents somebody else in business, usually under contract

aggregate *noun* **1.** the total obtained by adding subtotals together **2.** a collection of pieces of information

aggression *noun* the state of feeling violently angry towards someone or something

aggressive *adjective* **1.** describes a type of in-line skating, skateboarding, or snowboarding that focuses on performing stunts **2.** used for describing medical treatment that involves frequent high doses of medication

agile *adjective* able to move quickly and with suppleness, skill and control

agility *noun* a combination of physical speed, suppleness and skill

agitated *adjective* anxious, nervous, or upset and unable to relax

agonist *noun* **1.** a muscle whose action is balanced by that of another associated muscle **2.** a hormone, neurotransmitter or drug that triggers a response by binding to specific cell receptors

agonist co-contraction *noun* a situation in which both the muscle involved in performing a movement and its antagonist contract simultaneously, thought to increase joint stability for strong movements

aikido *noun* a martial art originating in Japan that involves throwing techniques that make use of an opponent's momentum to perform the throw and may also involve some strikes

aim *noun* a goal or objective

air *noun* (*in skateboarding, in-line skating and snowboarding*) a trick performed with the whole board or both the skates off the ground

air splint *noun* a splint consisting of an inflatable cylinder that surrounds an injured limb

air sports *noun* all sports that take place in the air, including aeronautics, ballooning, paragliding and hang-gliding

airway, breathing, circulation *noun* the three main checks that should be performed during first aid for a person who has collapsed. Abbreviation **ABC**

airway management *noun* the act of ensuring that an injured person has a clear and unobstructed airway when giving immediate care

airway patency *noun* the fact that an airway is unobstructed and functioning normally

ALA *abbreviation* alpha-lipoic acid

alactic *adjective* used for describing metabolism that generates energy without producing lactic acid by using already-present stores of ATP

albumin solution *noun* a substance used for masking banned substance abuse

alcohol *noun* **1.** a pure colourless liquid that is formed by the action of yeast on sugar solutions and forms the intoxicating part of drinks such as wine and whisky **2.** any drink made from fermented or distilled liquid

alcoholic *adjective* containing alcohol ■ *noun* a person who is addicted to drinking alcohol and shows changes in behaviour and personality as a result of this addiction

alcohol intake *noun* the amount of alcohol consumed by a person during a given period such as a week

alcuronium *noun* a drug used as a muscle relaxant

aldosterone *noun* a hormone, secreted by the adrenal gland, that regulates the balance of sodium and potassium in the body and the amount of body fluid

alert *adjective* used for describing someone who takes an intelligent interest in his or her surroundings

alert, verbal, pain, unresponsive *phrase* full form of **AVPU**

alertness *noun* the state of being alert and ready to respond to stimuli

Alexander technique *noun* a method of improving the way a person stands and moves that involves making them much more aware of how muscles behave

alimentary system *noun* same as **digestive system**

alipogenic *adjective* not forming fat

alkalaemia *noun* an excess of alkali in the blood

alkali *noun* a substance that neutralises acids and forms salts

alkalinisation *noun* the act of ingesting an alkaline substance in order to raise the pH of body fluids and thereby reduce the likelihood of doping markers being detected by tests

alkalosis *noun* a condition in which the alkali level in the body tissue is high, producing cramps

All-Africa Games *plural noun* a multi-sport event open to all nations of the African continent, first held in 1965

all comers *plural noun* everyone who wants to participate in a competition or sport

allergen *noun* a compound that reacts with the proteins of the skin and mucous membranes of some people to cause rashes, irritation, asthma and other unpleasant symptoms

allergic *adjective* having an allergy to something

allergy *noun* a sensitivity to particular substances that causes an unpleasant physical reaction

alley-oop *noun* **1.** (*in basketball*) a play in which a player jumps up to receive a pass over the basket and immediately puts the ball into the net from above **2.** (*in basketball*) a pass aimed to allow a player to jump up to receive it over the basket **3.** (*in snowboarding and surfing*) a rotation of 180° or more made in the air while moving in an uphill or upwards direction (*slang*) **4.** (*in skateboarding*) a trick performed in the opposite direction to which the skateboarder is moving (*slang*)

allogotrophia *noun* growth in one organ that occurs when nutrients from another organ leach into it

all-rounder *noun* somebody who is good at many things, especially in sports

all-star *adjective* made up of very famous and talented performers or players ■ *noun* US a member of an all-star team

all-terrain boarding *noun* a form of skateboarding using a modified board with larger wheels that enables the rider to travel over all types of terrain, especially down mountain slopes

aloe vera *noun* a soothing, moisturising extract of the leaves of a species of aloe, used in medicines and cosmetics

alpha-1 receptor *noun* a receptor that causes vasoconstriction when stimulated

alpha-2 receptor *noun* a receptor that inhibits noradrenaline production when stimulated

alpha agonist *noun* a substance that stimulates alpha-1 and alpha-2 receptors

alpha-blocker *noun* a substance that reduces the effects of alpha-1 and alpha-2 receptors, used for treating vascular disorders and increase blood flow

alpha-lipoic acid *noun* a sports supplement that maintains insulin sensitivity. Abbreviation **ALA**

Alpine racing *noun* skiing races on steep courses, especially downhill and slalom events

Alpine skiing *noun* skiing on steep mountain courses, rather than across country

alprostadil *noun* a drug that causes vasodilation, used for treating heart complaints

also-ran *noun* a horse or other entrant in a race that does not finish in any of the winning places

alternate metabolism *noun* the ability to switch quickly between aerobic and anaerobic metabolism, essential for team sports players who need repeated bursts of energy

alternate test *noun* a test for alternate metabolism capacity that measures power output and blood lactate levels during a physical test

altitude *noun* the height of an object above sea level

altitude sickness *noun* a reduction in the amount of oxygen in body tissues caused by being at high altitudes, which may affect athletes performing abroad

altitude training *noun* training for athletes at altitude to acclimatise them and prepare them for competition

alveoli *plural noun* tiny thin-walled air sacs found in large numbers in each lung, through which oxygen enters and carbon dioxide leaves the blood

amateur *noun* **1.** someone who does something for pleasure rather than payment **2.** someone with limited skill in, or knowledge of, an activity

ambidextrous *adjective* used for describing a person who can use both hands equally well and who is therefore not right- or left-handed

ambulant *adjective* used for describing a disabled athlete who does not use a wheelchair

amenorrhoea *noun* the absence of one or more menstrual periods, usual during pregnancy and after the menopause

American football *noun* a game played in the United States by two teams of 11 players wearing shoulder padding and helmets who carry, throw and kick an oval ball, with points scored by carrying the ball into a zone at the opponent's end of the field or by kicking the ball between vertical goalposts

AMI *abbreviation* athletic motivation inventory

amine *noun* any organic derivative of ammonia in which one or more hydrogen atoms is replaced with an alkyl group

amino acid *noun* a chemical compound that is broken down from proteins in the digestive system and then used by the body to form its own protein. ◊ **essential amino acids**

amino acid score *noun* same as **protein score**

amino acid supplement *noun* same as **protein supplement**

aminoaciduria *noun* the presence of abnormal levels of an amino acid in the urine

aminogram *noun* a diagram of the composition of an amino acid

amino group *noun* a group of substances that consists of amino acids and amines

aminopeptidase *noun* an enzyme that removes amino acids from a peptide or protein

aminophylline *noun* a drug that dilates the bronchioles to deliver more oxygen to the lungs, used for relieving asthma

ammonia *noun* a gas with an unpleasant smell that is easily soluble in water

ammonium salts *noun* a substance used as mild stimulant and diuretic

amortisation *noun* the act of exerting static strength while shifting between eccentric and concentric actions

amortisation phase *noun* the build-up phase prior to reaching the amortisation point

amortisation point *noun* the point at which an action changes from concentric to eccentric, or vice versa

amotivational syndrome *noun* a psychological condition characterised by a loss of the motivation to carry out socially accepted behaviours and tasks, usually associated with the use of marijuana

amphetamine *noun* a drug that stimulates the central nervous system, formerly used for treating depression and as an appetite suppressant

amphiarthrosis *noun* limited movement between bones that are connected by cartilage or ligaments, e.g. the vertebrae

amplitude *noun* (*in snowboarding*) the degree of height a rider can attain above the lip of a pipe

amputate *verb* to remove a limb or other appendage of the body, especially in a surgical operation

amputee *noun* a person who has had a limb or part of a limb removed for medical reasons

amylaemia *noun* an excess of starch in the blood

amyloid *noun* a non-nitrogenous food consisting mostly of starch

amyloid plaque *noun* a build-up of amyloids in bodily tissues, causing organ failure

amyotonia *noun* a lack of muscle tone

amyotrophic *adjective* characterised by degeneration of the muscles

amyotrophy *noun* a degeneration of the muscles caused by nerve disease

anabolic *adjective* building up muscle or tissue

anabolic agent *noun* a substance sometimes misused by athletes to increase muscle size

anabolic steroid *noun* a drug that encourages the synthesis of new living tissue, especially muscle, from nutrients

anabolism *noun* the part of metabolism that builds up muscle or tissue

anaemia *noun* a medical condition in which an unusually low level of red blood cells or haemoglobin makes it more difficult for the blood to carry oxygen, producing symptoms of tiredness and paleness of lips, nails and the inside of the eyelids

anaemic *adjective* having anaemia

anaemotrophy *noun* insufficient nourishment of the blood

anaerobic capacity *noun* the maximum amount of energy that can be produced by anaerobic metabolism

anaerobic exercise *noun* exercise that involves the exchange of energy in the muscles without the use of oxygen

anaerobic glycolysis *noun* the breakdown of muscle glucose without using oxygen to provide energy

anaerobic metabolism *noun* the breakdown of carbon and fats into energy without the presence of oxygen

anaerobic power *noun* same as **anaerobic capacity**

anaerobic respiration *noun* the series of biochemical processes which lead to the formation of ATP without oxygen

anaerobic threshold *noun* same as **onset of blood lactate accumulation**

anaerobic training *noun* training that increases the body's capacity for anaerobic exercise

analeptic *noun* a stimulant drug such as caffeine

analgesia *noun* treatment to control pain

analgesic *noun* a painkilling drug

Analysis and Performance in Sport *noun* an area of sports science study, which deals with the factors affecting an athlete's performance. Abbreviation **APS**

anamnesis *noun* someone's medical history, especially given in their own words

anaphylactic *adjective* relating to or caused by extreme sensitivity to a substance

anaphylactic shock *noun* a sudden severe, sometimes fatal reaction to something such as an ingested substance or a bee sting

anaphylaxis *noun* **1.** extreme sensitivity to a substance introduced into the body **2.** same as **anaphylactic shock**

anatomical *adjective* relating to the body, or to the structure of the body

anatomical cross-sectional area *noun* the area of the largest cross-section of an individual muscle, measured using MRI scanning. Abbreviation **ACSA**

anatomical position *noun* (*in anatomy*) the standard position of the body from which all directions and positions are derived, in which the body is assumed to be standing, with the feet together, the arms to the side, and the head, eyes and palms facing forward

anatomical short leg *noun* ◆ **short leg**

anatomy *noun* **1.** the structure of the body **2.** the branch of science that studies the structure of the bodies of humans and animals

anchor *noun* the team member who is responsible for the last leg in a relay race or who is at the back in a tug of war

androcentric *adjective* concerning or emphasising men or male interests

androcentrism *noun* the practice of giving male interests and actions more prominence, at the expense of females at a similar professional level

androgen *noun* either of the male sex hormones testosterone and androsterone that increase the male characteristics of the body

androgenic steroid *noun* a steroid that has a strong effect on testostorone production

androstenedione *noun* a dietary supplement that increases testosterone production, energy, strength and muscle development (NOTE: Unwanted side effects include disruption of hormonal balance, leading to aggressive behaviour, mood swings and hair loss.)

androsterone *noun* one of the male sex hormones

aneurin *noun* same as **vitamin B1**

angina *noun* a medical condition in which lack of blood to the heart causes severe chest pains

angina pectoris *noun* same as **angina**

angiology *noun* the branch of medicine that deals with blood vessels and the lymphatic system

angiotensin *noun* a hormone that causes blood pressure to rise, formed in the blood by a series of processes that can be influenced by drugs

angle *noun* the difference in direction between two lines or surfaces measured in degrees

angle of pull *noun* the angle between the muscle acting on a particular bone and the bone itself

angle of release *noun* the angle relative to the ground at which a ball is kicked, affecting its flight path

angular motion *noun* a turning movement of a body around a fixed axis

anhydrosis *noun* an unusually low production of sweat

animal heat *noun* same as **diet-induced thermogenesis**

ankle *noun* the joint that connects the foot to the leg

anklebone *noun* same as **talus**

ankle instability *noun* weakness in the ankle caused by previous injuries, increasing the likelihood of further sprains and fractures

ankle strap *noun* a supportive wrap that protects the ankle from injury during exercise

ankylose *verb* to cause bones to fuse and a joint to become stiff as a result of injury or disease, or intentionally through surgery, or to fuse and become stiff

ankylosis *noun* joint fusion or stiffness resulting in a loss of movement, caused by injury or disuse

annular ligament *noun* a ring-shaped ligament that surrounds an ankle joint or a wrist joint and holds other ligaments in place

annulus fibrosus *noun* the peripheral portion of the disc structure between vertebrae in the back, consisting of fibrous cartilage

anorectic *adjective* suppressing the appetite

anorectic drug *noun* a medicine or supplement that suppresses the appetite

anorexia athletica *noun* compulsive overexercising, often a feature of eating disorders other than anorexia nervosa

anorexia nervosa *noun* a psychological condition, usually found in girls and young women, in which a person refuses to eat because of a fear of becoming fat

anorexigenic *adjective* same as **anorectic**

anoxaemia *noun* a deficiency of oxygen in the blood flowing through the arteries

anoxia *noun* a complete absence of oxygen from the blood and bodily tissues

anserine bursa *noun* a bursa in the knee that lies behind the pes anserinus

anserine bursitis *noun* bursitis at the knee joint

antagonism *noun* **1.** the opposing force that usually exists between pairs of muscles **2.** the interaction between two or more chemical substances in the body that reduces the effect each substance has individually

antagonist *noun* a muscle that is the counterpart to the agonist in an active stretch, causing a lengthening movement rather than a contracting movement

antagonist co-contraction *noun* a situation in which both the muscle involved in performing a movement and its antagonist contract simultaneously, thought to increase joint stability for strong movements

antebrachial *adjective* relating to the forearm

anterior *adjective* used for describing a body part that is situated in the front of the body

anterior compartment *noun* a muscle compartment at the front of the lower leg

anterior cruciate ligament *noun* a ligament in the knee that connects the shin bone to the thigh bone, often torn in sports injuries. Abbreviation **ACL**

anterior dislocation *noun* dislocation of the shoulder joint in which the ball moves in front of the socket

anterior drawer test *noun* a test to assess ligament damage in the ankle, in which the joint is manipulated and bone movement assessed

anterior scalene *noun* a pair of muscles involved in tilting the neck

anthocyanin *noun* a water-soluble plant pigment responsible for blue, violet and red colours

anthropometer *noun* a device for measuring the dimensions of the human body

anthropometric *adjective* used for referring to statistical data that concerns the human body

anthropometry *noun* the gathering of physical data from people for the purposes of statistical analysis

antiadrenergic *adjective* counteracting the physiological effects of adrenaline

antibacterial *adjective* destroying bacteria

antibiotic *noun* a drug such as penicillin that is developed from living substances and stops the spread of microorganisms ■ *adjective* stopping the spread of bacteria

antibody *noun* a protein that is stimulated by the body to produce foreign substances such as bacteria, as part of an immune reaction

anticatabolism *noun* the prevention of the release of energy from food, which promotes muscle growth

anticholinergenic *noun* a substance that is used for blocking the neurone receptors of acetylcholine

anticholinesterase *noun* a substance that blocks nerve impulses by reducing the activity of the enzyme cholinesterase

anticipate *verb* to realise what may happen and do what is necessary to prepare to deal with it

anticipation *noun* the process of realising what may happen and doing what is necessary to prepare to deal with it

anticoagulant *noun* a natural or synthetic agent that prevents the formation of blood clots

antidiscrimination *adjective* intended to combat unfair treatment of individuals or groups, especially treatment based on prejudice about ethnicity, physical abilities, age, gender or sexual preference

antidiuretic hormone *noun* a hormone secreted by the pituitary gland which reduces the amount of water excreted in urine in response to dehydration or exercise. Abbreviation **ADH**

antigen *noun* a substance that stimulates the production of antibodies, e.g. a protein on the surface of a cell or microorganism

antihypertensive *noun* a substance that lowers blood pressure

anti-inflammatory *noun* a drug that reduces inflammation, e.g. aspirin

antioxidant *noun* a substance that makes oxygen less damaging, e.g. in the body or in foods or plastics

antiperistalsis *noun* a movement in the oesophagus or intestine which causes their contents to move in the opposite direction to usual peristalsis, so leading to vomiting

antispasmodic *adjective* controlling spasms ■ *noun* a drug or other agent that controls muscle spasms

antithrombin *noun* a substance in the blood that inhibits the action of thrombin, preventing blood clots

anuria *noun* a failure to produce urine

anxiety *noun* the state of being very worried and afraid

anxiety-prone *adjective* tending to suffer from anxiety and stress

anxiolytic *noun* a substance that reduces anxiety

aorta *noun* the main artery in the body, which sends blood containing oxygen from the heart to other blood vessels around the body

aortic valve *noun* a valve with three flaps, situated at the opening into the aorta

aplasia *noun* the absence or partial development of an organ, part of an organ or tissue

Apley test *noun* a test for knee injury in which the lower leg is gently rotated in different directions

apnoea *noun* the act of stopping breathing (NOTE: The US spelling is **apnea**.)

apocrine gland *noun* any body-odour-producing gland in which parts of the gland's cells break off with the secretions, e.g. a sweat gland

aponeurosis *noun* a band of tissue that attaches muscles to each other

apophysis *noun* a projection on a bone to which tendons are often attached

apophysitis *noun* inflammation of an apophysis

apparatus *noun* equipment used in a laboratory or hospital (NOTE: No plural: use *a piece of apparatus*; *some new apparatus*.)

appendicular *adjective* referring to body parts which are associated with the arms and legs

apperceive *verb* to analyse a situation using previous experience of similar situations, and react accordingly

apperception *noun* the ability to analyse a situation using previous experience of similar situations

appetite *noun* the feeling of wanting food

appetite suppressant *noun* a drug such as amphetamine that makes the user feel less hungry

apple-shaped *adjective* used for describing a person with a body that has fat deposits mostly around the abdominal area

applied psychology *noun* the branch of psychology in which theory is applied to real-life situations, e.g. in a training situation or in a medical setting

applied sports psychology *noun* sports psychology that involves the practical application of general theories in order to help individual athletes

apprehension test *noun* a test to assess the site and severity of injuries, performed by manipulating a patient's joints to see whether this causes pain

approach *noun* **1.** a way of dealing with a problem **2.** in golf, a shot made from the fairway towards a green **3.** same as **approach shot** ■ *verb* **1.** in golf, to make a shot from the fairway towards a green **2.** in tennis, to come in towards the net

approach shot *noun* in tennis, a shot hit deep into the opponent's court, designed to give the player time to approach the net for the next shot

apraxia *noun* a condition in which someone is unable to make proper movements

APS *abbreviation* Analysis and Performance in Sport

aptitude *noun* **1.** a natural tendency to do something well, especially one that can be further developed **2.** quickness and ease in learning

aquaplane *noun* a water-skiing board on which someone stands while being towed by a motorboat

aquarobics *noun* aerobic exercises done to music in a swimming pool

aquatics *noun* sports played in or on water

aqua training *noun* exercise carried out in water, designed both to support joints and also provide additional resistance

arch *noun* any of the several curved arrangements of bones and ligaments that form the foot, especially the medial arch on the inside of the foot

archery *noun* the activity of shooting with a bow and arrow

arch pain *noun* pain in the ligaments forming the medial arch of the foot, caused by activities such as running in unsupportive shoes

arch supports *plural noun* same as **orthotics**

arena *noun* an indoor or outdoor area surrounded by seating for spectators, where shows or sports events take place

arginine *noun* an amino acid that helps the liver form urea

arm *noun* the part of the body from the shoulder to the hand, consisting of the upper arm, the elbow and the forearm

arm blaster *noun* a piece of weightlifting equipment that holds the elbows in place during biceps curls

arm extension *noun* a backwards or downwards movement of the arm from the shoulder joint

arm flexion *noun* a forwards or upwards movement of the arm from the shoulder joint

arm horizontal extension *noun* a backwards horizontal movement of the arm from the front to the side of the body

arm horizontal flexion *noun* a forwards horizontal movement of the arm from the side to the front of the body

arm preference *noun* the tendency to favour one arm over another when performing particular movements

arnica *noun* a liquid preparation made from the dried flower heads of the perennial plant *Arnica montana*, used for treating bruises and sprains

Arnold press *noun* a type of dumbbell lift designed to work out the shoulders

aromatherapy *noun* the use of oils extracted from plants to alleviate physical and psychological disorders, usually through massage or inhalation

arousal *noun* (*in performance theory*) a stimulation that causes a person to perform

arrested progress *noun* a point in the process of learning a skill at which a plateau is reached and further progress is a struggle

arrhythmia *noun* a variation in the rhythm of the heartbeat

arterial plaque *noun* a build-up of cholesterol on the walls of arteries, leading to arteriosclerosis

arteriole *noun* a very small artery

arteriosclerosis *noun* a medical condition in which calcium deposits in the arteries cause them to harden

artery *noun* a blood vessel that takes blood from the heart to the tissues of the body

arthalgia *noun* pain in a joint

arthrectomy *noun* the surgical removal of a joint

arthritis *noun* a painful inflammation of a joint. ◊ **osteoarthritis, rheumatoid arthritis, reactive arthritis**

arthrodesis *noun* the fusion of two or more bones at a joint, restricting its movement

arthrodia *noun* movement of a joint in which one surface slides along another, as occurs between the vertebrae

arthrogram *noun* an x-ray image of a joint taken using arthrography

arthrography *noun* a method of x-raying joints in which air or coloured liquid is injected in order clearly to show up defects

arthropathy *noun* any disorder of a joint

arthroplasty *noun* a surgical operation to repair or replace a joint

arthroscope *noun* a medical instrument that is inserted into a part of the body and sends an image to an outside monitor, used for diagnosing injuries

arthroscopy *noun* a surgical examination of the inside of the body using an arthroscope

arthrosis *noun* the degeneration of a joint

articular *adjective* relating to joints

articular capsule *noun* same as **joint capsule**

articular cartilage *noun* a layer of cartilage at the end of a bone where it forms a joint with another bone

articular fibrocartilage *noun* discs of cartilage such as those between the vertebrae

articulate *verb* to be linked with another bone in a joint

articulation *noun* a joint in the body

artificial limb *noun* same as **prosthesis**

artificial resuscitation *noun* any method of forcing air into the lungs of a person who has stopped breathing, especially the method that involves blowing air into the mouth

asana *noun* a posture used in yoga

ascesis *noun* self-restraint and self-denial, especially in pursuit of a long-term goal

ascorbic acid *noun* vitamin C, found in fresh fruit

ASEAN ParaGames *plural noun* a multi-sport event for disabled athletes in association with the Southeast Asian Games, held directly afterwards

Ashes *noun* (*in cricket*) the trophy awarded to the winner of a series of test matches between England and Australia, or the name given to the series itself

ashtanga yoga *noun* a dynamic form of yoga that focuses on synchronising the breathing with each exercise to increase circulatory benefits

Asiad *noun* same as **Asian Games**

Asian Games *plural noun* a major multi-sport event that is open to athletes from all Asian nations and takes place every four years

aspartate *noun* an amino acid salt used as an ergogenic agent

aspiration *noun* the action of breathing food particles into the lungs when eating

aspirational *adjective* showing a desire or ambition to achieve something, especially self-improvement or material success

aspire *verb* to seek to attain a goal

assault course *noun* an area of land on which there are various obstacles to be climbed over, crawled under, and run through, used by soldiers for training and keeping fit

assertive *adjective* confident in stating a position or claim

assess *verb* to consider something carefully to make a judgment about it

assessment *noun* **1.** careful consideration of something to make a judgment about it **2.** a judgment based on evidence

assimilation *noun* the process in which the body takes in food substances or other nutrients

assist *noun* an act by a player in a sport that enables another member of the team to score or achieve a successful defensive move

assistant mover *noun* a muscle that is not the main muscle involved in a movement but provides a small amount of extra power or stability

assistant referee *noun* either of two people who help the referee at a football match and whose opinion may be sought if the referee is unsure

assisted stretching *noun* stretching using a partner to provide movement and balance that cannot be achieved by one person alone

associative *adjective* used for describing the attentional style of an athlete who tends to focus more on internal stimuli

associative coping, associative strategy *noun* a method of blotting out external distractions during competition by concentrating on your own thoughts and feelings

associative stage *noun* the middle stage of skill acquisition in which the sequence of movements has been learned but must be consciously refined though coaching

associator *noun* a type of athlete who needs to blot out external distractions for an extended period, e.g. a long-distance runner

astasia *noun* a severe lack of motor coordination resulting in an inability to stand upright

A-state *noun* an individual's response to a particular stressful situation, such as competing in a sport

astatic *adjective* unsteady because of poor muscle coordination

asthenic *adjective* used for describing someone who has a slender and lightly muscled build

asthma *noun* a lung condition, characterised by narrowing of the bronchial tubes, in which the muscles go into spasm and the person has difficulty breathing

asymptomatic *adjective* used for describing an injury or condition that does not present any symptoms

asynergy *noun* a failure of coordination between different muscle groups so that delicate, skilled, or rapid movements become impossible

ataxia *noun* a failure of the brain to control movements

ataxiameter *noun* a device for measuring a person's ability to balance

atenolol *noun* a drug used for the management of high blood pressure and angina

atheroma *noun* a fatty deposit that causes atherosclerosis

atherosclerosis *noun* a condition in which deposits of fats and minerals form on the walls of an artery, especially the aorta or one of the coronary or cerebral arteries, and prevent blood from flowing easily. Also called **coronary thrombosis**

athlete *noun* **1.** someone who has the abilities necessary for participating in physical exercise, especially in competitive games and races **2.** a competitor in track or field events

athlete profile *noun* a table of an athlete's key characteristics, used for devising training plans

athlete's foot *noun* an infectious skin disorder between the toes, caused by a fungus. Also called **tinea pedis**

athlete's kidney *noun* a condition found in some athletes who suffer repeated blows to the abdomen, in which the kidney is jarred and blood is found in the urine

athletic *adjective* **1.** relating to athletes, athletics or other sports activities **2.** used for describing a body type with a large skeletal structure and strong muscles **3.** used for describing a sports player who is faster or more agile than his or her opponent

athletic amenorrhoea *noun* the absence or irregularity of menstrual periods as a result of intense exercise, causing hormone levels to fluctuate

athleticism *noun* the fact of being athletic

athletic motivation inventory *noun* a list of qualities thought to be desirable in a potential athlete, e.g. openness to instruction, determination, self-control and the ability to work in a team. Abbreviation **AMI**

athletic pubalgia *noun* a tear in the muscles of the lower abdomen, caused by repeated bending and stretching

athletics *noun* **1.** sports activities carried out on a field, e.g. discus, high jump and long jump, or on a track, e.g. running **2.** the methods, systems and principles of training and practice for athletic activities **3.** *US* activities such as sports and exercises that require physical skill and strength

Atkins diet *noun* a plan to help people lose weight that suggests that they should eat a lot of protein and fat but little carbohydrate

atlas *noun* the topmost vertebra of the neck, above the axis, that connects the spine to the skull

atonic *adjective* displaying a lack of muscle tone or tension

atony *noun* a lack of tone or tension in the muscles

ATP *abbreviation* adenosine triphosphate

A-trait *noun* the personality trait that is a tendency to panic when put under stress

atrial natriuretic peptide *noun* a hormone released by the atria in response to elevated blood pressure that suppresses aldosterone and causes vasodilation, thereby decreasing blood pressure

atrioventricular node *noun* a mass of conducting tissue in the right atrium of the heart, which continues as the atrioventricular bundle and passes impulses from the atria to the ventricles. Also called **AV node**

atrium *noun* **1.** one of the two upper chambers in the heart **2.** a cavity in the ear behind the eardrum (NOTE: The plural is **atria**.)

atrophy *noun* the process of wasting away because of a lack of nutrients

attack *verb* to attempt to defeat, or score against, an opponent in a competitive game or sport

attention *noun* special care or treatment

attentional focus *noun* the ability to notice relevant stimuli in a performance situation and to ignore others that may be distracting

attentional style *noun* the stimuli to which a particular athlete pays attention, whether external, e.g. crowd noise or the presence of other athletes, or internal, e.g. the athlete's own feelings and physical sensations

attenuation *noun* a reduction in the effect or strength of something such as a virus, either because of environmental conditions or as a result of a laboratory procedure

attribute *noun* same as **quality**

audience *noun* a group of people assembled to watch and listen to an event

audience effect *noun* the effect that being watched while performing has on an athlete

auditory nerve *noun* same as **vestibulocochlear nerve**

Australian Rules *noun* an Australian game resembling rugby, played on an oval pitch with 18 to a team and a large oval ball that can be punched, kicked or carried

autochthonous *adjective* used for describing a physical function or disorder that originates in the part of the body where it is found

autogenic training *noun* a method of relieving stress by using meditation and other mental exercises to produce physical relaxation

autonomic *adjective* governing itself independently

autonomic nervous system *noun* the nervous system formed of ganglia linked to the spinal column, which regulates the automatic functioning of the main organs such as the heart and lungs and works when a person is asleep or even unconscious. ◊ **parasympathetic nervous system, sympathetic nervous system**

autonomous stage *noun* the last stage of skill acquisition in which the sequence of movements has been learned and refined and becomes unconscious

autotransfusion *noun* a blood transfusion using the patient's own blood, as in blood doping

auxology *noun* the study of human physical growth and development

auxotonic *adjective* occurring against increasing force as part of a muscle contraction

avascular necrosis *noun* a condition in which tissue cells die because their supply of blood has been cut

avena sativa *noun* a stimulant and nutritive supplement

average *noun* a measure of a player's or team's achievement, reached by dividing the number of opportunities for successful performances by how many times a successful performance was achieved

average heart rate *noun* heart rate shown as an average over the course of a particular activity

avitaminosis *noun* a disease caused by deficiency of a specific vitamin

AV node *noun* same as **atrioventricular node**

AVPU *noun* a scale of responsiveness applied on a person who has suffered a head injury, namely Alert, in which the person is fully conscious, Verbal, in which the patient responds to verbal stimuli, Pain, in which the patient responds to painful stimuli, and Unresponsive, in which the patient does not respond to any stimuli

avulsion *noun* the painful separation of a muscle from its attachment at the bone

avulsion fracture *noun* a bone fracture caused by the avulsion of an attached muscle

awareness *noun* the fact of being aware of something, e.g. of a change in an opponent's position or mood

away game *noun* a match played at a ground that is not the team's own ground

awkwardly *adverb* in a way that puts the body in an unnatural or painful position and seems likely to cause injury

axial *adjective* referring to an axis

axis *noun* **1.** an imaginary line through the centre of the body **2.** the second vertebra of the neck, below the atlas, connected to the skull

axon *noun* a nerve fibre that sends impulses from one neuron to another, linking with the dendrites of the other neuron

axon terminal *noun* the end of an axon that touches the dendrite of a neighbouring cell to allow signals to be sent between the two

ayurvedic medicine *noun* a traditional Hindu system of healing that assesses someone's constitution and lifestyle, and recommends treatment based on herbal preparations, diet, yoga and purification

azygous *adjective* single and not forming one of a pair

B

B *noun* a human blood type of the ABO system, containing the B antigen. Someone with this type of blood can donate to people of the same group or of the AB group, and can receive blood from people with this type or with type O.

back *noun* **1.** the part of the body from the neck downwards to the waist, consisting of the spine and the bones attached to it **2.** the side that is opposite to the front. ◊ **dorsum** **3.** a player in sports such as football or hockey whose role is mainly to prevent the other team from scoring ■ *verb* to bet money on the person, team or animal thought likely to win a race or competition

backache *noun* pain in the back, often without a specific cause

back bend *noun* an exercise in gymnastics in which a person bends over backwards from a standing position until the hands touch the floor

backboard *noun* (*in basketball*) the vertical board situated behind the basket that serves to rebound the ball into the basket or onto the court. Also called **board**

back check *verb* (*in ice hockey*) to skate back towards your own goal while trying to block an opponent with the body or a stick

back extension *noun* an exercise in which the upper body overhangs a platform, with the body face down, and is moved up and down using the back muscles, like a reverse sit-up

backfield *noun* (*in American football*) the area of the playing field behind the line of scrimmage

backflip *noun* a backward midair somersault with the arms and legs extended, performed in gymnastics, diving and board sports such as skateboarding and snowboarding

backhand *noun* in tennis and other racket games, a stroke made with the back of the hand turned towards the ball or shuttlecock as the arm moves outwards from a position across the body ■ *verb* to hit the ball with a backhand

back pass *noun* in football, a pass from an outfield player back to the goalkeeper. Goalkeepers are forbidden to handle back passes with their hands.

back-pedal *verb* to move the pedals of an exercise bike in the opposite direction to normal, in order to change the muscle groups being exercised

backspin *noun* the movement of a ball that spins backwards as it travels forwards, usually imparted by hitting the lower half of the ball

back stop *noun* a screen or barrier to stop a ball travelling out of the playing area

backstroke *noun* a method of swimming on the back in which the swimmer makes circular backward movements with each arm alternately while kicking the legs rhythmically up and down

back support *noun* a supportive wrap that protects the back from injury during exercise

backswing *noun* the backward movement of a player's club, bat or racket away from the eventual point of contact with the ball in preparation for playing the actual stroke

bad cholesterol *noun* cholesterol that is transported towards cells and tissue by low density lipoprotein (*informal*)

badminton *noun* an indoor game in which rackets are used to hit a shuttlecock back and forth across a high net

BADS *abbreviation* biologically active dietary supplement

baguazhang *noun* a Chinese martial art in which each movement is based upon the movements of one of 8 animals

bail *noun* (*in cricket*) either of the two short pieces of wood laid on top of the stumps to make the wicket

Baker's cyst *noun* a fluid swelling in the back of the knee caused by injury

balance *noun* **1.** the act of staying upright and in a controlled position, not stumbling or falling **2.** a state of emotional and mental stability in which somebody is calm and able to make rational decisions and judgments **3.** the proportions of substances in a mixture, e.g. in the diet

balance beam *noun US* same as **beam**

balanced diet *noun* a diet that contains the right quantities of basic nutrients

balanced tension *noun* the theory that a low level of stress can be beneficial to an athlete's performance

Balance of Good Health *noun* a piechart representation of the proportions in which food groups should be consumed for health

ball *noun* **1.** an object, usually round in shape and often hollow and flexible, used in many games and sports in which it is thrown, struck or kicked **2.** the soft part of the hand below the thumb **3.** the soft part of the foot below the big toe

ball-and-socket joint *noun* a joint such as the hip joint in which a bone with a rounded end fits into a concave area of the adjoining bone, allowing a wide range of movement

ballboy *noun* a boy who retrieves balls that go out of play during a tennis match and delivers them to the server when required

ballet *noun* a form of dance characterised by conventional steps, poses and graceful movements including leaps and spins

ball game *noun* **1.** any game played with a ball **2.** *US* a game of baseball

ballgirl *noun* a girl who retrieves balls that go out of play during a tennis match and delivers them to the server when required

ball hog *noun* (*in team sports*) a player who dominates the ball and does not allow other members of the team the opportunity to play

ballistic *adjective* relating to the movements of objects propelled through the air

ballistic movement *noun* a fast and intense movement involving a rapid muscular contraction

ballistics *noun* the study of movement, particularly of the trajectory of a flying object

ballistic stretching *noun* stretching using the momentum of a ballistic movement to enhance the effects, not recommended for most people as it carries a high risk of injury

balneotherapy *noun* physical therapy using immersion in water

bandage *noun* a long strip of thin or elasticated fabric that is wrapped around a wound or injured part of the body to protect or support it

bandaging *noun* same as **taping**

bandy *noun* a sport played on ice with sticks, similar to ice hockey but with rules close to those of football

Bankart lesion *noun* a tear to the labrum of the shoulder joint caused by repeated violent movement of the arm

banned substance *noun* a performance-enhancing substance, e.g. a steroid, stimulant or hormone, that professional athletes may not use (NOTE: Banned substances are detected in drugs testing, and usually lead to the athlete being disqualified from competition.)

bantamweight *noun* (*in professional boxing*) a weight category for competitors who weigh between 51 and 53.5 kg or 112 and 118 lb

barbell *noun* a metal bar with removable weights at each end, used in weightlifting

barbell curl *noun* a curl performed with both arms holding a barbell

barbell shrug *noun* an exercise in which a barbell is held with the arms loosely hanging at the front of the body, and the shoulders are slowly raised and lowered

barbiturate *noun* a drug with sedative and hypnotic properties

bariatrics *noun* the medical treatment of obesity

baroreceptor *noun* any of a group of nerves near the carotid artery that sense changes in blood pressure

barotrauma *noun* pain caused by pressure disturbances inside the ear canal, suffered by scuba divers

basal ganglia *plural noun* masses of grey matter at the base of each cerebral hemisphere that receive impulses from the thalamus and influence the motor impulses from the frontal cortex

basal metabolic rate *noun* the amount of energy used by the body in exchanging oxygen and carbon dioxide when at rest, formerly used as a way of testing thyroid gland activity. Abbreviation **BMR**

base *noun* **1.** in baseball, one of the four corners of the diamond-shaped infield that a batter must touch in order to score a run **2.** a substance that reacts with an acid to form a salt

baseball *noun* **1.** a game played with a bat and ball by two teams of nine players on a field with four bases marking the course the batters must take to score runs **2.** a hard leather-covered ball about 23 cm in circumference, used in the game of baseball

base hit *noun* in baseball, a hit that enables the batter to reach a base safely

base-jump *verb* to participate in the sport of basejumping

basejumping *noun* the extreme sport of parachuting from the tops of very tall natural objects or constructions such as cliffs, towers or buildings

baseline *noun* **1.** a boundary line at each end of a court that marks the limit of play in tennis, badminton or basketball **2.** on a baseball field, a line running from home plate to first base and from home plate to third base, and extending into the outfield as foul lines

3. in baseball, the area within which a base runner must stay when running between bases **4.** the point from which change can be measured

BASES *abbreviation* British Association of Sport and Exercise Sciences

base training *noun* general athletic training designed to improve overall fitness

basic food *noun* a type of food that leaves an alkaline residue after being metabolised. Compare **acid food**

basic skill *noun* a simple skill such as running, jumping or hand-eye coordination that is a basic requirement for involvement in many sports

basket *noun* **1.** (*in basketball*) a mounted horizontal metal hoop with a hanging open net, through which a player must throw the ball in order to score **2.** (*in basketball*) a goal scored by throwing the ball through the basket, which is worth 1, 2 or 3 points depending on circumstances

basketball *noun* **1.** a game played by two teams of five players who score points by throwing a ball through a basket mounted at the opponent's end of a rectangular court **2.** a large round ball of the type used in the game of basketball

bat *noun* **1.** an implement of varying shape used for striking the ball in many sports, e.g. cricket, table tennis and baseball **2.** a heavy stick or wooden club **3.** (*in cricket*) a batsman

baths *plural noun* reservoirs of water of various temperatures, sometimes with added minerals, in which the body is submerged for therapeutic purposes

baton *noun* a short stick or hollow cylinder passed by each runner in a relay team to the next runner

baton change *noun* the transfer of the baton in a relay race from one member of a competing team to the next runner

batsman *noun* **1.** (*in cricket or baseball*) a player who is batting **2.** a cricket player who specialises in batting, rather than bowling or fielding

batter *noun* especially in baseball, a player who bats

batting *noun* (*in cricket or baseball*) the action or ability of a player or team that hits with a bat

batting average *noun* US (*in baseball*) a measure of a batter's performance, calculated by dividing the total of base hits gained in a given period by the number of times at bat

BCAA *abbreviation* branched-chain amino acid

beam *noun* **1.** a long thick solid bar used as a support **2.** a narrow shaft of light or radiation **3.** a narrow horizontal wooden bar on legs that women gymnasts stand on to perform balancing exercises

beats per minute *noun* the number of heartbeats occurring within one minute. Abbreviation **BPM**

beef *noun* muscular strength or effort (*informal*)

beef protein *noun* isolated meat protein from beef, used as a bodybuilding supplement, to provide iron and to enrich other meats

beefy *adjective* strong and muscular (*informal*)

beginner *noun* someone who has just started to learn or do something

behavioural anxiety *noun* anxiety that is expressed through a person's behaviour

behavioural coaching *noun* skills coaching in which the athlete is given a breakdown of the components of the skill, with positive personal feedback as they master each part

behavioural medicine *noun* the interdisciplinary study of behavioural, psychosocial and biomedical knowledge relevant to the understanding of health and illness

behavioural sciences *noun* the study of human behaviour

behaviourism *noun* an approach to psychology that focuses on a person's behavioural responses to stimuli and the reasons for these

behaviour modification *noun* a formal method of changing somebody's habits and long-term behavioural patterns through education and guidance

behaviour therapy *noun* a form of psychotherapy with the goal of observable changes in problem behaviour rather than changes in mental state

belief *noun* confidence that someone or something is good or will be effective

belly *noun* the abdomen or the stomach (*informal*)

belt *noun* **1.** a belt awarded to a sports competitor, especially in boxing or the martial arts, as a trophy or a sign of having attained a particular grade **2.** somebody awarded a particular belt for an achievement, usually in boxing or one of the martial arts

bench *noun* **1.** a long seat in a gym, used for lying on when doing exercises **2.** a seat for a rower in a boat **3.** in team sports, the seats for players not taking part on the field or court **4.** the officials and players who are not taking part on the field or court ■ *verb* in team sports, to exclude or remove a member of a sports team from play

bench press *noun* an exercise in which a person lies on his or her back on a bench and lifts weights straight upwards from the chest

bench-press *verb* to be able to lift a particular weight in a bench press exercise

bend *verb* to curve from a straight shape

benefit *noun* something that has a good effect or promotes wellbeing

benign *adjective* generally harmless

Bennett's fracture *noun* a fracture of the first metacarpal, the bone between the thumb and the wrist

benzodiazepine *noun* a mild anxiolytic used by sportspeople

Bernoulli effect *noun* the difference in air pressure on either side of a spinning ball, which causes it to curve in the air

best *noun* **1.** someone or something of the highest quality or standard **2.** the highest quality or standard that someone or something is capable of **3.** the best time or score that someone has achieved in a sport or game

beta-1 agonist *noun* a substance that stimulates the beta-1 receptors

beta-1 receptor *noun* a receptor that causes the heart to beat more strongly when stimulated

beta-2 agonist *noun* a substance that stimulates the beta-2 receptors

beta-2 receptor *noun* a receptor that causes vasodilation when stimulated

beta-blocker *noun* a drug that reduces the effects of beta-1 and beta-2 receptors, sometimes misused by athletes to produce a calming effect

beta carotene *noun* an orange or red pigment in carrots, egg yolk and some oils, converted by the liver into vitamin A

beta-hydroxy beta-methylbutyrate *noun* a metabolite of leucine, used by body-builders to increase muscle gain. Abbreviation **HMB**

betting shop *noun* a shop or office that is licensed to take bets on the results of races and other sporting activities

BFC *abbreviation* body fat composition

BIA *abbreviation* bioelectrical impedance analysis

biacromial breadth *noun* an anthropometric measure of shoulder width

biarticulate *adjective* used for describing a muscle that spans two joints

biathlon *noun* a competition that combines cross-country skiing with rifle shooting at targets along the course

biaxial joint *noun* a joint that allows movement on two planes

bicarbonate loading *noun* the practice of taking large quantities of an alkali in order to neutralise lactic acid in the body and so slow fatigue

biceps *noun* any muscle formed of two parts joined to form one tendon, especially the muscles in the front of the upper arm **biceps brachii** and the back of the thigh **biceps femoris**. ◊ **triceps** (NOTE: The plural is **biceps**.)

biceps brachii *noun* the muscle at the front of the upper arm that bulges when contracted

biceps curl *noun* a curl performed with one arm, which contracts the biceps brachii muscle

biceps femoris *noun* a muscle in the side and back of the thigh that flexes the knee

bicipital *adjective* **1.** relating to a biceps muscle **2.** consisting of two parts

bicipital tendinitis *noun* inflammation of the tendon connecting the biceps brachii to the scapula, caused by repeated overarm movements

bicuspid valve *noun* same as **mitral valve**

bicycle *noun* a vehicle with two wheels and a seat that is moved by pushing pedals with the feet, and steered by handlebars at the front wheel ■ *verb* to travel by bicycle

bicycle motocross *noun* full form of **BMX**

bike *noun* same as **bicycle**

bikram yoga *noun* a form of yoga performed in a hot room to relax muscles and joints and also increase detoxification through sweating

bilateral *adjective* affecting both sides

bilateral integration *noun* the use of both sides of the body at once to perform a smooth and coordinated movement

biliocristal breadth *noun* an anthropometric measure of waist width

billiards *noun* an indoor game in which a felt-tipped stick is used to hit balls across a cloth-covered table into pockets

billiard table *noun* a rectangular table covered in smooth, close-fitting cloth, on which the game of billiards is played

binding *noun* one of the fastenings on a ski or snowboard that hold the ski to the boot

binge drinking *noun* the consumption of an excessive amount of alcohol in a short period of time for the purpose of becoming drunk

binge eating *noun* uncontrolled eating, especially when caused by bulimia

binge eating disorder *noun* a psychiatric disorder in which the person has a compulsion to overeat, but does not purge afterwards

binge-purge syndrome *noun* any disorder in which bingeing is followed by purging, e.g. bulimia

bioactive *adjective* producing an effect in living tissue or in a living organism

bioactivity *noun* the effect that a substance or agent has on an organism or living tissue

bioassay *noun* a test of the strength of a drug, hormone, vitamin or serum in which its effect on living animals or tissue is examined

bioavailability *noun* the extent to which a nutrient or medicine can be taken up by the body

bioavailable *adjective* used for describing the extent to which a nutrient or medicine can be taken up by the body

biochemical *adjective* relating to biochemistry

biochemistry *noun* the chemistry of living tissues

bioelectrical impedance analysis *noun* an accurate method of measuring body fat using an electrical current. Abbreviation **BIA**

bioenergetics *noun* a method of studying and understanding the human personality in terms of the body and its energetic processes, based on the belief that the body and the mind are functionally closely related

biofeedback *noun* the control of the autonomic nervous system by someone's conscious thought, as he or she sees the results of tests or scans

bioflavonoid *noun* any of various complex chemicals that are widely found in fresh raw fruits and vegetables, thought to protect the body's stores of vitamin C

biologically active dietary supplement *noun* a substance used for enriching food that contains nature-identical compounds in a concentrated form. Abbreviation **BADS**

biological value *noun* a measure of protein quality, expressed as the amount of it that is absorbed and retained in the body. Abbreviation **BV**

biomarker *noun* a distinctive indicator of a biological or biochemical process, e.g. a chemical whose occurrence shows the presence of a disease

biomaterial *noun* any material that performs, aids or replaces a natural function, e.g. one used as a medical implant

biomechanical analysis *noun* the assessment of the proper use of techniques in sport and exercise

biomechanics *noun* the study of body movements and of the forces acting on the musculoskeletal system, used in sport for analysing complex movements to improve efficiency and help avoid injury

biomedicine *noun* **1.** the use of the principles of biology, biochemistry, physiology and other basic sciences to solve problems in clinical medicine **2.** the study of the body's ability to withstand unusual or extreme environments

bionic *adjective* used for of a replacement human organ or limb, created using bionics

bionics *noun* the enhancement or replacement of human organs or limbs using modern technology, e.g. the provision of artificial limbs

biorhythm *noun* a regular process of change that takes place within living organisms, e.g. sleeping, waking or the reproductive cycle (NOTE: Some people believe that biorhythms affect behaviour and mood.)

bioscience *noun* a science that studies structures, functions, interactions or other aspects of living organisms, e.g. biology, ecology, physiology or molecular biology

biotin *noun* a type of vitamin B found in egg yolks, liver and yeast

bipennate *adjective* referring to a muscle with fibres which rise from either side of the tendon

birdie *noun* (*in golf*) a score in which the ball is hit into the hole using one stroke fewer than the accepted standard number of strokes (**par**) for that hole

black belt *noun* **1.** a belt worn by someone who has reached a high level of skill in a martial art such as judo or taekwondo **2.** someone at a high level of skill in a martial art, entitled to wear a belt that is black

black box model *noun* same as **behaviourism**

black eye *noun* an area of bruising around a person's eye

black heel *noun* same as **calcaneal petechiae**

black out *verb* to have sudden loss of consciousness

blackout *noun* a sudden loss of consciousness (*informal*)

blanket finish *noun* a situation in which the runners in a race finish very close to one another

bleachers *plural noun* US **1.** seats in an uncovered area of a sports stadium **2.** retractable tiered benches for spectators in an indoor sports arena

blinder *noun* an outstanding performance in a sport (*informal*)

blind side *noun* (*in rugby*) the side of the field that lies between a scrum and the nearer touchline

blindside 360 *noun* (*in wakeboarding and snowboarding*) a 360-degree turn in which the rider is facing away from and unable to see either the takeoff or the landing point

blind testing *noun* a way of testing the efficacy of supplements using a test group and a control group for the purposes of comparison

blister *noun* a swelling on the skin containing serum from the blood, caused by rubbing, burning or a disease such as chickenpox

blitz *verb* (*informal*) **1.** to defeat a person or team overwhelmingly in a game **2.** to concentrate a lot of effort on something to get it done

block *noun* **1.** the act of stopping a function **2.** something that causes an obstruction **3.** ⬩ **starting blocks**

blocked practice *noun* practice of a particular skill over and over until it is mastered, with no interruption, before moving on to the next skill

blocked skill *noun* a skill that cannot be mastered for psychological reasons or because of an injury impeding the appropriate body movements

blocker *noun* a substance that blocks an action. ◊ **alpha-blocker, beta-blocker**

blood *noun* a red liquid moved around the body by the pumping action of the heart

blood chemistry test *noun* a test of the level of a particular substance in the blood, usually a performance-enhancing drug

blood cholesterol *noun* the concentration of cholesterol in the bloodstream (NOTE: A high concentration can cause coronary heart disease.)

blood clot *noun* a thick mass of coagulated blood

blood clotting *noun* the process by which blood changes from being liquid to being semi-solid and so stops flowing

blood doping *noun* the banned practice of reinjecting an athlete with his or her own red blood cells shortly before a competition in order to enhance performance. Also called **blood retransfusion**

blood flow *noun* same as **circulation**

blood glucose *noun* sugar in the form in which it is carried in the blood, an excess of which can indicate diabetes

blood group *noun* same as **blood type**

blood homocysteine *noun* the concentration of homocysteine amino acids in the blood stream

blood lactate *noun* same as **lactate**

blood-pooling *noun* a situation in which blood collects in extremities, e.g. fingers or toes, and is not returned to the heart, resulting in a drop in blood pressure

blood pressure *noun* the pressure, measured in millimetres of mercury, at which the blood is pumped round the body by the heart

blood retransfusion *noun* same as **blood doping**

blood-shunting *noun* the diversion of blood towards areas of need within the body such as muscles, caused by vasodilation and constriction

blood sport *noun* a sport in which animals are killed, e.g. bull-fighting

bloodstream *noun* the flow of blood circulating through the blood vessels

blood sugar *noun* the amount of glucose in blood, regulated by insulin

blood sugar level *noun* the amount of glucose in the blood, which is higher after meals and in people with diabetes

blood test *noun* a scientific analysis of a sample of blood

blood type *noun* one of the different groups into which human blood is classified. Also called **blood group**

blood vessel *noun* any tube that carries blood round the body, e.g. an artery, vein or capillary

blood volume *noun* the total amount of blood in the body

blow-out fracture *noun* a fracture to the inside of the eye socket, caused by a sudden increase in pressure, as occurs, e.g., when being hit in the eye by a projectile

blue line *noun* either of two blue lines that divide an ice hockey rink into the defensive, neutral and offensive zones

BMX *noun* the riding or racing of bicycles designed for use on rough terrain or open country. Full form **bicycle motocross**

board *noun* **1.** same as **backboard 2.** same as **skateboard 3.** a general term for the flat piece of equipment used in sports such as snowboarding, surfing or wakeboarding

board sports *noun* a general term for sports that involve the use of a board, e.g. snow-boarding or skateboarding

bobsleigh *noun* a long racing sledge with steering, brakes, a seat for two or more people, and two pairs of runners, one in front and one at the back

boccia *noun* a Paralympic sport that is similar to boules

body *noun* **1.** the physical structure of a person, as opposed to the mind **2.** the main part of a person's body, not including the head or arms and legs **3.** ♦ **foreign body**

body bar *noun* a type of free weight

bodyboarding *noun* a form of surfing in which the participant is mainly lying down on the board

bodybuilding *noun* the practice of developing the muscles of the body through weightlifting and diet

bodycheck *noun* in some sports, especially ice hockey or soccer, an illegal act of using the body to obstruct an opposing player ■ *verb* in some sports, especially ice hockey or soccer, to use the body to obstruct an opposing player illegally

body composition analysis *noun* a method of testing the proportions of different fat and lean tissues that make up a person's body. Abbreviation **BCA**

body composition monitor *noun* a piece of personal equipment, like a set of bathroom scales, that also measures body fat percentage, body water percentage, muscle mass, bone mass and metabolic rate

body control *noun* the ability to use major and minor muscles to give the body stability, balance and poise

body culture *noun* a social atmosphere in which pressure is put on individuals to conform to a high standard of fitness or attractiveness

body fat *noun* tissue in which the cells contain fat that replaces the fibrous tissue when too much food is eaten

body fat composition *noun* the proportion of fat to lean tissues that makes up a person's body, determined using body composition analysis. Abbreviation **BFC**

body fluid *noun* a liquid in the body, e.g. water, blood or semen

body fuels *plural noun* same as **metabolic fuels**

body image *noun* the mental image that a person has of their own body. Also called **body schema**

body language *noun* the expression on your face, or the way you hold your body, interpreted by other people as unconsciously revealing your feelings

bodylink *noun* an interconnected set of devices that monitor your body during exercise, e.g. a heart-rate monitor, a timer and a mileometer

body mass index *noun* an index that expresses adult weight in relation to height, calculated as weight in kilograms divided by height in metres squared. Abbreviation **BMI** (NOTE: A body mass index of less than 25 is considered normal, and one of over 30 implies obesity.)

body schema *noun* same as **body image**

body water content *noun* the amount of water in body tissues

body weight *noun* a measure of how heavy a person is

body weight training *noun* weight training that involves using only the body's weight as the resistant force, as distinct from training in which external weights and equipment is used

body work *noun* physical manipulation of the human body, including all types of massage, carried out to improve general health or posture, or to treat injuries

bomb calorimeter *noun* a device for measuring the amount of heat released during chemical combustion

bonding *noun* the formation of a close emotional tie between people, e.g. the establishment of a relationship between members of a team

bone *noun* any of the numerous solid structures in the body that make up the skeleton

bone atrophy *noun* same as **bone loss**

bone chip *noun* a fragment of detached bone that slips into a nearby joint causing pain and swelling, caused by trauma

bone density *noun* same as **bone mass**

bone formation *noun* the creation of new bone fibres within the body from calcium carbonate and calcium phosphate

bone hypertrophy *noun* an increase in bone mass as a result of activity, especially weightbearing activity

bone loss *noun* the weakening of bone fibres caused by ageing or disease, causing conditions such as osteoporosis. Also called **bone atrophy**

bone marrow *noun* soft tissue in cancellous bone

bone mass *noun* the concentration of fibres in bone. Also called **bone density**

bone mineralisation *noun* the absorption of essential minerals into bone fibres

bone resorption *noun* the breakdown of the calcium in bone that is then reabsorbed into the bloodstream

bone scan *noun* the use of scintigraphy as a method of detecting bone fractures

bone strength *noun* the ability of bone to withstand pressure and shock without damage

bone structure *noun* **1.** the system of jointed bones that forms the skeleton **2.** the shape of a bone or set of bones

bonk *verb* (*in snowboarding*) to strike or collide with something while riding a snowboard

booby prize *noun* a prize given as a joke to the person or team coming last in a competition

book *verb* (*in team sports*) to penalise a player for a serious offence and make a note of his or her name. ◊ **yellow card**, **red card** (NOTE: When players are booked, the way in which they are penalised varies according to which sport they are playing and according to the severity of the action for which they were penalised. The punishment ranges from a simple warning to the player being permanently excluded from the game and possibly also banned from a number of future games.)

bookable *adjective* used for describing an offence in football for which a player may be booked or is likely to be booked

boom *noun* a beam to which the bottom edge of a sail is attached in order to hold the sail at an advantageous angle to the wind

boost *verb* to make something increase

Borg Scale *noun* a scale on which the rate of perceived exhaustion is rated, from very light to exhausting

Bosman ruling *noun* a legal ruling in football that allows European players to transfer to another club in the European Union at the end of their contract, without restriction by their current club, named after Jean-Marc Bosman, a Belgian player who, in 1990, won a lawsuit against his club RFC Liège and the restrictions they placed on him

boules *noun* an outdoor game of French origin, similar to bowls, traditionally played on open dusty ground with heavy metal balls that are tossed with a backhand action

boundary *noun* the outer limit of the playing area of a cricket pitch

bout *noun* a boxing or wrestling match

Bowen therapy *noun* a therapeutic technique that initiates healing and encourages emotional stability using manipulation of muscles and connective tissues

bowl *verb* **1.** (*in cricket*) to send a ball, usually overarm, to a batsman **2.** (*in cricket*) to get a batsman out by bowling

bowler *noun* **1.** (*in cricket*) a player who bowls the ball **2.** someone who plays bowls

bowling *noun* **1.** same as **ten-pin bowling 2.** a game played by rolling a ball so that it either hits pins, as in tenpin bowling, or moves close to another ball, as in bowls **3.** (*in cricket*) the action of launching the ball at a batsman

bowls *noun* a game in which heavy wooden balls are rolled on a flat surface towards a smaller target ball

box *noun* **1.** a relatively private enclosed area at a sports venue that contains the best and most luxurious seats **2.** in many sports, a marked-off part of the playing area used for a special purpose, or subject to special rules **3.** (*in football*) the penalty area (*informal*) **4.** a protective plastic covering for a sportsman's genitals, worn especially in cricket ■ *verb* to fight using the techniques of boxing, or fight someone in a boxing match

boxing *noun* the sport of fighting with the fists with padded gloves, with the aim of knocking out the opposing boxer, or inflicting enough punishment to cause the other boxer to retire or be judged defeated

boxing ring *noun* a square raised platform with roped-in sides, used as the fighting arena in boxing matches. Each fighter has a designated corner diagonally opposite the other.

box splint *noun* a solid plastic splint for immobilising an injured patient's leg

BPM *abbreviation* beats per minute

brace *noun* any type of splint or appliance worn for support, e.g. to hold an injured knee

brachial *adjective* relating to the arm

brachialis *noun* a muscle in the upper arm that flexes the elbow

brachial plexus *noun* the group of nerves that serve the shoulder muscles, attached at the base of the neck

brachial plexus neurapraxia *noun* an injury to the nerves serving the arm, caused by a trauma of the kind that occurs in contact sports, producing a stinging or burning sensation

brachium *noun* an arm, especially the upper arm between the elbow and the shoulder (NOTE: The plural is **brachia**.)

brachoradialis *noun* a muscle in the inside of the forearm that flexes the elbow

bracing *noun* **1.** the act of fitting a brace to support some part of the body after injury **2.** the act of stiffening the major muscles to balance or stabilise oneself

bracketed morality *noun* an outlook during a sporting competition in which the usual morals of everyday life are suspended

bradyarrhythmia *noun* a slow resting heart rate that is also arrhythmic

bradycardia *noun* a slow rate of heart contraction, shown by a slow pulse rate of less than 70 beats per minute

bradykinesia *noun* an unusual slowness of muscle movement, symptomatic of depression or a neural disorder

bradykinin *noun* a peptide produced in the blood when tissues are injured that plays a role in inflammation

bradypnoea *noun* unusual slowness in breathing

brain *noun* the part of the central nervous system situated inside the skull

brain bucket *noun* a protective helmet worn when engaging in sports such as climbing or motorcycling (*slang*)

brain damage *noun* injury to the brain tissue that can impair its ability to function, often but not necessarily resulting in long-term impairment or disability

branched-chain amino acid *noun* an amino acid that is an essential part of muscle protein, often used in bodybuilding supplements. Abbreviation **BCAA**

bravura *noun* great skill that is shown when something is done in an exciting or innovative way

brawn *noun* muscular strength (*informal*)

brawny *adjective* muscular and strong-looking

break *verb* 1. to damage a hard body part such as a bone, or sustain such a break 2. (*in tennis*) to win a game in which the other player is serving 3. (*in cricket*) to change direction after bouncing 4. (*in cricket*) to hit and knock over a bail from the wicket 5. to separate after being in a boxing or wrestling clinch 6. to increase speed suddenly in a race 7. same as **counterattack** ■ *noun* (*in tennis*) the winning of a game in which the other player is serving

breaking point *noun* the point at which someone loses the ability to deal physically, psychologically or emotionally with a stressful situation

break point *noun* in tennis, a point that, if won, results in the player who is not serving winning the game

breastbone *noun* a bone that is in the centre of the front of the thorax and to which the ribs are connected. Also called **sternum**

breaststroke *noun* a swimming stroke in which both arms are extended and pulled back together in a circular motion while both legs are thrust out and pulled back together

breathe *verb* to take air into your lungs through your mouth or nose and let it out again, a process that is necessary to oxygenate the blood and keep tissue healthy

breathing *noun* same as **respiration**

breathless *adjective* finding it difficult to breathe enough air, e.g. after exertion

breathlessness *noun* difficulty in breathing enough air

bridge *noun* 1. the top part of the nose where it joins the forehead 2. an artificial tooth or set of teeth that is held in place by being joined to natural teeth 3. a part joining two or more other parts

brisk *adjective* done quickly and energetically

briskly *adverb* in a quick and energetic manner

British Association for Nutritional Therapy *noun* a not-for-profit organisation that provides lists of accredited nutrition practitioners. Abbreviation **BANT**

British Association of Sport and Exercise Sciences *noun* a professional body that represents all those working in the sports and exercise industries. Abbreviation **BASES**

British Nutrition Foundation *noun* an organisation that works in partnership with scientific institutions, the government and the food industry to disseminate nutritional information. Abbreviation **BNF**

brittle bone disease *noun* same as **osteoporosis**

bronchiole *noun* a very small air tube in the lungs leading from a bronchus to the alveoli

bronchodilator *noun* a drug that makes the bronchi wider, used in the treatment of asthma and allergy

bronchus *noun* either of the two air passages that lead from the trachea into the lungs, where they split into many bronchioles (NOTE: The plural is **bronchi**.)

bronze medal *noun* a medal that is awarded to a person who is placed third in a competition, especially a sporting event

broomball *noun* (*in Canada*) a game similar to ice-hockey played without skates, using brooms adapted to the game and a large ball instead of a puck

brown adipose tissue, brown fat *noun* fat stored in the body that is metabolically active and burned if needed. Compare **white adipose tissue**

bruise *noun* a dark painful area on the skin where blood has escaped under the skin following a blow. Also called **contusion** ■ *verb* to cause a bruise on part of the body

bruised *adjective* painful after a blow and showing the presence of blood under the skin

bruised ribs *plural noun* a deep bruise over the ribs, usually caused by a heavy blow as during contact sports

brush up *verb* to refresh or renew knowledge of or skill in something

buckle fracture *noun* a fracture commonly found in children, in which one side of the bone is shattered while the other side is unaffected

buff *adjective US* physically fit and strong, especially through exercise and a controlled diet (*informal*)

buffer *noun* a substance that keeps a constant balance between acid and alkali

buff up *verb US* to become or make yourself physically fit and strong through exercise and diet (*informal*)

build *noun* the general size and shape of a person's body

bulimia nervosa *noun* a psychological condition in which a person overeats uncontrollably and follows this with behaviour designed to prevent weight gain, e.g. vomiting, use of laxatives or excessive exercise

bulk *noun* **1.** large size or mass **2.** the body of someone who is large or overweight

bulk up *verb* to visibly increase muscle mass through exercise

bullseye *noun* the centre of a target in a sport such as archery, which usually carries the highest score

bully-off *noun* formerly, a way of starting a hockey match in which two opposing players hit sticks over the ball before each tries to hit it first

bung *noun* an illicit fee paid to a football player, manager or agent to facilitate a player transfer (*slang*)

bungee jumping *noun* a sport in which a person dives from a high place using an elastic cord tied to the ankles as a restraint

bunion *noun* an inflammation and swelling of the big toe, caused by tight shoes which force the toe sideways so that a callus develops over the joint between the toe and the metatarsal

bunionette *noun* a bunion on the little toe

burdock *noun* a detoxifying supplement

burn *noun* **1.** an injury to skin and tissue caused by light, heat, radiation, electricity or chemicals **2. the burn** a sensation of burning that occurs during strenuous exercise, and the positive psychological sensation associated with it

burner *noun* same as **brachial plexus neurapraxia**

burning foot syndrome *noun* neuralgic pain in the feet caused by severe deficiency of protein and B vitamins

burnout *noun* a feeling of depression, fatigue and lack of energy caused by stress and overworking the body

bursa *noun* a cushioning pocket of lubricating fluid that prevents two bones from rubbing together at a joint

bursitis *noun* inflammation of a bursa, especially in the shoulder

butterfly, butterfly stroke *noun* a swimming stroke in which both arms are lifted simultaneously above and over the head while both feet are kicked up and down

buzzer *noun* a device that makes a buzzing sound to signal that a game has finished

B vitamin *noun* a water-soluble vitamin belonging to a group that is essential to the working of some enzymes (NOTE: The B vitamins are B1 thiamine, B2 riboflavin, B6 pyridoxine, B12 cobalamin, B5 pantothenic acid, folic acid and biotin.)

bye *noun* **1.** the right to proceed to the next round of a competition without contesting the present round, often through nonappearance of an opponent **2.** (*in golf*) an informal match contested over remaining holes, once the main competition is over **3.** (*in cricket*) a run scored off a ball that has not been hit by a batsman, awarded to the team as a whole rather than to an individual batsman

C

cable crossovers *plural noun* an exercise using a machine with resistant cables that are pulled forward and crossed over the chest

cable rower *noun* a rowing machine with resistant cables that are pulled, recreating the sensation of pulling oars

cachexia *noun* severe wasting caused by serious illness

cadence *noun* the beat or measure of something that follows a set rhythm, e.g. in dance or when setting the number of strokes per minute to be achieved by a rowing crew

caecal slap syndrome *noun* a condition, suffered by long-distance runners, in which part of the intestine rubs against the abdominal muscles, causing pain and internal bleeding

caffeine *noun* a stimulant found in coffee, tea and cola nuts

caffeinism *noun* a condition caused by an excessive amount of caffeine in the body, resulting in symptoms of high blood pressure, diarrhoea, palpitations, accelerated breathing and insomnia

cage *noun* **1.** (*in athletics*) a wire-mesh structure used to enclose the area from which the discus and hammer are thrown **2.** (*in baseball*) a screen behind home plate that stops thrown or fouled balls **3.** (*in basketball*) the basket (*informal*) **4.** (*in ice hockey*) the goal (*informal*)

cal *abbreviation* calorie

calcaneal *adjective* relating to the heel of the foot

calcaneal apophysitis *noun* inflammation of the heel caused by repeated heel strikes, as with running, or by wearing unsupportive shoes during sport

calcaneal petechiae *noun* ruptured blood vessels in the heel that give it a blackened appearance, caused by repeated heel strikes and sudden stops and starts, as in many sports

calcaneus *noun* the large bone forming the heel of the foot, to which the Achilles tendon is attached

calcific bursitis *noun* a condition in which calcium is deposited on the bursa and tendons of the shoulder, causing inflammation

calcitonin *noun* a hormone produced by the thyroid gland, believed to regulate the level of calcium in the blood. Also called **thyrocalcitonin**

calcitriol *noun* a form of Vitamin D used to control or reverse bone loss

calcium *noun* a metallic chemical element that is a major component of bones and teeth and is essential for various bodily processes, e.g. blood clotting (NOTE: The chemical symbol is **Ca**.)

calf *noun* a muscular fleshy part at the back of the lower leg

calf raise *noun* an exercise in which the person stands with their heels overhanging a step, and raises and lowers the whole body on the toes, toning the calf muscles

calf stretch *noun* a stretch performed standing and braced against a wall, in which one leg is extended backwards and the person leans forward to stretch the back of the calf

calf support *noun* a supportive wrap used for protecting the calf from injury during exercise

call *verb* **1.** to make an official decision in a sporting event or a game **2.** to postpone or stop a sporting event because of bad weather or other unsuitable conditions **3.** to commentate on radio or television on a sporting event, especially a horse race ■ *noun* **1.** a decision made by a referee **2.** a declaration made during a game, e.g. the choice of heads or tails when a coin is tossed

Callanetics a trade name for a system of exercise made up of small precise movements that are designed to tone and strengthen the muscular system

callipers *plural noun* an instrument with movable legs used for measuring body fat

callisthenics *plural noun* energetic physical exercises designed to improve fitness and muscle tone, including press-ups, sit-ups and star jumps

callus *noun* **1.** an area of thick hard skin formed as a response to repeated contact or pressure, especially on the hands or feet **2.** a mass of tissue that forms round a broken bone as it starts to mend, leading to consolidation

calmodulin *noun* a calcium-binding protein found in the cells of most living organisms that controls many enzyme processes

caloric deficit *noun* a situation in which you are burning more calories than you consume, leading to weight loss

caloric surplus *noun* a situation in which you are consuming more calories than you burn, leading to weight gain

calorie *noun* a unit of measurement of energy in food. Abbreviation **cal**

calorie-controlled *adjective* used for describing a diet that is low in calories for the purpose of losing weight

calorie-dense *adjective* used for describing food and drink that is high in calories with comparatively few essential nutrients

calorie goal *noun* the number of calories that should be eaten each day according to an individual weight loss or exercise regime

calorie intake *noun* the numbers of calories consumed in a day

calorific *adjective* used for describing food and drink that contains many calories and is therefore likely to be fattening

calorific balance *noun* a situation in which the amount of energy being expended equals the amount being taken in through the diet

calorimeter *noun* a piece of equipment that measures the amount of heat given out or taken in during a process such as combustion or a change of state

calorimetry *noun* the science of measuring the heat given off in a thermal reaction

camogie *noun* an Irish stick and ball game that is a form of hurling played by women. Camogie was developed in 1900 by women in Dublin and the game has become increasingly popular with more than 400 clubs affiliated to the Camogie League.

cAMP *noun* a derivative of ATP that plays an important role in glycogenolysis and lipolysis. Full form **cyclic adenosine monophosphate**

Canada Games *plural noun* a two-week multi-sport event that takes place every two years in Canada, in which the 13 provinces each enter a team of athletes

cancellous *adjective* describes bone that has a mesh of hollows on the inside, as opposed to being compact or dense

cancer *noun* a malignant growth or tumour that develops in tissue and destroys it, can spread by metastasis to other parts of the body and cannot be controlled by the body itself

cancer cell *noun* a mutated cell in the body that quickly multiplies, forming a tumour that may spread into surrounding tissue

canoe *noun* a lightweight boat, pointed at each end, that can be paddled by one or two people and can carry passengers. Canoes were originally made from natural materials, but modern canoes are made of aluminium or of moulded plastic and fibreglass. ■ *verb* to paddle a canoe, often as a sport or hobby

canoeing *noun* the sport, hobby, or activity of paddling a canoe

canoeist *noun* somebody who canoes, especially as a sport or a hobby

cap *noun* **1.** a covering that protects something **2.** a player who has been selected for a special team such as a national cricket, football or rugby team ■ *verb* to select a player for a special team such as a national side, for which a cap is awarded

capacitate *verb* to make someone able, fit or qualified to do something (*formal*)

capacity *noun* **1.** the ability to do something easily **2.** the amount of something that a container or organ can hold **3.** the amount of something that can be produced or the amount of work that can be done

capillaries *plural noun* extremely narrow thin-walled blood vessels that form a network throughout the body, enabling the exchange of substances between the blood and the tissues

capitellum *noun* a rounded enlarged part at the end of a bone, especially this part of the upper arm bone (the **humerus**) that forms the elbow joint with one of the lower bones, the radius (NOTE: The plural is **capitella**.)

capitular *adjective* describing the rounded end of a bone

capitulum *noun* the rounded end of a bone that articulates with another bone, e.g. the distal end of the humerus (NOTE: The plural is **capitula**.)

capoeira *noun* a martial art and dance form, originally from Brazil, that is used to promote physical fitness and grace of movement

capsule *noun* ♦ **joint capsule**

capsulitis *noun* ♦ **adhesive capsulitis**

capsulorrhaphy *noun* ♦ **Dutoit staple capsulorrhaphy**

captain *noun* the leader of a team in a sport or game

captopril *noun* a drug that blocks the action of angiotensin, used for controlling high blood pressure

carb *noun* a carbohydrate, or a high-carbohydrate food (*informal*)

carb blocker *noun* a sports supplement that helps weight loss by blocking the breakdown of carbohydrates

carb loading, carbohydrate loading *noun* a controversial practice of first starving the body of carbohydrates, then following a high-carbohydrate diet just before an athletic event in an attempt to boost performance

carbohydrase *noun* an enzyme that aids the breakdown of a carbohydrate

carbohydrate *noun* an organic compound derived from sugar, the main ingredient of many types of food

carbon dioxide *noun* a colourless gas produced by the body's metabolism as the tissues burn carbon, and breathed out by the lungs as waste (NOTE: Its chemical symbol is CO_2.)

carbonic anhydrase *noun* an enzyme in living tissue such as blood cells that contains zinc and aids the transfer of carbon dioxide from the tissues to the lungs

carboxyhaemoglobin *noun* a compound of carbon monoxide and haemoglobin formed when a person breathes in carbon monoxide from tobacco smoke or car exhaust fumes

carcinogen *noun* a substance that causes cancer

cardiac *adjective* of the heart, or relating to the heart

cardiac arrest *noun* a condition in which the heart muscle stops beating

cardiac asthma *noun* difficulty in breathing caused by heart failure

cardiac compression *noun* artificial rhythmic compression of someone's heart in order to restore or maintain blood circulation after the person has collapsed

cardiac conducting system *noun* the nerve system in the heart which links an atrium to a ventricle, so that the two beat at the same rate

cardiac contusion *noun* a bruise on the heart caused by a heavy blow to the chest, which can lead to arrhythmia and haemorrhage

cardiac cycle *noun* the repeated beating of the heart, formed of the diastole and systole

cardiac hypertrophy *noun* enlargement of the heart, either caused by a thickening of the ventricular walls or by an enlargement in ventricular capacity

cardiac index *noun* the cardiac output per square metre of body surface, usually between 3.1 and 3.8l/min/m^2 (litres per minute per square metre)

cardiac monitor *noun* an apparatus for measuring and recording the electrical impulses of the muscles of the heart as it beats

cardiac muscle *noun* a muscle in the heart that makes the heart beat

cardiac output *noun* the volume of blood pumped by the heart, measured in litres per minute

cardiac pacemaker *noun* an electronic device that is implanted on a patient's heart or worn attached to the chest and stimulates and regulates the heartbeat

cardiac rate *noun* same as **heart rate**

cardiac reflex *noun* the reflex that controls the heartbeat automatically

cardio *noun* same as **cardiovascular training**

cardio- *prefix* relating to or involving the heart

cardioaccelerator *noun* a drug or other agent that increases the heart rate

cardiogenic *adjective* resulting from activity or disease of the heart

cardioinhibitory *adjective* slowing the heart rate or otherwise interfering with its normal speed, rhythm, output or efficiency

cardiology *noun* a branch of medicine dealing with the diagnosis and treatment of heart disorders and related conditions

cardiomegaly *noun* pathological enlargement of the heart

cardiomyocyte *noun* a cell of muscular tissue in the heart

cardiomyopathy *noun* a disorder of the heart muscle

cardiopulmonary resuscitation *noun* an emergency technique to revive someone whose heart has stopped beating that involves clearing the person's airways and then alternating heart compression with mouth-to-mouth respiration

cardiorespiratory endurance *noun* the body's ability to carry out prolonged exercise, taking into account both muscle strength and aerobic capacity

cardioselective *adjective* used for describing substances that have a strong effect on heart function

cardiovascular *adjective* relating to the heart and the blood circulation system

cardiovascular disease *noun* reduced function of the heart and arteries caused by excessive intake of saturated fats. Abbreviation **CVD**

cardiovascular endurance *noun* the ability of the cardiovascular system to deliver sufficient blood to the muscles to sustain intense activity for any period of time

cardiovascular training *noun* exercise that raises the heart rate and increases circulation, strengthening the cardiovascular system and burning fat. Also called **cardio**

cardioversion *noun* a procedure to correct an irregular heartbeat by applying an electrical impulse to the chest wall

carnitine *noun* a derivative of lysine

carnosine *noun* a sports supplement

carotid artery *noun* either of the two main arteries that carry blood to the head and neck

carotid body *noun* tissue in the carotid sinus which is concerned with cardiovascular reflexes

carotid pulse *noun* a pulse taken from one of the carotid arteries in the neck

carotid sinus *noun* an expanded part attached to the carotid artery, which monitors blood pressure in the skull

carpal *adjective* relating to the wrist

carponavicular fracture *noun* a fracture to the wrist caused by forcefully bending the hand back during a fall

carpus *noun* the set of bones by which the hand is connected to the lower arm. Also called **wrist** (NOTE: The plural is **carpi**.)

cartilage *noun* the tough elastic tissue that is found in the nose, throat and ear and in other parts of the body

cartilage deformity *noun* ♦ **perichondrial haematoma**

cartilaginous joint *noun* **1.** same as **synchondrosis 2.** same as **symphysis**

case-control study *noun* an epidemiological research method in which people who have developed a disease such as cancer are studied alongside people who have not, and the differences and possible causes analysed

casein *noun* a protein found in milk

case study *noun* an analysis of a particular case or situation used as a basis for drawing conclusions in similar situations

CASMT *abbreviation* cognitive-affective stress management training

cast *noun* an enclosed support for an injured body part that holds it rigid while the tissues heal

casting *noun* the act of fitting a cast to support a limb after injury

catabolism *noun* the part of metabolism that releases energy from food

catalyst *noun* a substance that produces or helps a chemical reaction without itself changing

catalytic enzyme *noun* an enzyme that produces a chemical reaction or helps one to take place

catastrophic injury *noun* a sports injury that is debilitating and results in a temporary or even permanent inability to play

catch *verb* (*in cricket*) to cause the batsman hitting the ball to be out by catching the ball before it reaches the ground ■ *noun* a move in ball games such as cricket or rounders in which a player catches a ball hit by another before it touches the ground, forcing that person to retire

catcher *noun* the baseball player who stands behind home plate, signals for pitches and catches pitched balls that have not been hit by the batter

catch out *verb* (*in cricket, rounders or baseball*) to catch a ball hit by a player while it is still in the air, forcing the player or the player's team to retire

catchweight *adjective* used for describing a contest in a sport such as wrestling or horseracing that has no weight restrictions

catecholamine *noun* a compound belonging to a class that act as neurotransmitters or hormones

catharsis hypothesis *noun* the idea that playing sport provides a safe outlet for negative emotions such as frustration and aggression

cathepsin *noun* an enzyme that hydrolyses proteins

catheter *noun* a tube passed into the body along one of the passages in the body

cathexis *noun* the concentration of a great deal of psychological and emotional energy on one particular person, thing or idea

cauliflower ear *noun* same as **perichondrial haematoma**

causalgia *noun* pain in a limb as a result of localised nerve damage

causal modelling *noun* (*in psychology*) a method of analysing and explaining the causes of a particular behaviour

caving *noun* the activity or sport of exploring and climbing in underground caves and passages

cavus foot *noun* a condition in which a person has high, tight arches that do not allow the foot to roll when it strikes the ground. Also called **claw foot**

ceiling *noun* an upper limit or point that cannot be passed

ceiling level *noun* the highest possible level of fitness that can be attained by a person

cellular respiration *noun* the process by which glucose is converted to pyruvic acid and then to ATP in the body

cellulite *noun* fatty deposits beneath the skin that give a lumpy or grainy appearance to the skin surface, especially on the thighs or buttocks

cellulitis *noun* a usually bacterial inflammation of connective tissue or of the subcutaneous tissue

central *adjective* at the centre

central fatigue *noun* exhaustion caused by the depletion of glycogen in the body and by increased secretion of serotonin, which removes the desire to exercise

central nervous system *noun* the brain and spinal cord that link all the nerves in the body

central obesity *noun* the condition of being 'apple-shaped', with subcutaneous fat being deposited mainly around the abdomen

centre *noun* **1.** in some sports, an attacking player or position in the middle of the field or court **2.** in Australian Rules football, a player who occupies a position in the centre circle ■ *verb* in some sports, to pass, hit or kick a ball or puck from the edge of the playing area towards the middle

centreback *noun* (*in sports such as football and hockey*) the player or position in the middle of the back line

centre forward *noun* (*in sports such as football and hockey*) the player or position in the middle of the forward attacking line

centre half *noun* (*in football and hockey*) the player or position in the middle of the half line

centre of gravity *noun* **1.** the point at which a body can be balanced. Abbreviation **CG 2.** the point through which the force of gravity acts

centre of percussion *noun* same as **sweet spot**

centrifugal force *noun* the force of acceleration away from the axis around which an object rotates

centripetal force *noun* a force that pulls a rotating or spinning object towards a centre or axis

centrum *noun* the central part of an organ (NOTE: The plural is **centra**.)

century *noun* (*in cricket*) 100 runs scored by one batsman

cephalic *adjective* relating to the head

cephalosporin *noun* a broad-spectrum antibiotic used for treating fungal infections of the skin

cerebellum *noun* a region of the brain that plays an important role in sensory perception and motor output, located in the lower back part of the brain

cerebral cortex *noun* the outer layer of grey matter which covers the cerebrum

cerebral haemorrhage *noun* abnormal bleeding from a blood vessel in the brain that may lead to a stroke if left untreated. The most common cause is a ruptured artery caused by high blood pressure or degeneration of the blood vessel concerned.

cerebral hemisphere *noun* either of the two symmetrical halves of the front part of the brain

cerebral palsy *noun* (*in disabled sport events such as the Paralympics*) a category for athletes with a lack of muscular control caused by damage to the brain

cerebrospinal *adjective* involving both the brain and the spinal column

cerebrospinal fluid *noun* the colourless fluid in and around the brain and spinal cord that absorbs shocks and maintains uniform pressure

cerebrotonic *adjective* having a quiet, unassertive personality

cerelose *noun* a commercial preparation of glucose

ceruloplasmin *noun* a copper-transporting protein present in the blood

cervical *adjective* relating to the neck

cervical collar *noun* a rigid collar that supports the neck during rehabilitation for a spinal injury

cervical radiculitis *noun* a pinched nerve in the neck

cervical rib *noun* an extra rib sometimes found attached to the vertebrae above the other ribs, sometimes the cause of thoracic outlet syndrome

cervical spondylosis *noun* a degenerative disorder of the vertebrae in the neck, caused by repetitive bending

cervical vertebrae *plural noun* the seven bones that form the neck

chafe *verb* to rub something, especially to rub against the skin

chaining *noun* a way of learning a complex series of movements, using the same order as the movements will be performed

chalasia *noun* relaxation of the lower oesophageal sphincter causing gastric reflux

chalk *noun* a chalky preparation applied to the hands to improve grip, used by weight-lifters, gymnasts and others

challenge *noun* a test of someone's abilities, or a situation that tests someone's abilities in a stimulating way

challenging *adjective* demanding physical or psychological effort of a stimulating kind

champion *noun* someone who competes in and wins a contest, competition or tournament, either alone or as a member of a team

championship *noun* **1.** a contest, competition or tournament that is held to decide who will be the overall winner **2.** the designation or period of being a champion

change over *verb* **1.** (*in team sports*) to switch to opposite ends of a playing field, usually halfway through a match **2.** (*in a relay race*) to pass on the responsibility for participation to another team member by handing over a baton or touching

changeover *noun* (*in tennis*) the

character *noun* **1.** the way in which a person thinks and behaves **2.** the set of qualities that make somebody or something distinctive, especially somebody's qualities of mind and feeling

charley horse *noun* a severe muscular cramp, especially of the upper leg

cheat *verb* to break the rules of a game in an attempt to gain an unfair advantage ■ *noun* someone who breaks rules or uses trickery to gain an unfair advantage

cheat rep *noun* a rep performed using improper form, e.g. by using other muscle groups or relying on momentum or gravity to help perform the motion

check *verb* in sports such as ice hockey, to move directly into the path of an opponent, usually making physical contact, in order to block his or her progress

check over *verb* to examine someone carefully to establish his or her state of health

chelated *adjective* used for describing a dietary supplement that has been treated to make it easier for the body to absorb

chelated mineral *noun* an essential mineral that has been treated to make it more absorbable by the body when used as a dietary supplement

chemical energy *noun* the energy released or absorbed in a chemical reaction during the decomposition or formation of compounds

chemical score *noun* a measure of protein quality, expressed as its limiting amino acid content as compared to egg protein

chemoprophylaxis *noun* the use of medication to prevent disease

chemoreceptor *noun* a cell which responds to the presence of a chemical compound by activating a nerve, e.g. cells in the carotid body reacting to lowered oxygen and raised carbon dioxide in the blood

chemzyme *noun* a substance that acts like an enzyme to increase the effectiveness of a drug

chest *noun* the upper front part of the body between the neck and stomach. Also called **thorax**

chest press *noun* an exercise in which the arms are pushed away from the chest against some resistance, e.g. by lifting a weight when lying on the back

chicane *noun* (*in motorsport*) a sharp double bend created by placing barriers on the circuit

chin *noun* same as **pull-up** ■ *verb* to perform chins

chinaman *noun* (*in cricket*) a slow off-break bowled by a left-handed bowler to a right-handed batsman

Chinese medicine *noun* a very old system of diagnosis, treatment and prevention of illness developed in China that uses medicinal herbs, minerals and animal products in addition to acupuncture, massage and exercise

chin raise *noun* same as **chin**

chin-up *noun* US same as **pull-up**

chip *noun* **1.** same as **chip shot 2.** a space or crack left in something hard or brittle after a small piece has been broken off or out of it ■ *verb* **1.** to hit or kick a ball or puck so that it travels a short distance in a high arc **2.** (*in golf*) to play a chip shot **3.** to become damaged by having a small piece or small pieces break off

chip shot *noun* **1.** a short-range kick or shot in which the ball or puck rises sharply into the air **2.** (*in golf*) a short approach shot, used for lofting the ball onto the green

chiropractic *adjective* used for describing medical treatment based on the theory that diseases and disorders are caused by a misalignment of the bones, especially in the spine, that obstructs proper nerve functions

chiropractor *noun* a person who treats musculoskeletal disorders by making adjustments primarily to the bones of the spine

chitosan *noun* a substance derived from the shells of crab, lobster and other crustaceans, used as dietary supplement

chloride shift *noun* the reversible exchange of bicarbonate and chloride ions from blood serum to red cells during the transport of carbon dioxide

chlorine *noun* a powerful greenish gas, used for sterilising water

chlorothiazide *noun* a drug that relieves fluid retention, used in the treatment of high blood pressure

chocamine *noun* an anorectic supplement

choke *verb* to lose nerve or confidence and falter in the middle of doing something

chokehold *noun* a hold in some martial arts that restricts the opponent's breathing, causing loss of consciousness

cholecalciferol *noun* same as **vitamin D3**

cholesterol *noun* a fatty substance found in fats and oils, also produced by the liver and forming an essential part of all cells

cholinergic *adjective* used for describing a neurone or receptor that responds to acetylcholine

cholinesterase *noun* an enzyme which breaks down a choline ester

chondral *adjective* relating to or consisting of cartilage

chondroitin *noun* a substance that, when combined with glucosamine, rebuilds damaged cartilage

chondromalacia *noun* a condition in which cartilage becomes eroded by constant friction against a hard surface

chondromalacia patellae *noun* pain caused by friction against the cartilage surface at the back of the patella. Abbreviation **CMP**

chop *verb* to hit a ball with a quick sharp downward movement of a racket or bat, often in order to give the ball backspin

chorea *noun* a sudden severe twitching, usually of the face and shoulders, which is a symptom of disease of the nervous system

choreoathetosis *noun* a movement disorder characterised by fidgeting and slow writhing movements

christie *noun* (*in skiing*) a type of turn used for stopping or rapidly changing direction, in which the skier twists sharply aside while keeping the skis parallel to each other

chromatography *noun* a substance analysis technique used for urine testing of athletes

chromium *noun* a metallic trace element (NOTE: The chemical symbol is **Cr**.)

chromium deficiency *noun* a rare condition resulting in poor metabolisation of sugar

chromium picolinate *noun* a sports supplement that maintains insulin sensitivity

chromosome *noun* a rod-shaped structure in the nucleus of a cell that consists of DNA and carries genes

chronic *adjective* **1.** used for describing a disease or condition that lasts for a long time. Compare **acute 2.** used for describing severe pain

chronic fatigue syndrome *noun* same as **ME**

chronic fibrosis *noun* scarring to connective tissue caused by repeated damage

chronic injury *noun* an injury from the past that still causes pain or restricted movement, requiring ongoing treatment

chronic toxicity *noun* high exposure to harmful levels of a toxic substance over a period of time

chronological age *noun* somebody's real age, as opposed to the age suggested by his or her mental or physical development

chronoscope *noun* an electronic instrument that is designed to measure very small intervals of time with extreme precision

chrysin *noun* an oestrogen inhibitor

cicatrisation *noun* the process of healing to form a scar, or the scar that is formed

cinder track *noun* a running track covered with a layer of fine ash to improve grip and make the surface softer

circuit training *noun* a form of sports training that involves performing different exercises in rotation

circular effect of aggression *noun* the theory that taking part in sport does not provide an outlet for aggressive feelings but increases a person's tendency towards aggression

circulation *noun* the flow of blood around the body. Also called **blood flow**

circulatory system *noun* a system of arteries and veins, together with the heart, that makes the blood circulate around the body

circumduction *noun* the action of moving a limb so that the end of it makes a circular motion

circumflex nerve *noun* a sensory and motor nerve in the upper arm

citrate synthase *noun* an enzyme that is involved in the Krebs cycle

citric acid cycle *noun* same as **Krebs cycle**

classic *noun* a major sporting event, e.g. a horse race or golf tournament

claudication *noun* the fact of limping or being lame

clavicle *noun* either of two long thin bones that join the shoulder blades to the breastbone. Also called **collarbone**

claw foot *noun* same as **cavus foot**

clay pigeon *noun* a clay disc thrown into the air from a machine called a trap as a target for shooting with shotguns

clean and jerk *noun* a two-part lift in weightlifting, in which the bar is lifted firstly to the chest and then above the head

clean and snatch *noun* same as **snatch**

clean-living *adjective* never doing anything that might be considered immoral or unhealthy

clearance *noun* in games, the process of clearing the ball from the defence area

cleats *plural noun* same as **spikes**

clenbuterol *noun* a banned substance that acts as a growth agent

cliff-jumping *noun* the sport of jumping from a high point such as a cliff into water

climb *verb* to go up mountains or rocks on foot or using hands and feet as a sport

climber *noun* **1.** somebody who climbs rocks or mountains as a sport **2.** a player or team who is steadily gaining in rank or status

climbing *noun* the sport of climbing mountains or rocks

clinical nutrition *noun* the use of nutrition as a means of treating illnesses

clinical psychologist *noun* a psychologist who treats human mental and behavioural problems as opposed to doing research on them

clinical psychology *noun* the branch of psychology that deals with the diagnosis and treatment of psychological and behavioural problems

clinical trial *noun* a trial carried out in a medical laboratory on a person or on tissue from a person

clonic cramp *noun* cramping of the muscles in which they are seen to twitch and jerk uncontrollably

closed fracture *noun* a fractured bone that has not pierced the skin

closed skill *noun* a skill in which the same movement is performed every time, with no adaptation to circumstances, such as in diving or gymnastics. Compare **open skill**

closed stance *noun* in sports such as baseball or golf, a stance in which the front foot is closer to the line of play than the rear foot

clot *verb* to change from a liquid to a semi-solid state, or to cause a liquid to do this ■ *noun* a soft mass of coagulated blood in a vein or an artery

club *noun* **1.** a stick or bat used in some sports, especially golf, to hit a ball **2.** an association of people with a common interest **3.** an organisation formed for the pursuit of a sport

CMP *abbreviation* chondromalacia patellae

coach *noun* someone who trains sports players or athletes ■ *verb* to train someone in a sport

coaching *noun* the activity or profession of training sports players or athletes

co-active sport *noun* any sport in which each athlete performs separately, with no team element, e.g. marathon running

coapt *verb* to join or bring displaced parts close together in their correct alignment, e.g. the edges of a wound or broken bone

coaptation *noun* the action or process of joining or closing parts together, e.g. the edges of a wound or broken bone

coasteering *noun* a sporting activity that takes place along a coast and combines scrambling, rock climbing, traversing, swimming and cliff jumping

cobalamin *noun* same as **vitamin B12**

coccydynia *noun* pain in the coccyx

coccyx *noun* the lowest bone in the backbone (NOTE: The plural is **coccyges**.)

cocktail *noun* a combination of two or more drugs or therapeutic agents given as a single treatment

co-contraction *noun* ♦ **agonist co-contraction**

code *noun* a system of accepted laws and regulations that govern procedure or behaviour within a particular sport

codeine *noun* an opiate drug used to relieve pain

coeliac disease *noun* an allergic disease, mainly affecting children, in which the lining of the intestine is sensitive to gluten, preventing the small intestine from digesting fat

coenzyme *noun* a non-protein compound that combines with the protein part of an enzyme to make it active

coenzyme A *noun* a complex compound that acts with specific enzymes in energy-producing biochemical reactions. Abbreviation **CoA**

coexistent *adjective* used for describing multiple injuries that exist at the same time

cognitive *adjective* relating to the process of acquiring knowledge by the use of reasoning, intuition or perception

cognitive-affective stress management training *noun* stress management training that focusses on the mental processes that trigger emotional responses and looks to develop strategies for recognising and coping with these. Abbreviation **CASMT**

cognitive anxiety *noun* stress that derives from an athlete thinking consciously about what may go wrong, which may be detrimental to performance

cognitive appraisal *noun* a study of an athlete's attitude and mental state undertaken by a sports psychologist, usually used for diagnosing burnout

cognitive assessment *noun* a set of logic questions used in a sports concussion assessment tool, e.g. a series of numbers or words that are read out and should be repeated backwards

cognitive attribution model *noun* a sports psychology model of the way in which athletes view failure or success, in light of how much personal control they had over all the competition variables

cognitive-behavioural *adjective* relating to the way in which mental processes determine actions, and how these can be modified and used for improving performance

cognitive dissonance *noun* a state of psychological conflict or anxiety resulting from a contradiction between a person's simultaneously held beliefs or attitudes

cognitive learning *noun* skills learning that emphasises participation and reasoning on the part of the learner

cognitive psychology *noun* the branch of psychology that deals with unobservable mental processes

cognitive stage *noun* the first stage of skill acquisition in which the sequence of movements must be learned through coaching and practice

cohesion *noun* the force of attraction between the molecules of a solid or liquid that holds them together

cohesive *adjective* sticking, holding, or working together as a united whole

cohort study *noun* a study of people over an extended period of time

cold therapy *noun* same as **ice therapy**

cold water immersion *noun* exposure to cold water that results in a lowering of the core body temperature, a risk faced by enthusiasts of water sports such as canoeing

colforsin *noun* a vasodilatory sports supplement

collagen *noun* a thick protein fibre that forms bundles that make up the connective tissue, bone and cartilage

collapse *verb* 1. to fall down in a semi-conscious state 2. to be suddenly and quickly overwhelmed by an opponent or opposing team

collarbone *noun* same as **clavicle**

collateral ligaments *plural noun* large ligaments that stabilise the joints at the knee and elbow

collective *adjective* made or shared by everyone in a group

collective aims *plural noun* goals that all members of a team share

collective behaviour *noun* behaviour exhibited by people working as part of a team, when they are influenced by one another and enjoy a degree of anonymity

Colles fracture *noun* a fracture of the lower end of the radius with displacement of the wrist backwards, usually caused when someone has stretched out a hand to try to break a fall

colon *noun* the main part of the large intestine, running from the caecum at the end of the small intestine to the rectum

colon cancer *noun* cancer of the colon or bowel, against which regular exercise in later life is thought to give protection

colours *plural noun* the clothing worn by a jockey or an athlete that indicates the horse's owner or the team to which the athlete belongs

combat *noun* a physical struggle between opposing individuals or forces

combat sport *noun* a sport in which one person fights another, e.g. wrestling, boxing and the martial arts

combination *noun* (*in boxing*) two or more punches quickly delivered one after the other

comfort level, comfort zone *noun* the set of physical or psychological circumstances in which someone feels most at ease and free from physical discomfort or stress

command style *noun* a coaching technique in which the coach gives direct instructions and the athlete has little personal input

commentary *noun* a spoken description of a sporting event being broadcast on radio or television as it happens

commentary box *noun* a booth at a sports stadium from which a television or radio commentator makes a broadcast

commentator *noun* a broadcaster for radio or television who describes sporting events as they happen

comminute *verb* to break, or cause a bone to break, into small parts

comminuted fracture *noun* a fractured bone in which there are several breaks or cracks or extensive fragmentation

commissure *noun* a structure that joins two similar tissues, e.g. a group of nerves that crosses from one part of the central nervous system to another

Commonwealth Games *plural noun* a sports contest held every four years involving participants from countries of the Commonwealth

Commonwealth Youth Games *plural noun* a smaller version of the Commonwealth Games aimed at young people

commotio cordis *noun* sudden heart failure caused by a heavy blow to the chest, usually occurring while participating in a contact sport

commotio retina *noun* a heavy blow to the eye causing bruising, swelling and retinal damage

community *noun* a group of people who live and work in a district

community medicine *noun* the branch of medicine devoted to the provision of public health care

compartment *noun* a group of related muscles that are found together in a particular area of the body

compartment syndrome *noun* a condition in which a particular set of muscles are overused

compensate *verb* **1.** to make good the failure of an organ by making another organ, or the undamaged parts of the same organ, function at a higher level **2.** to emphasise a particular ability or personality characteristic in order to make the lack of another one seem less bad

compensatory movement *noun* a second movement that compensates for any potential bad effects caused by a primary muscle movement, e.g. loss of balance

compete *verb* to try to win or do better than others

competence *noun* the ability to do something well, measured against a standard, especially ability that you get through experience or training

competent *adjective* having enough skill or ability to do something well

competing response theory *noun* the idea that offering an external reward such as a trophy for winning a competition may distract the competitor from the joy of winning for its own sake, lessening motivation

competition training *noun* athletic training that specifically prepares the athlete for the competition situation

competitive *adjective* **1.** involving competition **2.** tending to want to do something better than others or achieve more than others

competitive individualism *noun* the belief that competition is a natural and healthy way of distributing rewards to those who try hardest and have the most natural ability, and that it brings out the best in a person

competitiveness *noun* the quality of being competitive

competitive state anxiety *noun* a feeling of stress caused by competition, especially when the athlete does not feel able to meet the challenges

Competitive State Anxiety Inventory-2 *noun* full form of **CSAI-2**

competitive stress *noun* stress caused by an athlete feeling unable to meet the demands of the competition

complacency *noun* the state of being self-satisfied or overly self-confident, which may lead to longer reaction times in relation to unexpected stimuli

complaint *noun* a physical disorder, usually something minor

complementary action of proteins *noun* the act of eating different types of protein in the same meal so as to raise their biological value

complementary medicine *noun* a range of therapies based on the holistic treatment of physical disorders, generally addressing the causes of diseases rather than their symptoms and also taking steps in the prevention of disease. The term embraces therapies such as acupuncture, herbal medicine and homeopathy.

complete blood count *noun* a diagnostic test used to identify the levels of all blood-cell types in a quantity of blood

complete protein *noun* a protein that contains all of the essential amino acids

complex carbohydrate *noun* any carbohydrate with large molecules containing many linked sugar units, broken down more slowly by the body

complex performance *noun* an extended athletic performance such as participation in a team game, where several physical and mental skills are required

composition *noun* the make-up or structure of something

compound fracture *noun* a fractured bone that has pierced the skin, exposing the break

compress *noun* a wad of cloth soaked in hot or cold liquid and applied to the skin to relieve pain or swelling, or to force pus out of an infected wound

compression *noun* **1.** the act of squeezing or pressing **2.** a serious condition in which the brain is compressed by blood or cerebrospinal fluid accumulating in it or by a fractured skull

compression neuropathy *noun* a condition in which the nerves become pinched by a nearby swelling or by constant pressure, e.g. the pressure of gripping bicycle handlebars, causing pain, tingling and numbness

compressor *noun* a device such as a pump that compresses air in order to increase its pressure

compulsive *adjective* driven by an irresistible inner force to do something

compulsory *adjective* required by law or an authority ■ *noun* an exercise or routine that participants in a sport such as gymnastics or figure skating must perform as part of a competition

computerised tomography scan *noun* full form of **CT scan**

comradeship *noun* the feelings or bonds that unite close friends or colleagues, e.g. loyalty, friendship or a common cause

conative *adjective* used for describing behaviour that is based on willpower or the drive to succeed

concede *verb* **1.** to accept and acknowledge defeat in a contest without waiting for the final result **2.** to allow an opponent or opposing team to gain a goal or points

concentric *adjective* involving a shortening of the muscle

concentric action *noun* an action performed by contracting a muscle

concentric strength *noun* the force exerted by a muscle while it is contracting

conceptual competence *noun* the ability to make decisions based on a set of concrete observations and known facts

concussion *noun* **1.** an injury to the brain, often resulting from a blow to the head, that can cause temporary disorientation, memory loss, or unconsciousness **2.** an injury to an organ of the body, usually caused by a violent blow or shaking

condition *noun* **1.** the particular state of someone or something **2.** a particular illness, injury or disorder ■ *verb* to undertake a fitness plan to improve general health, appearance or physical performance

conditioned *adjective* **1.** having reached a particular or high level of fitness, quality or performance **2.** brought on unconsciously by a stimulus that triggers a reaction because of a learned association with something else

conditioned response *noun* a response to a stimulus as a result of associating it with an earlier stimulus

conditioning *noun* the work or programme used to bring somebody or something to a good physical state

conduct *noun* the way a player behaves on a sports field or in another arena

conduction *noun* the process of passing heat, sound or nervous impulses from one part of the body to another

conductive *adjective* relating to conduction

condyle *noun* a rounded end of a bone that articulates with another

condyloid *adjective* rounded like the protruding surface at the end of a bone

cone *noun* a plastic object used to mark out playing areas in a field or sports hall

conference *noun* an association or league of sports teams that compete with each other

confidence *noun* a belief in your ability to succeed

confrontation *noun* a face-to-face meeting or encounter, especially a challenging or hostile one

congenital *adjective* existing at or before birth

congenital anomaly *noun* a medical condition that arises during the development of the foetus and is present at birth

congestive heart failure *noun* a form of heart failure in which the heart is unable to pump away the blood returning to it fast enough, causing congestion in the veins

conjugated protein *noun* a protein containing at least two double or triple chemical bonds alternating with single bonds

conjunctivitis *noun* inflammation of the eye caused by infection, injury or allergy

connective tissue *noun* tissue that forms the main part of bones and cartilage, ligaments and tendons, in which a large proportion of fibrous material surrounds the tissue cells

conscience *noun* the sense of what is right and wrong that governs someone's thoughts and actions, urging him or her to do right rather than wrong

consolidation *noun* the increasing of the strength, stability or depth of a person's or group's success or position

constant resistance exercise *noun* an exercise using weights in which the load does not change during the course of the exercise

constitution *noun* general physical and sometimes psychological make up, especially the body's ability to remain healthy and withstand disease or hardship

constitutive rule *noun* one of a set of basic rules that define a sport

constrict *verb* to become narrower, or make something, especially a blood vessel, narrower

constrictor *noun* a muscle that squeezes an organ or makes an organ contract

contact sport *noun* any sport in which physical contact between players is an integral part of the game, e.g. boxing, rugby or taekwondo

contaminated *adjective* made impure by the presence of substances that are harmful to living organisms

contamination *noun* **1.** the act of making something impure by touching it or by adding something to it **2.** a state of impurity caused by the presence of substances that are harmful to living organisms

contentious *adjective* causing or likely to cause disagreement and disputes between people with differing views

contest *noun* an organised competition for a prize or title, especially one in which the entrants appear or demonstrate their skills individually and the winner is chosen by a group of judges

contest arena *noun* the place in which an athlete performs in competition, which may differ in important ways from the training arena

contextural interference *noun* the effect of performing a skill in a different context to the one in which it is usually performed, e.g. in competition

continuity theory *noun* the idea that, to adjust to retirement from professional sport, it is best to wind down gradually, replacing old roles with new ones such as taking up coaching or commentating

continuous passive motion *noun* a technique, used in the rehabilitation of injured limbs, in which the limb is moved and manipulated passively without using the muscles

continuous reinforcement *noun* behavioural reinforcement that is given every time the correct behaviour is exhibited

continuous skill *noun* an activity that has no real beginning, middle and end and can go on for any length of time, e.g. swimming or cycling

continuous training *noun* steady exercise at a medium intensity with no bursts of activity or rest periods. Compare **interval training**

contract *noun* a formal or legally binding agreement, e.g. one setting out terms of employment ■ *verb* **1.** to become smaller and tighter, or make a muscle or part of the body smaller and tighter **2.** to make a formal or legally binding agreement with someone to do something

contractile *adjective* able or tending to shrink, tighten or become narrower

contractile time *noun* the time taken for a muscle to become fully tense from a state of complete relaxation

contractile tissue *noun* the fibres in muscle that can contract, composed of actin and myosin

contraction *noun* a tightening movement that makes a muscle shorter, makes the pupil of the eye smaller or makes the skin wrinkle

contractor *noun* something that contracts, e.g. a muscle

contract-relax stretching *noun* stretching in which the muscle is fully contracted then stretched out, usually with the aid of a partner

contracture *noun* a permanent tightening of a muscle caused by fibrosis

contraindication *noun* a sign that a particular exercise should not be performed, e.g. pain or stiffness

contrast baths *plural noun* a set of hot and cold baths used to administer alternating heat and cold therapy for an injured limb

contrecoup *noun* an injury to one side of an organ, especially the brain, as a result of a blow that causes it to swing inside the retaining cavity

control *noun* skill in using something or in performing

control group *noun* a group of people who are not being treated but whose test data are used as a comparison in a study

controlling aspect *noun* in competing response theory, the degree to which an athlete is motivated by external rewards at the expense of internal motivation

contusion *noun* same as **bruise**

convalescence *noun* gradual return to good health after an illness or medical treatment, or the period spent recovering

convergence *noun* the turning inwards of both eyes in order to look at something nearer than the previous object viewed

conversational index *noun* a measure of how easy an athlete finds it to speak while exercising at various intensities, which indicates their anaerobic threshold

conversion *noun* (*in rugby*) a kicking of the ball over the crossbar following a try, or the score made with a successful kick

conversion disorder *noun* a neurosis marked by the appearance of physical symptoms such as partial loss of muscle function without physical cause but in the presence of psychological conflict

convert *verb* **1.** (*in rugby*) to add to the points awarded for a try by following it with a successful kick of the ball over the crossbar **2.** to take advantage of an opportunity offered by an opponent, such as by winning a break point in tennis

convulsion *noun* a violent shaking of the body or limbs caused by uncontrollable muscle contractions, which can be a symptom of brain disorders and other conditions

convulsive *adjective* undergoing or producing uncontrollable jerking of the body or limbs

cool down *verb* to become less warm after exertion

cool-down *noun* a session of gentle activity and stretching after exercise to relax the muscles

coordination *noun* the ability to use two or more parts of the body at the same time to carry out a movement or task

coordinative structure *noun* a group of muscles that are functionally interlinked

COPE model *noun* a model designed to help athletes manage their stress, in which the elements are Control over emotions, Organisation of stimuli, Planning of a suitable response and Execution of the response

coping skills *plural noun* learned methods of managing strong feelings in response to events, so that they do not detract from a generally positive mindset

coping strategy *noun* ◆ coping skills

copper *noun* a metallic trace element (NOTE: The chemical symbol is **Cu**.)

copper gluconate *noun* a metabolisable form of copper used as a supplement to treat deficiency

coracoid *noun* a bony projection on the shoulder blade in most mammals

coracoid projection *noun* a knob on the shoulder blade to which the biceps brachii muscle is attached

corded *adjective* having tensed or well-developed muscles visible as ridges or ripples

core stability *noun* the fact of having strong abdominal and back muscles so as to maintain proper posture when doing other exercises

core temperature *noun* the optimum internal body temperature of a person, which it is dangerous to raise or lower

Cori cycle *noun* the way in which excess lactic acid produced by muscles is converted back to glucose so that it can be reused for energy production

cork *noun* a heavy bruise to the quadriceps

corneal abrasion *noun* a tiny scratch on the surface of the eyeball, often incurred during contact or ball sports

corner *noun* **1.** the part of the playing field or surface where two boundaries meet **2.** a free kick or shot from a corner of the field, given to the attacking team when a defending player plays the ball over the goal line **3.** (*in boxing and wrestling*) any of the four parts of a ring where the ropes are attached to the posts, especially the two where the competitors rest between rounds

coronal plane *noun* a plane at right angles to the median plane, dividing the body into dorsal and ventral halves

coronary *adjective* used for describing the arteries that supply blood to the heart muscles

coronary artery *noun* either of the two arteries that supply blood to the heart muscles

coronary circulation *noun* blood circulation through the arteries and veins of the heart muscles

coronary heart disease *noun* any disease that affects the coronary arteries and may lead to strain on the heart or to a heart attack. Abbreviation **CHD**

coronary ligament strain *noun* a strain to the ligament in the knee

coronary occlusion *noun* a blockage of the coronary arteries, disrupting the blood flow to the heart

coronary thrombosis *noun* same as **atherosclerosis**

coronary vein *noun* a vein of the group that drains blood from the muscles of the heart

corrective activity *noun* a training exercise designed to correct a problem with a learned skill

corrective therapy *noun* professional coaching or counselling to correct undesirable behaviour

corrugator *noun* a muscle that wrinkles the skin when it contracts

cortex *noun* the outer layer of an organ, as opposed to the soft inner medulla

corticosteroid *noun* **1.** any steroid hormone produced by the cortex of the adrenal glands **2.** a drug that reduces inflammation, used in treating asthma, gastrointestinal disease and in adrenocortical insufficiency

corticotrophin *noun* a hormone secreted by the pituitary gland that stimulates the adrenal glands

cortisol *noun* same as **hydrocortisone**

cortisone *noun* a hormone secreted in small quantities by the adrenal cortex

costal *adjective* relating to the ribs

costochondrial separation *noun* a sports injury in which one or more ribs becomes detached from the sternum, usually caused by a heavy blow to the chest

costochondritis *noun* inflammation of the point at which the ribs are attached to the sternum

counsel *verb* to give someone advice and support on personal or psychological matters, usually in a professional context

counselling *noun* a method of treating mental disorders in which a specialist talks with a person about his or her condition and how to deal with it

counter *verb* (*in boxing and other full-contact sports*) to defend oneself against a punch or kick from an opponent, and deliver a punch or kick in return

counterattack *verb* to make an attacking move from a defensive position

counterconditioning *noun* a process of psychological conditioning that attempts to replace somebody's undesired habitual response to a particular situation with a desired learned response

countering *noun* a method of encouraging positive thinking by identifying present negative triggers and thoughts, and building new responses to these

coup de grâce *noun* the final action that assures victory or success

course *noun* an area where a race is run or where a sport in which players progress over the area is played

court *noun* the playing area in some sports, e.g. basketball and tennis

cox *noun* the member of a rowing crew who faces forward, steers the boat and directs the speed and rhythm of the rowers

coxa *noun* the hip joint (NOTE: The plural is **coxae**.)

coxal *adjective* relating to the hip

coxa vara *noun* an unusual development of the hip bone, making the legs bow

coxitis *noun* inflammation at the hip joint

cradle *noun* **1.** a frame placed beneath bedclothes covering a patient to keep him or her from touching a sensitive part of the body, e.g. after an injury or operation **2.** (*in cricket*) a shallow curved frame used in catching practice

cramp *noun* a painful involuntary spasm in the muscles, in which the muscle may stay contracted for some time

cramping *noun* the occurrence of cramps during or after exercise

cranial nerves *plural noun* the nerves, twelve on each side, that are connected directly to the brain, governing mainly the structures of the head and neck

craniosacral therapy *noun* gentle manipulation of the bones of the face, skull and spine, intended to relieve conditions including migraine, sinusitis and musculoskeletal problems

crash *verb* **1.** to collide **2.** to suffer a total loss of physical or mental energy, often because of exhaustion or stress

crash course *noun* a course of study or training done intensively over a short period of time in order to learn the basics of a subject, skill, or activity quickly

crash diet *noun* a dietary plan that drastically reduces calorie intake for a short period, leading to rapid but unsustainable weight loss

crash helmet *noun* a hard padded helmet worn by cyclists, racing drivers and others to protect the head in case of an accident

crawl *noun* a fast swimming stroke in which the swimmer lies face down and uses a flutter kick and an overarm stroke

crease *noun* **1.** (*in cricket*) any of various lines that demarcate the wicket, especially the **popping crease 2.** the rectangular area in front of an ice hockey goal **3.** the semicircular area surrounding a lacrosse goal

creatine *noun* a compound of nitrogen found in the muscles, produced by protein metabolism and excreted as creatinine

creatine kinase *noun* an enzyme that breaks down phosphocreatine into creatine and phosphoric acid, releasing energy

creatine monohydrate *noun* a form of creatine sold as a bodybuilding supplement

creatine phosphate *noun* a store of energy-giving phosphate in muscles

creatinine *noun* a substance that is the form in which creatine is excreted

creativity *noun* the ability to use the imagination to develop new and original techniques or make unorthodox plays to successfully deal with difficult situations

creep effect *noun* a condition in which a vertebral disc is put under repeated pressure, causing it to leak tissue and become tight and hardened

crepitus *noun* **1.** a harsh crackling sound heard through a stethoscope in a person with inflammation of the lungs **2.** a scratching sound made by a broken bone or rough joint

crew *noun* the rowers and cox of a racing boat

cricket *noun* an outdoor sport played by two teams of 11 players using a flat bat, a small hard ball, and wickets. A player scores by batting the ball and running, while the defenders can get a player out by bowling and hitting the wicket, catching a hit ball, or running the player out.

crista *noun* a ridge, e.g. the border of a bone

criterion-referenced test *noun* a situation in which a competitor must achieve a predetermined standard or score, rather than beat a competitor's score

critical power *noun* a level of intensity that is the highest that a person can exercise at without becoming exhausted

criticise *verb* to say what is wrong with something

criticism *noun* a spoken or written opinion or judgment of what is wrong or bad about someone or something

cromoly *noun* a steel alloy that is light and durable, used to make sports equipment such as bicycle frames

croquet *noun* an outdoor game, usually played on a lawn, in which the players use long-handled wooden mallets to hit large wooden balls through a series of hoops

cross *noun* **1.** a pass that sends the ball across the field in a team game such as hockey **2.** a punch thrown at a boxing opponent from the side, in response to and evading the opponent's jab or lead ■ *verb* in football and some other games, to make a pass that sends the ball across, rather than up or down, the field

crosscheck *verb* (*in hockey, ice hockey and lacrosse*) to obstruct an opposing player by using both hands to thrust a playing stick across his or her body

cross-country *noun* a sporting activity or event such as running, cycling or racing that is done off the roads

cross-country skiing *noun* skiing on long narrow skis across open countryside on fairly level ground

crosscourt *adjective* hit or thrown from one side of a playing court towards the other, especially in tennis or basketball

crossfield *adjective* kicked or thrown from one side of a playing field towards the other, especially in football or rugby

cross-frictional massage *noun* a form of massage in which the pressure is applied across the fibres of the muscle

cross-sex effect *noun* the fact of having members of the opposite sex in the audience, and the effect that this may have on an athlete's performance

cross-train *verb* to learn one or more tasks or skills at a time, or teach someone one or more skills

crosstrainer *noun* **1.** an athlete who trains for more than one competitive sport at a time **2.** an exercise machine intended to help develop many different groups of muscles ■ *plural noun* **crosstrainers** sports shoes designed for more than one sporting activity

cross training *noun* fitness training in different sports, e.g. running and weight-lifting, usually undertaken to enhance performance in one of the sports

crowd control *noun* methods of coping with large groups of people such as at a sports game, making sure that they each have space and can move freely

cruciate ligament *noun* any ligament shaped like a cross, especially either of two ligaments behind the knee that prevent the knee from bending forwards

cruiserweight *noun* (*in professional boxing*) a weight category for competitors whose weight does not exceed 86 kg or 190 lb

crunch *noun* a form of sit-up in which the body is only partially raised, intended to strengthen the abdominal muscles

crural *adjective* relating to the thigh, leg or shin

crural length *noun* the ratio of thigh length to total leg length, relevant in some athletic events that involve jumping

crutches *plural noun* a pair of long sticks with handgrips and rests for the forearm or armpit, used for support by a person who is unable to walk unassisted

cryokinetics *noun* the combination of massage and ice therapy in the rehabilitation of a sports injury

cryotherapy *noun* same as **ice therapy**

CSAI-2 *noun* a method used to measure levels of competitive state anxiety, which looks at both the athlete's general tendency towards stress (A-trait) and the their tendency to suffer stress under pressure (A-state). Full form **Competitive State Anxiety Inventory-2**

CT scan *noun* a system of examining the body in which a narrow X-ray beam, guided by a computer, photographs a thin section of the body or of an organ from several angles, using the computer to build up an image of the section. Full form **computerised tomography scan**

cubital *adjective* relating to the elbow

cuboid subluxation *noun* misalignment of the middle bone of the foot, often caused by landing awkwardly from a jump

cue *noun* **1.** (*in games such as snooker and pool*) a long tapering stick used for striking the cue ball **2.** a stimulus or pattern of stimuli, often not consciously perceived, that results in a specific learned behavioural response

cue ball *noun* in billiards, snooker or pool, the white ball struck with the cue so that it strikes the object ball in turn

cuff *noun* an inflatable band fastened around a patient's arm when measuring blood pressure

cuneiform *adjective* used for describing any of three wedge-shaped bones of the ankle

cup *noun* **1.** a sporting competition in which the winner's prize is a large ornamental cup **2.** *US* an athletic support reinforced with plastic or metal, worn to protect the male genitals during team sports

Cup Final *noun* the final match in a knockout sports competition, especially in football

cup holder *noun* a team that won the cup in the previous staging of a sporting competition or tournament

cup tie *noun* a match in a knockout competition for which the prize is a cup

curl *noun* a weight training exercise in which a weight held in the hand or hands is lifted by curling the forearm towards the upper arm

curl bar *noun* a weighted shaped bar designed for use when performing curls

curling *noun* a team game played on an ice rink, in which a heavy polished stone with a handle is slid towards a circular target (**000**)

curl-up *noun* a type of sit-up performed slowly with great attention to technique and form

cursorial *adjective* having a body or body parts particularly well-adapted for running

curveball *noun* in baseball, a ball that when pitched drifts to the left if thrown by a right-handed pitcher and to the right if thrown by a left-handed pitcher

curved last *noun* same as **performance last**

curvilinear *adjective* moving along a curved path or line

Cushing response *noun* a raise in blood pressure combined with a slowing heart rate, a classic symptom of intercranial pressure caused by a head trauma

custom drug *noun* a drug that targets a specific condition, especially a drug that is tailored to an individual patient's genetic requirements

cut *verb* **1.** to hit a ball with a racket in such a way that it spins as it flies through the air **2.** to strike a cricket ball square on the offside with the bat more or less parallel to the ground

cutaneous *adjective* relating to the skin

cutting up *noun* the practice of reducing bodily water retention in order to improve muscular definition. Also called **drying out**

CV training *abbreviation* cardiovascular training

cyanocobalamin *noun* same as **vitamin B12**

cyanosis *noun* a condition characterised by a blue colour of the peripheral skin and mucous membranes, a symptom of lack of oxygen in the blood, e.g. in heart or lung disease

cycle *noun* **1.** a series of events that recur regularly **2.** same as **bicycle** ■ *verb* to ride a bicycle

cycling *noun* the sport of riding a bicycle

cyclocross *noun* the sport of racing bicycles across rough country

cyst *noun* an unusual growth in the body shaped like a pouch, containing liquid or semi-liquid substances

cysteine *noun* a sulphur-containing amino acid that is converted to cystine during metabolism

cystine *noun* an amino acid

cystinuria *noun* a genetic disease involving high levels of cysteine in the urine, causing the formation of kidney stones

cytoplasm *noun* a substance inside the cell membrane that surrounds the nucleus of a cell

cytoplasmic streaming *noun* the movement of cytoplasm within living cells resulting in the transport of nutrients and enzymes

D

dactylion *noun* the tip of the middle finger, an anatomical site used in anthropometrical measurements

daily dozen *noun* a set of physical exercises done each day (*informal*)

dan *noun* **1.** one of the numbered black-belt levels of proficiency in martial arts such as judo and taekwondo. Also called **dan grade 2.** somebody who has achieved a dan

dancercise *noun* aerobic exercise in the form of dance

DanceSport *noun* dancing as a competitive activity

dark horse *noun* a little-known competitor who achieves unexpected success in a race or other sporting contest

darts *noun* an indoor game in which players take turns throwing arrow-shaped missiles (**darts**) from a set distance at a circular board (**dartboard**) placed at about eye level on a wall

DCO *abbreviation* doping control officer

dead *adjective* **1.** not sensitive **2.** in some sports, used to describe a ball that has crossed the boundary of the playing area

dead arm *noun* a situation in which the shoulder socket briefly dislocates before slipping back in, causing pain and numbness in the arm

dead ball *noun* a ball that temporarily cannot be used for the purposes of the game, usually because it has gone outside the playing area

dead heat *noun* a race or other competition in which two or more contestants finish together or with the same score

dead leg *noun* a situation in which the quadriceps muscle is crushed against the bone by a heavy blow, causing pain and restricted movement

deadlift *noun* **1.** a weightlifting event in which a weight is raised from the floor to the level of the hips and lowered again in a controlled manner **2.** an exercise in which a barbell is lifted from the floor, emphasising proper posture

dead space *noun* same as **respiratory dead space**

debridement *noun* the removal of dead or damaged tissue from a injury site to promote rapid healing

decalcification *noun* same as **bone loss**

decalcify *verb* to lose calcium or a calcium compound, or remove calcium or a calcium compound from bones or teeth

decathlete *noun* an athlete who competes in a decathlon

decathlon *noun* a contest in which athletes compete in ten different events and are awarded points for each to find the best all-round athlete. The events are long jump, high jump, pole vault, shot put, discus, javelin, 110-metre hurdles, and running over 100 metres, 400 metres, and 1,500 metres.

decelerate *verb* to reduce speed, or make something do this

deceleration *noun* the act or process of reducing speed or making something go more slowly

deceleration injury *noun* an injury such as whiplash that occurs when a moving body suddenly stops

decider *noun* something that settles the outcome of a contest or argument, especially, in sport, a game played to determine the ultimate winner

decision *noun* a win in a boxing match that is awarded to the fighter who is given the higher total of points by the judges

deck *noun* a platform on which physical exercises are performed, e.g. in a gym

declare *verb* (*in cricket*) to end an innings before all the batsmen have been dismissed, having decided, as the batting side or the captain of it, that the team has probably made enough runs

decompensation *noun* a situation in which the heart is faced with an increased workload and is unable to cope

decompression *noun* **1.** the expansion of small nitrogen bubbles in body tissues that occurs as a person rises from a scuba dive, which can be harmful if not controlled **2.** a surgical procedure carried out to reduce pressure in an organ or part of the body caused, e.g., by fluid on the brain, or to reduce the pressure of tissues on a nerve

decompression sickness *noun* damage to bodily tissues caused by decompression when rising from a scuba dive too quickly, with symptoms including skin rashes, extreme fatigue, joint pain, breathing difficulties and unconsciousness

decondition *verb* to lose physical fitness through lack of exercise or illness, or cause someone to do this

decongestant *noun* a drug that reduces congestion and swelling, sometimes used for unblocking the nasal passages

dedication *noun* the quality of being committed to achieving a goal

deep *adjective* located, coming from or reaching relatively far inside the body

deep-range conditioning *noun* conditioning that builds up strength in minor muscles, allowing greater flexibility

deep stroking massage *noun* a form of deep-tissue massage in which stroking pressure is applied along the length of the muscle, removing accumulated fluids. Abbreviation **DSM**

deep-tissue *adjective* affecting the deeper layers of muscle tissue

defeat *verb* to win a victory over an opposing player or team ■ *noun* the fact or an instance of losing to an opposing player or team in a competition

defence *noun* **1.** in sports, the method or manoeuvres that prevent the other team from scoring **2.** the sports team members who have responsibility for defence (NOTE: The US spelling is **defense**.)

defend *verb* **1.** to resist the attacks of an opposing player or team and try to prevent them from scoring **2.** to try to retain a sporting title by competing in the relevant competitions **3.** to protect the goal and goal area from the attacks of the opposition

defender *noun* **1.** a player whose role is to try to prevent the opposition from scoring or getting into a scoring position **2.** the holder of a title that is being challenged

defensive *adjective* **1.** concentrating more on preventing an opponent from gaining an advantage than on scoring **2.** *US* relating to those players who have responsibility for defence

deferent *adjective* going away from the centre

deferred gratification *noun* a situation in which a person sacrifices short-term comfort for long-term goals, which will bring greater satisfaction

defibrillator *noun* a machine that administers a controlled electric shock to the chest or heart to correct a critically irregular heartbeat that cannot drive the circulation

deficiency *noun* **1.** a lack of something necessary, especially a nutrient **2.** a failure to reach the required standard in something

deficiency disease *noun* a disease caused by lack of an essential element in the diet such as vitamins or essential amino and fatty acids

deficient *adjective* **1.** lacking a particular quality or nutrient, especially one that is expected or necessary **2.** not meeting the required standard

defined *adjective* used for describing of a person's physique that shows good muscle tone

definition *noun* the quality of being clearly or sharply visible

Défi sportif *noun* an annual multi-sport event held in Montreal, open to athletes with disabilities

deft *adjective* moving or acting in a quick, smooth and skilful way

degenerative arthritis *noun* same as **osteoarthritis**

dehydrate *verb* to lose water

dehydration *noun* a dangerous lack of water in the body resulting from inadequate intake of fluids or excessive loss through sweating, vomiting or diarrhoea

deionised water *noun* purified water that has been through a process that removes mineral salts. Also called **demineralised water**

delayed onset muscle soreness *noun* pain in the muscles felt for one or two days after unusually intense exercise. Abbreviation **DOMS**

deleterious *adjective* having a harmful or damaging effect on someone or something

delinquency *noun* antisocial or illegal behaviour or acts, especially by young people. ◊ **hooliganism**

delinquent *noun* someone, especially a young person, who has acted antisocially

deltoid *noun* a thick triangular muscle that covers the shoulder joint

delts *plural noun* the deltoid muscles (*informal*)

demineralised water *noun* same as **deionised water**

democratic coaching *noun* a coaching style in which the athlete or team are actively involved in training decisions

demographic *adjective* relating to the details of a population

demographics *noun* the study of human populations

demonstration sport *noun* a sport that is contested in the Olympics on a trial basis and has yet to be accepted as a permanent medal sport

dendrite, dendron *noun* a branched extension of a nerve cell that receives electrical signals from other neurons and conducts those signals to the cell body

denervate *verb* to deprive an organ or body part of nerves, either by cutting them or by blocking them with drugs, e.g. to control pain

denervation *noun* the stopping or cutting of the nerve supply to a part of the body

densitometry *noun* the measurement of the density of bodily organs and tissues such as bones

dental injury *noun* damage caused to the teeth by a collision or facial injury

deoxyribonucleic acid *noun* full form of **DNA**

Department of Health *noun* a UK government department in charge of health services. Abbreviation **DH**

dependence *noun* the fact that a person is addicted to a substance

depolarisation *noun* the reversal of the normal electrical polarity of a nerve or muscle cell membrane during the passage of a nerve impulse or muscle contraction

depressed fracture *noun* a fracture of a flat bone such as those in the skull where part of the bone has been pushed down lower than the surrounding parts

depression *noun* **1.** a psychiatric disorder showing symptoms such as persistent feelings of hopelessness, dejection, poor concentration, lack of energy, inability to sleep and, sometimes, suicidal tendencies **2.** the act of lowering a limb

depressor *noun* **1.** a muscle that pulls part of the body downwards **2.** same as **depressor nerve**

depressor nerve *noun* a nerve that reduces the activity of an organ such as the heart and lowers blood pressure

depth perception *noun* the ability to perceive objects and their spatial relationship in three dimensions

deranged *adjective* used for describing the jaw when it has been moved out of alignment by a heavy blow

descriptive feedback *noun* feedback, given by a coach on an athlete's performance, that involves a detailed description of the performance

desensitisation *noun* a method of stress management in which the athlete visualises the potentially stressful situation while in a calming environment

desensitise *verb* to make something less sensitive to something such as pain, e.g. by stretching a muscle more over a period of time

designer drug *noun* a medicine that has been synthesised with the aim of producing a specific effect, e.g. muscle growth

desmin *noun* a filament found in skeletal and smooth muscle tissues

detached retina *noun* an injury to the eye in which the retina becomes loose, usually affecting vision and caused by a heavy blow

detachment training *noun* athletic training that helps athletes to ignore unnecessary stimuli such as crowd noise when performing

deteriorate *verb* to become worse

detox *noun* (*informal*) **1.** a medical facility in which alcoholics or drug addicts are detoxified **2.** the detoxification of an alcoholic or drug addict

detoxication *noun* the process in which toxic compounds in the body are metabolised into ones that can be excreted

detoxification *noun* **1.** the process of removing a toxic substance from something or counteracting its toxic effects **2.** the process of subjecting yourself to withdrawal from a toxic or addictive substance such as alcohol or drugs

detoxify *verb* to subject somebody or yourself to withdrawal from a toxic or addictive substance such as alcohol or drugs

detraining *noun* the effects seen when an athlete stops training, including loss of flexibility, agility and skills

deuce *noun* (*in tennis, badminton and other racket sports*) a situation in which a player must score two successive points to win after the score is tied

dexterity *noun* ease and skill in physical movement, especially in using the hands and manipulating objects

dexterous *adjective* characterised by ease and skill in physical movement, especially in using the hands and manipulating objects

dextrose *noun* same as **glucose**

DHA *noun* a polyunsaturated essential fatty acid found in cold-water fish and some algae that has been linked to the reduction of cardiovascular disease and other health benefits. Full form **docosahaexanoic acid**

diabetes *noun* a disorder in which the amount of glucose in the blood is too high because the body does not produce enough of the hormone insulin needed to convert the glucose from food into energy

dialogue *noun* a formal discussion or negotiation in which both parties put their views

diamond *noun* **1.** the area of a baseball field bounded by home plate and the three bases **2.** an area for playing baseball including the infield and the outfield

diamorphine *noun* the drug heroin when used medicinally as a painkiller

diapedesis *noun* a condition in which blood leaks through the apparently unruptured walls of blood vessels into surrounding tissue, as a reaction to severe inflammation or injury

diaphragm *noun* a thin layer of tissue stretched across an opening, especially the flexible sheet of muscle and fibre that separates the chest from the abdomen and moves to pull air into the lungs in respiration

diaphysis *noun* the long central part of a long bone. Also called **shaft**

diarrhoea *noun* a condition in which someone frequently passes liquid faeces

diarthrosis *noun* free movement of a joint that is not restricted by cartilage or ligaments

diastasis *noun* **1.** a condition in which a bone separates into parts **2.** dislocation of bones at an immovable joint

diastole *noun* the part of the process involved in each beat of the heart when its chambers expand and fill with blood. The period of diastole lasts about 0.4 seconds in an average heart rate. Compare **systole**

diastolic *adjective* relating to the diastole

diastolic blood pressure *noun* the pressure of blood in a person's artery when the heart contracts, shown written over the systolic blood pressure reading. Compare **systolic blood pressure**

diathermy *noun* heat treatment used for relieving sports injuries using microwaves or short waves

diet *noun* **1.** the amount and type of food eaten **2.** the act of eating only particular types of food, in order to become thinner, to cure an illness or to improve a condition

dietary *adjective* relating to food eaten

dietary fat *noun* fat from food, which is an essential nutrient and also transports other nutrients such as fat-soluble vitamins

dietary fibre *noun* food materials that cannot by hydrolysed by digestive enzymes and are therefore important for digestive health, found in fruit and grains. Also called **roughage**, **non-dietary polysaccharides**

dietary guidelines *plural noun* public advice on healthy eating

dietary intake *noun* the amount of a nutrient that a person receives through their diet

dietary reference value *noun* the amount of a particular nutrient that is recommended per person per day by official bodies

dietary supplement *noun* ♦ supplement

diet drink *noun* a drink that is low in calories or is a reduced-calorie version of a popular drink

dieter *noun* someone who is on a diet, especially a weight-loss diet

dietetic *adjective* relating to diets

dietetic foods *plural noun* food designed for people with specific nutritional requirements

dietetics *noun* the study of food and its nutritional value

diethylpropion *noun* an anorectic drug used for treating obesity

diet-induced thermogenesis *noun* an increase in heat production in the body after eating. Abbreviation **DIT**

differential relaxation *noun* the ability to consciously relax muscles that are not being used for a particular movement so as not to waste energy

diffident *adjective* lacking self-confidence

diffusion *noun* **1.** the process of mixing a liquid with another liquid, or a gas with another gas **2.** the passing of a liquid or gas through a membrane

digastric *adjective* used for describing a muscle, especially the muscle on either side of the lower jaw, in which two fleshy parts are connected by a tendon

digest *verb* to break down food in the stomach and intestine and convert it into elements that can be absorbed by the body

digestibility *noun* the percentage of a food that is digested and absorbed

digestible *adjective* possible to digest

digestion *noun* the act of breaking down food in the stomach and intestine and converting it into elements that can be absorbed by the body

digestive enzyme *noun* an enzyme in the digestive system that aids the biochemical breakdown of food in the body

digestive system *noun* the set of organs that comprises the stomach, liver and pancreas, responsible for the digestion of food. Also called **alimentary system**

digital *adjective* relating to the fingers or toes

digital scales *plural noun* personal weighing scales that give a digital reading

digital skipping rope *noun* a skipping rope with a digital monitor in the handle that counts the number of rotations

dilatation *noun* the widening of a cavity or passage such as the aorta, increasing the volume of blood that is pumped

dilator *noun* **1.** an instrument used for widening the entrance to a bodily cavity **2.** a drug used for making part of the body expand

diluent *noun* a substance used for diluting a liquid, e.g. water

dinghy *noun* a small boat, especially one with one mast and sails, used for recreation or racing

dip *noun* an exercise on parallel bars in which the elbows are bent until the gymnast's chin is level with the bars, and the body raised by straightening the arms

diploe *noun* a layer of spongy bone tissue filled with red bone marrow, between the inner and outer layers of the skull

diplopia *noun* double vision, often caused by a heavy blow to the head or eye region

dipsesis *noun* an unusually great thirst, or a craving for unusual drinks

dipsetic *adjective* provoking thirst

dipsogen *noun* something that provokes thirst

dipyridamole *noun* a drug that widens the blood vessels, used for treating angina and preventing the formation of blood clots

direct free kick *noun* ♦ **free kick**

dirt track *noun* a track of earth mixed with gravel and cinders that is used for horse racing or motorcycle racing

disability *noun* a condition in which part of the body does not function in the usual way and makes some activities difficult or impossible. ◊ **learning disability**

disability sport *noun* a sport such as boccia that is suitable for, or specially designed or adapted for, athletes with disabilities

disarticulate *verb* to separate something at the joints, or come apart at the joints

disc *noun* a flat round structure. ◊ **intervertebral disc**

disciplinary hearing *noun* a formal investigation by a sports federation into banned substance use by an athlete under their jurisdiction

discipline *noun* **1.** the ability to behave in a controlled and calm way even in a difficult or stressful situation **2.** mental self-control used in directing or changing behaviour, learning something or training for something **3.** a particular field of activity within a wider context, e.g. the discipline of javelin within athletics or of the parallel bars within gymnastics

disclaimer *noun* a statement refusing to accept responsibility for something, e.g. a denial of legal liability for any injury associated with a product

discomfort *noun* a feeling of mild pain

discounting principle *noun* (*in performance feedback*) the tendency of an athlete to reject the advice of a coach if it is felt that the coach has a generally negative or unfair viewpoint

discrete skill *noun* a skill that has an easily discernible beginning, middle and end, e.g. hitting a ball

discriminate *verb* to treat one person or group unfairly, usually because of prejudice about race, ethnicity, age, religion or gender

discrimination *noun* the act of treating one person or group unfairly, usually because of prejudice about race, ethnicity, age, religion or gender

discus *noun* **1.** a weighted disc thrown in competitions by an athlete who spins with outstretched arms to launch it from the flat of his or her hand **2.** an athletics event in which the contestants compete to throw a discus as far as possible

disinhibition *noun* conditioning that reverses the inhibitory effect of something such as the Golgi organs

disinhibition training *noun* training carried out to desensitise the Golgi organs in skeletal muscle tendons, so that they can be stretched further

dislocate *verb* to displace a bone from its usual position at a joint, or to become displaced

dislocated *adjective* used for describing a joint that is out of alignment, usually as a result of a fall or heavy blow

dislocation *noun* a condition in which a bone is displaced from its usual position at a joint. Also called **luxation**

disordered eating *noun* unusual eating habits that may present a risk to health, without exhibiting all the symptoms of a recognised eating disorder

disorientation *noun* feeling lost or confused, especially with regard to direction or position, sometimes as a result of a head injury

dispensable amino acids *plural noun* same as **non-essential amino acids**

displaced *adjective* used for describing an organ or bone that is not in the correct position

displaced fracture *noun* a fracture in which the pieces of bone move out of alignment with each other

displaced intervertebral disc *noun* a disc which has moved slightly, so that the soft interior passes through the tougher exterior and causes pressure on a nerve

displacement *noun* **1.** the fact of being moved out of the usual position **2.** the inappropriate transference of feelings from one situation to another, such as when taking out aggression caused by an earlier incident on an innocent person

disqualification *noun* the state of being disqualified from competition

disqualified *adjective* of a sports team or athlete, prevented from taking part in a competition because of a rules violation

disqualify *verb* to prevent a sports team or athlete from taking part in a competition because of a rules violation

dissociation *noun* the act of ignoring irrelevant stimuli such as crowd noise when competing so as to better concentrate on the game

dissociative *adjective* used for describing the attentional style of an athlete who tends to focus more on external stimuli

dissociator *noun* a type of athlete who needs to concentrate on external stimuli and blot out internal thoughts or sensations in order to perform, e.g. a player of team sports

distal *adjective* used for describing a body part situated away from the main trunk of the body

distance *noun* a measurement of the space between two points

distance running *noun* running that is over a considerable distance, e.g. marathon running

distend *verb* to expand, swell, or inflate as if by pressure from within, or cause something to do this

distended *adjective* made larger by gas such as air, by liquid such as urine, or by a solid

distension *noun* a condition in which something is swollen

distraction injury *noun* a stain or rupture caused by incorrect responses to neural stimuli, e.g. contracting a muscle when it should be stretched, caused by fatigue or stress

disuse *noun* the fact or condition of not being used, applied, or followed, especially for a long time

diuresis *noun* an increase in the production of urine

diuretic *noun* a substance that increases the production of urine

dive *verb* **1.** to perform a pattern of acrobatic movements in the air ending in a headfirst plunge into water, especially as a sport **2.** to swim below the surface of a stretch of water, often with special breathing apparatus

diving board *noun* a raised board at the edge of a swimming pool from which to dive into the water

diving reflex *noun* a reflex in which the heart rate slows and blood vessels of the skin narrow on immersion in cold water to conserve oxygen

division *noun* a group of teams of roughly similar standard in a sports league

division of labour *noun* the way in which a team divides tasks up between the players for maximum efficiency

dizziness *noun* the feeling that everything is going round because the sense of balance has been affected

dizzy *adjective* feeling that everything is going round because the sense of balance has been affected

DNA *noun* a chemical substance that is contained in the cells of all living things and carries their genetic information. Full form **deoxyribonucleic acid**

docosahaexanoic acid *noun* full form of **DHA**

dominant *adjective* important or powerful

DOMS *abbreviation* delayed onset muscle soreness

dopamine *noun* a substance found in the medulla of the adrenal glands, which also acts as a neurotransmitter

dopaminergic system *noun* part of the central nervous system responsible for motivational, emotional and cognitive processes, e.g. learning and attention

dope *noun* **1.** a drug given illegally to affect performance **2.** an illegal drug, especially cannabis (*slang*) ■ *verb* to add a drug to food or drink secretly in order to affect performance

dopehead *noun* somebody who takes illegal drugs regularly or who is physiologically or mentally dependent on them (*slang*)

dopester *noun* US somebody who is able to supply information and analysis about current events and forecasts for the future, especially in the fields of sport and politics (*informal*)

doping *noun* the use of illegal drugs, e.g. steroids, in sport

doping control officer *noun* an official who oversees the selection of athletes for drugs testing. Abbreviation **DCO**

doping control station *noun* an office where urine samples are given by athletes for drugs testing

doping marker *noun* ♦ **marker 2**

dormant *adjective* inactive for a time. Compare **active**

dorsal *adjective* **1.** relating to the upper back. Opposite **ventral 2.** relating to the back of the body

dorsiflexion *noun* flexion towards the back of part of the body, e.g. raising the foot at the ankle. Compare **plantar flexion**

dorsum *noun* the back of any part of the body

dose-related response *noun* a human response to a stimulant that varies according to the amount it is exposed to

double *noun* **1.** success in two events or competitions in the same year or series or against the same opponent **2.** (*in cue games*) a stroke that makes the ball rebound against a cushion and land in the opposite pocket **3.** (*in baseball*) a hit that enables a batter to reach second base

double-blind testing *noun* a form of blind testing in which the researchers are not aware which subjects are receiving the supplement and which are receiving a placebo until the results have been collected and analysed. Compare **single-blind testing**

double fault *noun* (*in tennis*) two consecutive serves that land outside the service box or in the net, with the result that the server loses a point

double-fault *verb* (*in tennis*) to make two consecutive faulty serves and lose a point as a result

double pull *noun* the twin action produced by agonist and antagonist muscles contracting and lengthening simultaneously

doubles *plural noun* a racket game played between two pairs of players

Douglas bag *noun* a piece of equipment for measuring VO2 and other breathing assessments

downhill *noun* a skiing race against the clock down a long mountainside course with several hundred yards between marker flags

drag *noun* the resistance experienced by a body moving through a fluid medium, especially by a swimmer when travelling through the water

drag racing *noun* the sport or activity of racing cars with specially modified bodies and engines over a distance of a 1/4 of a mile at extremely high speeds

draw *noun* **1.** the act of selecting at random which contestants are to play each other in a sporting contest, or the resulting list of matches to be played **2.** a contest that ends with both sides having the same score or with neither side having won ■ *verb* **1.** to finish a game with the scores for the opposing sides level or with neither side having won **2.** (*in golf*) to hit a ball so that it curves in flight following the direction of the golfer's swing instead of travelling straight

dream team *noun* the best possible combination of people to perform a task

dressing *noun* a bandage or other sterile covering put on a wound to protect it from infection or further damage

dribble *verb* to move a ball along using small repeated movements of the foot, the hand or a stick ■ *noun* a movement or run made while dribbling a ball, especially in football or basketball

drill *noun* a sequence of tasks or exercises repeated over and over until they can be performed faultlessly, as used in teaching sports skills ■ *verb* to make someone repeat a sequence of exercises or procedures over and over again in order to learn it

drive *verb* **1.** in some sports, to kick or hit a ball forcefully **2.** (*in golf*) to hit a long shot from either a tee or a fairway when covering the principal distance between holes **3.** (*in basketball*) to dribble the ball through a particular area of the court towards the basket **4.** (*in cricket*) to strike the ball very hard and straight with the bat held vertically ■ *noun* **1.** energy and determination that helps someone achieve what he or she wants to do **2.** in some sports, a forceful shot or stroke in hitting a ball **3.** (*in golf*) a long shot played from either a tee or fairway, when covering the principal distance between two holes **4.** (*in basketball*) a fast direct run towards the basket while dribbling the ball

drop *verb* **1.** to let something such as a ball fall **2.** to lose a match, game or part of a game

drop goal *noun* (*in rugby*) a goal scored by dropping the ball and then kicking it

drop handlebars *plural noun* (*on a racing bicycle*) handlebars that curve downwards, enabling the rider to adopt a more aerodynamic posture

drop kick *noun* **1.** (*in rugby or American football*) a method of kicking a ball on the half-volley by dropping it from the hands **2.** (*in amateur wrestling*) an illegal move in which one wrestler attacks another by leaping into the air and striking an opponent with both feet

drop shot *noun* in racket games, a shot in which the ball drops abruptly to the ground just after passing over the net or hitting the wall

drubbing *noun* a total or humiliating defeat over an opponent or opposing team (*informal*)

drug-nutrient interaction *noun* the effect of a medication on the proper function, absorption or use of a nutrient

drug-testing programme *noun* a systematic attempt to test some or all of the athletes in a sporting competition for banned substances

drying out *noun* same as **cutting up**

DSM *abbreviation* deep stroking massage

duathlete *noun* an athlete who takes part in a duathlon

duathlon *noun* a sports event in which athletes compete in two endurance events, e.g. cross-country skiing and rifle shooting, or running and swimming

dumbbell *noun* an exercise weight in the form of a metal bar with a metal disc or ball at each end

dumbbell bench press *noun* a bench press performed using dumbbells

dumbbell flyes *plural noun* flyes performed using dumbbells, often lying down

dumbbell lunge *noun* a lunge performed using dumbbells to give extra weight

dumbbell pullover *noun* a pullover performed using a dumbbell held in each hand

dumbbell rack *noun* a sturdy piece of gym equipment for holding dumbbells securely

dumbbell triceps extension *noun* an exercise in which a dumbbell is raised and lowered behind the back with the arms held over the head

dummy *noun* in football, rugby or a similar game, a feigned pass or other move intended to deceive an opponent, especially a tackler ■ *verb* to make a dummy in football, rugby or a similar game

duration *noun* the length of time for which something continues

duration-related response *noun* a human response to a stimulant that varies according to the time spent exposed to it

Dutoit staple capsulorrhaphy *noun* treatment for a weak shoulder joint that repeatedly dislocates, in which the glenoid labrum is stapled to the shoulder socket

dynamic balance *noun* the act of balancing while on a moving surface

dynamic conditioning *noun* the conditioning of muscles through sports that involve free movement

dynamics *noun* the branch of mechanics that deals with motion and the way in which forces produce motion

dynamic stretching *noun* stretching that involves some movement but does not force the muscle past its range of motion

dynamogeny *noun* the supposed effect on a runner of having faster athletes alongside them, stimulating nervous energy that gives them greater speed

dynamometer *noun* an instrument for measuring the force of muscular contraction

dynamometry *noun* the act of measuring the force of muscular contraction

dysbaria *noun* any disorder caused by differences between the atmospheric pressure outside the body and the pressure inside, e.g. when diving

dysdiadochokinesia *noun* the inability to carry out rapid movements, caused by a disorder or lesion of the cerebellum

dysfunctional *adjective* used for describing an organ or other part or system of the body that is unable to function regularly as a result of disease or impairment

dyshydria *noun* an unusual production of sweat, either excessive or insufficient

dyskinesia *noun* impairment of control over ordinary muscle movement, often resulting in spasmodic movements or tics

dysorexia *noun* a disorder of the appetite, e.g. anorexia nervosa or persistently uncontrolled eating

dysplasia *noun* an unusual development of tissue

dyspnoea *noun* a disruption to a person's usual breathing, e.g. unusual shortness of breath or pain experienced when breathing

dyspraxia *noun* difficulty in carrying out coordinated movements

dysreflexia *noun* any disorder of the reflexes

dysrhythmia *noun* an unusual rhythm, either in speaking or in electrical impulses in the brain

dyssynergia *noun* a lack of muscular co-ordination caused by a brain disorder

dystaxia *noun* a lack of muscular co-ordination

dysthymia *noun* persistent depression that has symptoms such as fatigue, low self-esteem, insomnia and appetite disturbances but is not severe enough to amount to a psychosis

dystonia *noun* a neurological disorder that causes involuntary muscle spasms and twisting of the limbs

dystrophin *noun* a protein found in muscle that is missing in people with muscular dystrophy

dystrophy *noun* the wasting of an organ, muscle or tissue owing to lack of nutrients in that part of the body

dysvitaminosis *noun* a disease caused by either a deficiency or excess of a particular vitamin

E

early response *noun* same as **ineffective anticipation**

East Asian Games *plural noun* a multi-sport event for athletes from the northeast Asian area, including China, Mongolia and North and South Korea, held every four years

easy set *noun* a set of exercises that are not challenging, used as a warm-up

easy wicket *noun* (*in cricket*) a wicket on which the ball bounces predictably and a batsman can score runs relatively easily

eating disorder *noun* an illness that causes the usual pattern of eating to be disturbed, e.g. anorexia or bulimia

Eating Disorders Association *noun* an organisation that provides support and information for people suffering from eating disorders and their families. Abbreviation **EDA**

eburnation *noun* the conversion of cartilage into a hard mass with a shiny surface like bone

ECA stack *noun* a thermogenic sports supplement containing ephedrine, caffeine and aspirin

eccentric action *noun* an action performed by extending a muscle

eccentric contraction *noun* a situation in which a muscle is tense, but lengthening, as of the arm muscles when slowly lowering a heavy weight

eccentric strength *noun* the force exerted by a muscle while it is extending

ecchymosis *noun* a dark area on the skin made by blood that has escaped into the tissues after a blow. Also called **bruise**

ECG *noun* a graph showing the behaviour of the heart by recording its electrical voltage, produced by a device called an electrocardiograph. Full form **electrocardiogram**

echinacea *noun* a herbal remedy prepared from the pulverised leaves and stems of purple coneflowers, thought to bolster the immune system

écorché *noun* an anatomical model of part or all of the human body with the skin removed, to allow study of the muscle structure

ectomorph *noun* a body type that is tall, thin and possibly underweight. Compare **endomorph**

edge *noun* an advantage over somebody, e.g. a competitor ■ *verb* **1.** to move gradually sideways, or make something move in this direction by pushing it **2.** to strike a ball or other object with the edge of a cricket bat **3.** to put weight down on the outer or inner side of a ski so that its edge cuts into the snow

EFA *abbreviation* essential fatty acid

effective anticipation *noun* reaction to an anticipated stimulus before it is actually given, resulting in quicker reaction times

effector *noun* **1.** a nerve ending in muscles or glands that is activated to produce contraction or secretion **2.** a muscle movement or other bodily action that brings about a desired effect

effector muscle *noun* a muscle that performs an intended action

efferent *adjective* carrying something away from part of the body or from the centre. Opposite **afferent**

efferent nerve *noun* same as **motor nerve**

efficacy *noun* the ability of an individual to use their skills to achieve something

efficiency *noun* **1.** the ability to make a physical movement with a minimum of unnecessary effort **2.** a comparison of the effective or useful output to the total input in any system

efficient *adjective* referring to the ability to act or produce something with a minimum of waste, expense or unnecessary effort

effleurage *noun* a form of massage in which the skin is stroked in one direction to increase blood flow

effort *noun* mental or physical energy that is exerted in order to achieve a purpose

effort headache *noun* a short-lived headache that is brought on by strenuous physical exercise

effusion *noun* a fluid-filled swelling in the body caused by injury

elapsed time *noun* the measured amount of time or actual duration of a sporting event such as a race

elastic *adjective* able to stretch and contract

elastic bandage *noun* a stretchy bandage used for supporting a weak joint

elastic fibre *noun* a smooth long thin fibre in connective tissue, composed mainly of the fibrous protein elastin

elastic strength *noun* the ability to contract a muscle swiftly in order to overcome a resistance

elastic tissue *noun* body tissue that is composed mainly of elastic fibres and is found in the skin, the walls of arteries, and some ligaments and tendons

elastin *noun* a fibrous protein resembling collagen that is the main constituent of the elastic fibres of connective tissue

elbow support *noun* an elastic wrap that protects the elbow from injury during exercise

electrical impedance analysis *noun* same as **bioelectrical impedance analysis**

electrical muscle stimulation *noun* a form of training in which an electrical current is passed through muscles to force them to contract. Abbreviation **EMS**

electrical stimulation *noun* same as **TENS**

electrocardiogram *noun* full form of **ECG**

electrocardiograph *noun* an apparatus for measuring and recording the electrical impulses of the muscles of the heart as it beats

electrolyte *noun* a substance in cells, blood or other organic material that helps to control fluid levels in the body and maintain normal pH levels

electrolyte balance *noun* the levels of electrolytes in the blood, which should be neither too high, to avoid overloading the kidneys, nor too low, to avoid weakness and malnutrition

electrolyte drink *noun* same as **sports drink**

electromyogram *noun* a chart showing the electric currents in active muscles. Abbreviation **EMG**

electromyograph *noun* a machine for producing a graphical tracing of the electrical activity picked up via electrodes inserted into muscle tissue

electromyopathy test *noun* a medical test for the proper conduction of electrical signals from nerves to muscles

electrophysiology *noun* the study of electrical impulses in the human body

electrotherapeutic treatment *noun* treatment of injuries using a mild electrical current applied to the body

electrotherapy *noun* the treatment of a disorder, e.g. some forms of paralysis, by using low-frequency electric current to try to revive the muscles

eleuthero *noun* a stimulant sports supplement that may increase metabolism

elevate *verb* to raise something or to lift something up

elevated *adjective* 1. raised to a higher place or position 2. increased

elevation *noun* the act of raising a limb to a higher point

eleven *noun* a team of 11 players, e.g. a football team or cricket team

elicit *verb* to get a response or measurement by performing an action that will provoke it, e.g. by stretching a painful limb to find the source of pain

eliminate *verb* to defeat a player or team and put them out of a competition

elimination tournament *noun* a series of games, bouts or contests in which a player or team is removed from competition after being defeated

elite *adjective* more talented, privileged or highly trained than others

elitism *noun* the belief that some people or things are inherently superior to others and deserve pre-eminence, preferential treatment, or higher rewards because of their superiority

elitist *adjective* a person who believes in elitism

elliptical trainer *noun* an exercise machine that works both the upper and lower body simultaneously

emaciation *noun* bodily wasting caused by malnutrition

embolism *noun* a condition in which an artery is blocked by a blood clot, interrupting normal blood circulation

embrocation *noun* same as **liniment**

emetatrophia *noun* bodily wasting caused by an inability to keep food down

eminence *noun* something that protrudes from a surface, e.g. a lump on a bone or swelling on the skin

emotional eating *noun* the consumption of food in response to feelings of stress or sadness, rather than hunger

empty calorie *noun* food that contains energy but no nutrients

EMS *abbreviation* electrical muscle stimulation

enarthrosis *noun* movement of a joint in all directions by a ball-and-socket arrangement, e.g. that at the hip and shoulder joints

encapsulate *verb* to enclose a nutrient, enzyme or other desirable substance within a vehicle such as a lipid, so that it is most efficiently delivered to its source

encapsulated *adjective* enclosed in a capsule or in a sheath of tissue

encephalin *noun* either of two chemicals with opiate qualities that are secreted in the brain and spinal cord and act to relieve pain

enclosure *noun* an area of ground at a sports event set aside for specific spectators or competitors

end *noun* **1.** half of a playing field or court, defended by one side **2.** (*in American football*) a player positioned at each end of the offensive or defensive line **3.** (*in curling and bowls*) a phase of play in a particular direction across the rink, green or other playing area

end line *noun* a line at the end of a court or field that marks the boundary of a playing area

endocardium *noun* a membrane which lines the heart

endocrine gland *noun* any gland of the body that secretes hormones directly into the blood or lymph, e.g. the thyroid, pituitary, pineal and adrenal glands

endocrine system *noun* the adrenal glands, pancreas and sexual organs collectively, which secrete hormones regulating growth, metabolism, tissue function and reproductive processes

endocrinology *noun* the study of the endocrine system, its function and effects

endogenous *adjective* originating or growing within an organism or tissue

endomorph *noun* a body type that is short, stocky and easily puts on weight. Compare **ectomorph**

endomysium *noun* connective tissue around and between muscle fibres

endorphin *noun* a peptide produced by the brain that acts as a natural painkiller. ◊ **encephalin**

endosteum *noun* a membrane lining the bone marrow cavity inside a long bone

endurance *noun* the ability or power to bear prolonged exertion, pain or hardship

endurance athlete *noun* an athlete who has a high level of aerobic fitness

endurance training *noun* exercises designed to increase an athlete's level of aerobic fitness

enduro *noun* a long race, especially one involving motorcycles or cars, in which the emphasis is on endurance rather than speed

energy *noun* the force or strength to carry out activities

energy balance *noun* a mathematical relationship between the number of calories a person consumes and the number they expend

energy bar *noun* a bar-shaped snack made of ingredients intended to boost physical energy

energy-dependent *adjective* used for describing a sport that involves a great deal of movement or effort and is therefore reliant on energy metabolism, e.g. running or swimming

energy drink *noun* same as **sports drink**

energy expenditure *noun* the amount of energy used during a particular activity such as running or walking

energy level *noun* the amount of energy that a person has over the course of the day, related to such factors as blood sugar levels, activity and how rested they are

energy requirements *plural noun* the number of calories needed to sustain the daily activity of an individual

energy supplement *noun* a supplement designed to give a person more energy, which may contain caffeine, B vitamins, sugar or herbal preparations

energy therapy *noun* a holistic method of healing using energy supposedly contained in and surrounding the human body, mind and spirit

energy value *noun* the amount of energy produced by a given amount of a particular food

enrich *verb* **1.** to improve the nutritional quality of food **2.** to improve the living conditions of farm animals, e.g. by providing them with larger living areas

enriched *adjective* used for describing food that has had vitamins and minerals added to make it more nutritious

enrichment *noun* the act of adding vitamins, minerals or other nutrients such as milk proteins to food, to make it more nutritious

enterovirus *noun* any virus that lives in the gastrointestinal tract but may multiply there and invade other parts of the body, e.g. poliomyelitis

enthesis *noun* the point at which a tendon joins to a bone

enthesitis *noun* inflammation of, or damage to, an enthesis

enthesopathy *noun* an inflammation or disease of an enthesis

enzyme *noun* a protein substance produced by living cells that aids a biochemical reaction in the body

enzyme activation assay *noun* a test of enzyme activity in red blood cells that reveals vitamin deficiencies

enzyme defect *noun* a metabolic disorder caused by a deficiency of a particular enzyme

enzyme precursor *noun* same as **proenzyme**

ephedra *noun* a plant used as a stimulant and slimming aid, containing ephedrine

ephedrine *noun* a drug that relieves asthma and blocked noses by causing the air passages to widen

epicardium *noun* the inner layer of the pericardium which lines the walls of the heart, outside the myocardium

epicritic *adjective* used for describing nerve fibres in the skin that are sensitive to fine distinctions in touch and temperature stimuli

epidemiological study *noun* a statistical study of medical conditions that affect a portion of a population, their causes, symptoms and possible preventative measures

epiglottis *noun* a flap of cartilage at the root of the tongue which moves to block the windpipe when food is swallowed, so that the food does not go down the trachea

epimysium *noun* a connective tissue binding striated muscle fibres

epinephrine *noun* same as **adrenaline**

epineurium *noun* a sheath of connective tissue round a nerve

epiphysis *noun* the rounded end of a long bone

epistaxis *noun* same as **nosebleed**

EPO *abbreviation* erythropoietin

equaliser *noun* a goal scored which makes the scores of each team equal

equestrian *adjective* relating to horses or riding ■ *noun* somebody who is skilled at riding horses or performing on horseback

equestrianism *noun* same as **horseriding**

erector spinae muscles *plural noun* the group of muscles in the lower back which flex and move the spine

erg, ergo *noun* same as **ergometer**

ergogenic *adjective* used for describing a stimulant that gives greater energy or improved mental capacity

ergograph *noun* a piece of equipment that records the work of one or several muscles

ergolytic *adjective* having a negative effect on muscle capacity

ergometer *noun* an instrument for measuring muscle power or work done by muscles, e.g. when exercising

ergonomic *adjective* designed for maximum comfort, efficiency, safety, and ease of use, especially in the workplace

ergospirometry *noun* the act of performing spirometry during exercise to measure gas metabolism

erythema *noun* same as **rubor**

erythrocyte *noun* a mature red blood cell

erythropoietin *noun* a banned substance that artificially increases the red blood cell count in the body, increasing oxygen transfer. Abbreviation **EPO**

essential amino acid index *noun* a measure of protein quality, expressed as its total amino acid content as compared to egg protein

essential amino acids *plural noun* the eight amino acids that are essential for growth but cannot be synthesised and so must be obtained from food or medicinal substances

essential fatty acid *noun* an unsaturated fatty acid that is essential for growth but cannot be synthesised and so must be obtained from food or medicinal substances. Abbreviation **EFA**

e-stim *abbreviation* electrical stimulation. ◊ **TENS**

estimated average requirement *noun* the amount of a particular nutrient that is estimated to be consumed per person per day by official bodies. Abbreviation **EAR**

estrane *noun* a steroid hormone derived from testosterone

ethical *adjective* **1.** concerning ethics, or reasonable or acceptable from a moral point of view **2.** used for describing a drug that is available on prescription only

EU *abbreviation* European Union

euplastic *adjective* referring to tissue which heals well

eurhythmics *noun* a system of physical exercise, therapy and musical training in which the body moves rhythmically and gracefully in interpretation of a piece of music

EuroGames *plural noun* a multi-sport event open to participants from all European nations, with an emphasis on gay and lesbian acceptance

European Union *noun* a group of European countries linked together by the Treaty of Rome, basing their cooperation on the freedoms of movement of goods, capital, people and services. Abbreviation **EU**

eusitia *noun* the state of having a normal appetite

Eustachian tube *noun* a bony passage extending from the middle ear to the nasopharynx that has a role in equalising air pressure on both sides of the eardrum

eustress *noun* a feeling of tension that is positive and enjoyable, as in fierce competition

eutrophia *noun* a normal state of nutrition

evaluate *verb* **1.** to examine and calculate the quantity or level of something **2.** to examine someone who is ill or injured and calculate the medical treatment they require

evaporative heat loss *noun* bodily cooling achieved by the evaporation of sweat from the skin

event *noun* **1.** an action or activity **2.** an organised activity in which several players or teams compete against each other

eversion *noun* the act of turning towards the outside or turning inside out

evodiamine *noun* a thermogenic stimulant used by athletes

exchange diet *noun* a weight-loss plan in which the types of food eaten do not matter as long as they add up to the correct number of calorie

exchange lists *plural noun* tables that show which foods contain equivalent numbers of calories, for use in planning an exchange diet

excitable *adjective* used for describing a nerve or tissue that is able to respond to a stimulus

excite *verb* to stimulate or increase the rate of activity of an organ, tissue or other body part

excretion *noun* the act or process of discharging waste matter from the tissues or organs

executor *noun* someone who performs an action or task

exercise *noun* **1.** physical or mental activity, especially the active use of the muscles as a way of keeping fit, correcting a deformity or strengthening a part **2.** a particular movement or action designed to use and strengthen the muscles ■ *verb* **1.** to undertake physical exercise in order to keep fit and healthy **2.** to subject the body, or part of it, to repetitive physical exertion or energetic movement in order to strengthen it or improve its condition

exercise adherence *noun* motivation to exercise and stay physically fit for its own sake

exercise ball *noun* a large inflated ball used in exercises to strengthen muscles and improve flexibility and balance

exercise bike *noun* a fitness machine in the form of a stationary bicycle that is pedalled vigorously for exercise

exercise challenge *noun* a medical test in which an athlete performs aerobic exercise while his or her breathing patterns are monitored, designed to diagnose exercise-induced asthma

exercise class *noun* same as **fitness class**

exercise headache *noun* same as **effort headache**

exercise-induced anaphylaxis *noun* a condition in which an athlete experiences anaphylaxis-like symptoms after exercise, often linked to food consumption

exercise-induced asthma *noun* asthma that is caused by exercise such as running or cycling. Abbreviation **EIA**

exercise intensity *noun* the degree to which a workout is difficult for the exerciser

exercise machine *noun* a machine that is specially designed to allow a person to perform a particular exercise or tone a particular area

exercise music *noun* music with about 120 beats per minute that is suitable for accompanying aerobics and other exercises

exercise platform *noun* a low step-like platform used for performing step aerobics

exercise prescription *noun* a personal fitness plan or guidelines given by a professional for health reasons

exercise program *noun* same as **fitness program**

exerciser *noun* **1.** a piece of equipment used for exercising the body **2.** someone who exercises racehorses

exergonic reaction *noun* a chemical reaction in which energy is released

exert *verb* to make a strenuous physical or mental effort

exertion *noun* physical activity

exfoliate *verb* to remove or shed a thin outer layer from something such as a bone during surgery

exhalation *noun* **1.** the act of breathing out **2.** air that is breathed out ▶ opposite **inhalation**

exhale *verb* to breathe out. Opposite **inhale**

exhibition game *noun* a sports contest played purely as a display of skill and an entertainment for spectators, with no prizes or competition points at stake

exocrine gland *noun* a gland that releases a secretion through a duct to the surface of an organ, e.g. the sweat and salivary glands

exogenous *adjective* developing or caused by something outside the organism. Compare **endogenous**

exogenous nitrogen *noun* nitrogen in the body that comes from dietary sources, as opposed to metabolic nitrogen

exostosis *noun* a benign growth on the surface of a bone

expectation *noun* **1.** a confident belief or strong hope that a particular event will happen **2.** a standard of conduct or performance expected by or of somebody

expenditure *noun* the act of using energy

expiration *noun* the act or process of breathing out

expiratory loop *noun* the volume of air that is expired at each point during a full forced expiration. A normal expiratory loop should involve a gradual tapering of the amount expired towards the end.

expire *verb* same as **exhale**

extended length conditioning *noun* same as **deep-range conditioning**

extensible *adjective* capable of being stretched

extension *noun* **1.** the stretching or straightening out of a joint **2.** the stretching of a joint by traction

extensor *noun* a stretchy band that is pulled between feet and arms to exercise muscles

externaliser *noun* a personality type in which the individual believes that what happens to them is controlled to a large degree by external variables. Compare **internaliser**

externally paced *adjective* used for describing skills that are performed under pressure in reaction to some outside change in situation

external obliques *plural noun* a pair of abdominal muscles that run diagonally inwards from the outer ribs to the pelvis

external overload *noun* a situation in which an athlete cannot block out distracting external stimuli and his or her performance suffers

external rotation *noun* movement of a ball-and-socket joint so that the limb turns outwards

extra time *noun* an additional fixed period played at the end of a match if the scores are equal at full time and a decisive result is needed

extravasate *verb* to leak, or cause blood or other fluid to leak, from a vessel into surrounding tissue as a result of injury, burns or inflammation

Extreme Games *plural noun* an international sports contest, modelled on the Olympic Games, involving competitions in extreme sports

extreme sport *noun* a sport considered more dangerous and thrilling than ordinary sports and often involving hazardous airborne stunts and tricks

extrinsic motivation *noun* motivation to achieve a goal out of a desire to win a prize

extroverted *adjective* **1.** interested in people and things other than oneself **2.** turned inside out

eyebath *noun* a small dish into which a solution can be put for bathing the eye

eye tracking *noun* the act of watching a moving ball

F

faceguard *noun* a protective grille worn to protect the face in certain sports, e.g. baseball and American football

face off *verb* (*in ice hockey, lacrosse and similar sports*) to start or restart play by dropping the puck or ball between two opposing players

face shield *noun* a piece of protective sports equipment that covers the head and face and protects them from flying objects

facet *noun* a flattish surface on a bone

facet joint *noun* the joint between each vertebra, formed of an intervertebral disc

facet joint syndrome, facet syndrome *noun* a condition in which a joint in the vertebrae becomes dislocated

facial nerve *noun* the seventh cranial nerve, which governs the muscles of the face, the taste buds on the front of the tongue and the salivary and lacrimal glands

fad diet *noun* a diet that is fashionable and often unusual or extreme, followed for a short time

faddy *adjective* tending to have strongly held likes and dislikes about food

fade *verb* **1.** to lose strength **2.** (*in golf*) to hit a ball so that, in a right-handed shot, it curves slightly from left to right, or be hit in this way ■ *noun* (*in golf*) a shot in which the ball curves slightly from left to right in the air

fail *verb* **1.** not to be successful in doing something **2.** to become weaker and less likely to recover

failure *noun* a lack of success in or at something

failure-orientated *adjective* used for describing a competing athlete who is keen to win in order to avoid the disappointment of failure, rather than for the joy of succeeding

fairway *noun* the closely mown area on a golf hole that forms the main avenue between a tee and a green

faith healer *noun* a healer who attempts to treat illness or disorders through prayer, sometimes also by touching the affected person

fakie *adverb* (*in skateboarding*) while moving backwards on the board

fall *noun* in wrestling, a scoring move in which a wrestler forces the opponent's shoulders to the floor for a specific period ■ *verb* to drop or be dropped or lowered

fallen arches *plural noun* a condition in which the arches in the sole of the foot are not high

false rib *noun* one of the bottom five ribs on each side that are not directly attached to the breastbone

false start *noun* a situation in which a competitor in a race breaks a regulation governing the starting procedure and the race has to be restarted

famine response *noun* same as **ketosis**

faradise *verb* to stimulate a nerve or muscle using an alternating current

faradism *noun* the therapeutic application of an alternating electric current to stimulate nerve and muscle function

fartleck training *noun* same as **interval training**

fascicle *noun* a bundle of branches, leaves or stems arising from the same point

fast break *noun* in team sports, a swift counterattack made in an attempt to score before the opposing players have the chance to recover their defensive positions

fast fibre *noun* same as **fast twitch fibre**

fasting *noun* the practice of going without food

fast twitch fibre *noun* a type of muscle fibre that contains high levels of ATP and is able to contract swiftly

fat burning *noun* the consumption of fat reserves by the body for energy, reducing visible body fat, usually achieved by increasing activity levels or decreasing calorie intake

fat content *noun* the amount of fat in a foodstuff, usually measured in grams

fat-free *adjective* used for describing foods that contain no animal or vegetable fat

fat-free mass *noun* all body tissues not containing fat, including bone, muscle, organs, hair, blood and retained water

fatigue *noun* very great tiredness

fatigue fracture *noun* same as **stress fracture**

fat-soluble vitamins *plural noun* vitamins A, D, E and K, which are not soluble in water

fatty acid *noun* same as **essential fatty acid**

featherweight *noun* (*in professional boxing*) a weight category for competitors whose weight does not exceed 57.1 kg or 126 pounds

FEC *abbreviation* forced expiratory capacity

federation *noun* a group of various bodies or parties that have united to achieve a common goal

feeble *adjective* lacking physical or mental strength or health

feedback *noun* comments in the form of opinions about and reactions to something such as athletic performance, intended to provide useful information for future development

feint *noun* a deceptive move in a competitive sport

felodipene *noun* a drug used for treating high blood pressure

female athlete triad *noun* a syndrome sometimes suffered by dedicated female athletes, consisting of the three interrelated health problems of disordered eating, amenorrhoea and bone loss

femoral *adjective* relating to the thigh

femoral neck stress fracture *noun* a fracture of the femur occurring to the narrowest part of the bone, caused by high-impact activities such as running

femoral nerve *noun* a nerve which governs the muscle at the front of the thigh

femoral pulse *noun* a pulse taken from a major artery in the thigh

femur *noun* the bone in the top part of the leg that joins the acetabulum at the hip and the tibia at the knee. Also called **thighbone** (NOTE: The plural is **femora**.)

femur width *noun* an anthropometric measure of thigh breadth

fence *verb* to fight using a slender sword, formerly in combat, now as a competitive sport

fencing *noun* the art or practice of fighting with slender swords, formerly in combat, now as a competitive sport

FEV1 *noun* a measure of the amount of air that a person can forcefully expire in one second. Full form **forced expiratory volume 1**

fibre *noun* 1. a structure in the body shaped like a thread 2. same as **dietary fibre**

fibrillation *noun* rapid chaotic beating of the heart muscles in which the affected part of the heart may stop pumping blood

fibroma *noun* a nonmalignant tumour of fibrous connective tissue such as cartilage

fibromyalgia *noun* a disorder causing aching muscles, sleep disorders, and fatigue, associated with raised levels of the brain chemicals that transmit nerve signals (**neurotransmitters**)

fibrosis *noun* a thickening and scarring of connective tissue most often following injury, infection, lack of oxygen or surgery

fibrositis *noun* a painful inflammation of the fibrous tissue that surrounds muscles and joints, especially the muscles of the back

fibrous joint *noun* a joint where fibrous tissue holds two bones together so that they cannot move, as in the bones of the skull

fibula *noun* the thinner of the two bones in the lower leg between the knee and the ankle. Compare **tibia** (NOTE: The plural is **fibulae**.)

fibulare *noun* one of the three ankle bones in the feet that form a joint with the fibula

field *noun* 1. an open expanse of ground kept or marked out as a playing area for a particular sport 2. all the participants in a race or other competitive event 3. all the participants in a race or competitive event except the leader, winner, or favourite 4. a particular arrangement of cricket fielders around the wicket ■ *verb* 1. in cricket, rounders or baseball, to retrieve, pick up or catch a ball in play, usually after it has been struck by the person batting 2. in cricket, rounders or baseball, to act as a fielder

field captain *noun* a leader of a team who decides on tactics and strategy and is authorised to discuss penalties with officials

fielder *noun* in cricket, rounders or baseball, a player who is positioned on the field of play to catch or retrieve the ball when it is struck by the person batting

field event *noun* an athletics event that takes place on an open area not on a track, e.g. the discus, javelin, long jump, or high jump

field goal *noun* 1. (*in American football*) a score worth three points, made by kicking the ball over the crossbar from a point about ten yards behind the line of scrimmage 2. (*in basketball*) a goal made during normal play by throwing the ball through the basket, worth two points, or three points if scored from beyond a specific distance

field sports *plural noun* outdoor country sports that involve killing or capturing animals, especially hunting, shooting, and fishing

field testing *noun* testing for something such as biomechanical analysis, carried out at the athlete's usual training ground, for maximum authenticity of results. Compare **lab testing**

fighter *noun* a competitor in a full-contact sport such as boxing or taekwondo

fight-or-flight reaction *noun* a set of physiological changes, including an increase in heart rate, blood pressure and the flow of epinephrine, that constitutes the body's instinctive response to impending danger or other stress

figure skating *noun* a form of competitive skating in which skaters trace patterns on the ice and perform spins, jumps, and other manoeuvres

fine motor skills *plural noun* the coordination of several small muscles to achieve a complex or subtle movement, as occurs, e.g., when making a facial expression. Compare **gross motor skills**

finish *noun* the final part of a race, especially a sprint, acceleration or challenge, near the finishing line

finishing line *noun* a real or imaginary line that marks the end of a race

fins *plural noun* broad flat rubber extensions worn on the feet to aid in swimming or diving. Also called **flippers**

firepower *noun* the capability or potential of a person, team or organisation for effective action

first eleven *noun* in football, cricket and other team sports with eleven players per team, the best of several teams competing for the same club at different levels

first fifteen *noun* in rugby, the best of several teams competing for the same club at different levels

fish oil *noun* oil obtained from fish, considered beneficial to health because it contains essential fatty acids and vitamins A and D

fit *adjective* strong and physically healthy (NOTE: **fitter – fittest**)

fitness *noun* the fact of being strong and healthy

fitness belt *noun* a belt that makes use of electronic massage to tone the muscles of the abdomen

fitness centre *noun* same as **leisure centre**

fitness class *noun* a group session of exercise such as yoga, spinning or aerobics, led by a fitness instructor

fitness equipment *noun* equipment used for exercise, including exercise machines, weights, benches and storage racks

fitness goal *noun* a target that a person hopes to achieve through a fitness program, e.g. increased flexibility, cardiovascular fitness or muscle development

fitness instructor *noun* a professional who gives other people advice and training for fitness, often employed by a leisure centre or gym, or who works as a personal trainer

fitness level *noun* how fit a person is, from absolute beginner to trained athlete

fitness program *noun* a suitable and coordinated program of exercise undertaken in order to meet a particular fitness goal

fitness rings *plural noun* a type of extensor

fitness testing *noun* professional assessment of a person's fitness level in order to develop a suitable exercise program

Fitt's and Posner's stages *plural noun* a theory developed in 1967 that describes the three stages of skill acquisition. ◊ **cognitive stage, associative stage, autonomous stage**

five-a-day *noun* the government-recommended guideline of eating at least 5 portions of fruit and vegetables a day for health

five-a-side *noun* football with five players in each team, including the goalkeeper, usually played indoors

fixator *noun* **1.** a muscle that immobilises a bone or joint, allowing movements to be performed without straining these **2.** a metal rod placed through a bone to keep a part of the body rigid

fixed joint *noun* a joint in the body where the bones are fused, not allowing any movement, as is the case with the bones of the skull

fixed weight *noun* a weight that is attached to a weightlifting machine. Compare **free weight**

fixture *noun* a sports event or its date

flame-out *noun* a form of burnout that occurs for a short period of time, usually after a heavy training season or competition

flat feet *plural noun* feet in which the arches are very low or non-existent. Compare **high-arched feet**

flat racing *noun* horse racing over level ground, without fences to be jumped

flavonoid *noun* a natural compound derived from phenol, belonging to a group that includes many plant pigments

flesh *noun* the soft part of the body covering the bones

flesh wound *noun* a wound that only affects the fleshy part of the body

fletching *noun* the feathered end on an arrow used in archery, which helps to stabilise it in flight

flex *verb* **1.** to bend something, especially a joint in the body **2.** to move or tense a muscle, or become tense or contracted

flexibility *noun* **1.** the amount or extent to which something can be bent **2.** the extent to which something can change or respond to a variety of conditions or situations

flexibility training *noun* regular exercise that increases the body's flexibility, e.g. yoga or Pilates

flexible *adjective* able to bend or be bent repeatedly without damage or injury

flexion *noun* the act of bending a joint

flexor *noun* a muscle that bends a joint or limb when it is contracted

flick *noun* (*in hockey*) a penalty shot taken from the penalty spot

flick-on *noun* (*in football and hockey*) a light touch on a moving ball with the foot, head or a stick, intended to guide it towards a teammate

flippers *plural noun* same as **fins**

float *noun* a buoyant rectangular board that supports the arms and top of the body of a swimmer, used for learning to swim and for kicking training

floating rib *noun* either of the two lowest ribs on each side, which are not attached to the breastbone

floor exercise *noun* an event in a gymnastics competition that consists of a series of tumbling exercises in a timed routine performed on a mat

floor guard *noun* a covering that protects a gymnasium floor from damage

fluid balance *noun* the maintenance of the balance of fluids in the body during training

fluid replacement *noun* the act of replacing lost fluids and salts after heavy exercise, sometimes by using a special sports drink

fluids *plural noun* all liquids that rehydrate the body, including water, cordials, fruit juice, tea and coffee

flush *verb* to artificially increase the size of muscles before a bodybuilding competition by using special exercises to fill them with blood

flutter kick *noun* a swimming technique that consists of moving the legs rapidly up and down in short strokes

flyes *plural noun* exercises performed using weights held in either hand, in which the arms are held horizontal and swung from the front to the sides of the body

fly-half *noun* (*in rugby*) a player who plays behind the forwards and the scrum half, provides a link between them and the three-quarter backs, and often has control of the team's tactics. Also called **stand-off half**

flying disc *noun* same as **Frisbee**

flying start *noun* a start of a race in which competitors cross the starting line at racing speed

flyweight *noun* (*in professional boxing*) a weight category for competitors whose weight does not exceed 51 kg or 112 lb

foam *noun* **1.** a mass of bubbles of air or gas in a liquid film **2.** a light, porous, semi-rigid or spongy material used for thermal insulation or shock absorption

focus *noun* **1.** concentrated effort or attention on a particular thing **2.** the aim of something, e.g. a fitness programme or a competitive tactic **3.** the centre of an infection (NOTE: The plural is **foci**.)

folate *noun* **1.** same as **folic acid 2.** a salt or ester of folic acid

folic acid *noun* a vitamin in the vitamin B complex found in milk, liver, yeast and green vegetables such as spinach, essential for creating new blood cells

follow through *verb* to continue the movement of an arm or leg past the point of contact or of release after hitting, throwing or kicking a ball or other object

follow-through *noun* the continuation of the movement of an arm or leg past the point of contact or of release after hitting, throwing or kicking a ball or other object

food additive *noun* same as **additive**

food allergy *noun* a reaction caused by sensitivity to particular foods, some of the commonest being nuts, strawberries, chocolate, milk, eggs and oranges

food combining *noun* the practice of eating different types of food at different times in the belief that this aids digestion and weight loss

food composition *noun* the percentages of each nutrient present in a particular foodstuff

food diary *noun* a note of all food eaten by a person over a particular period, used by a dietetic professional to assess their diet

food energy *noun* the amount of digestible energy provided by food

food exchange diet *noun* same as **exchange diet**

food group *noun* a general category under which foods are grouped, e.g. fats, proteins, dairy, fruits, vegetables and grains

food intolerance *noun* a sensitivity to, or an inability to digest, a particular food, ingredient or substance, which means that it should be excluded from the diet

food stacking *noun* the idea of eating nutrients in a particular order to allow them to be digested in the most efficient manner

football *noun* **1.** *UK* a game in which 2 teams of 11 players try to kick or head a round ball into the goal defended by the opposing team. Also called **soccer 2.** any game in which two teams kick or carry a ball into a goal or over a line, e.g. rugby, Australian Rules or Gaelic football **3.** the large round ball used in the game of football

football boots *plural noun* a pair of strong shoes with studs, worn for playing football

football ground *noun* a place where football matches take place, including the field on which the game is played, the area where the spectators sit or stand, and any associated buildings

football pitch *noun* the rectangular field on which football is played

football strip *noun* the clothing, of a distinctive colour or combination of colours, worn by the members of a particular football team and sometimes by their supporters

foot-eye coordination *noun* the ability to perform tasks that involve coordinating the movement of the feet and eyes, as does, e.g., kicking a ball

foot fault *noun* in tennis, a fault committed by a server whose foot touches any part of the baseline or court before the ball has been hit

foot loop *noun* an extensor fixed at one end to the floor

footwear *noun* coverings worn on the feet, especially shoes, boots, sandals or slippers, but often including socks or stockings

foramen *noun* a natural opening inside the body, e.g. the opening in a bone through which veins or nerves pass (NOTE: The plural is **foramina**.)

forced expiratory capacity *noun* the amount of air that can be forcibly expelled in the first few seconds of a forced vital capacity test. Abbreviation **FEC**

forced expiratory volume 1 *noun* full form of **FEV1**

forced rep *noun* a repetition of an exercise that is difficult and uncomfortable, designed to push the body to build more muscle

forced vital capacity *noun* the amount of air that can be expelled after inhaling the maximum possible amount into the lungs

force platform *noun* a piece of equipment like a set of scales that measures the force exerted by the athlete during a jump or action, used for performance testing

forecourt *noun* the part of the court nearest the net or front wall in games such as tennis, badminton and handball

forehand *noun* (*in racket games*) a basic stroke played with the palm of the racket hand facing forwards ■ *adjective, adverb* (*in racket games*) played with the palm of the racket hand facing forwards, or relating to a stroke played in this way ■ *verb* in racket games, to hit the ball with a forehand stroke

foreign body *noun* an unwanted substance or object in a place in the body where it does not belong, often introduced from an external location and causing irritation or contamination

form *noun* **1.** the condition of a player, team or athlete with regard to fitness, health and ability to perform well **2.** the posture and positioning in which a person does something such as lift a weight **3.** (*in some martial arts*) a formal series of movements, used either for training or to demonstrate technique

form drill *noun* an exercise that is designed to improve form and technique in a particular activity

forming *noun* the first stage of team development according to the Tuckman model, in which the team is put together and their goals and objectives set out

formula diet *noun* a diet of simple substances that do not need digesting

fortified *adjective* same as **enriched**

forward *noun* an attacking player in some team sports, e.g. football, rugby, hockey and basketball

forward pass *noun* (*in rugby*) an illegal pass in which the ball goes forward

forward roll *noun* in gymnastics, a movement in which the body is rolled over in a forward direction, placing the head on the ground and bringing the feet over the head

fossa *noun* a shallow hollow in a bone or the skin

foul *noun* an illegal action against an opposing player, or an action that breaks the rules of a sport ■ *verb* to act illegally against an opposing player, or break a rule of a sport

foul line *noun* **1.** (*in baseball*) either of the lines extending from home plate through first and third bases to the end of the playing field **2.** (*in basketball*) either of two lines on a court from which players get unobstructed chances to score a basket after they have been fouled. Also called **free-throw line 3.** (*in some other sports*) a boundary beyond which a ball or player is not permitted, e.g. the line in ten-pin bowling where the player must stop before releasing the ball

foul play *noun* **1.** unfair action or behaviour **2.** action that is contrary to the rules of a sport

four-four-two *noun* (*in football*) one of the most common outfield team formations comprising four defenders, four midfielders and two attackers

fracture *noun* a break in a bone

frame *noun* **1.** the particular size and shape of someone's body **2.** a solid support for something

frame of mind *noun* someone's psychological state, attitude or mood at a specific time

franchise *noun* US **1.** a professional sports team that is a member of an organised league (*informal*) **2.** an agreement or licence to own a sports team **3.** a player who is valuable and important to a team (*informal*)

freediving *noun* the extreme sport of submerging into deep water for as long as possible without the aid of oxygen tanks

free fatty acids *plural noun* fatty acids in the blood that are unattached to any other molecule, an important source of fuel. Abbreviation **FFA**

freeheel skiing *noun* a form of skiing in which the heel is not fixed down to the skis. Also called **telemark skiing**

free kick *noun* in football, a kick of a stationary ball awarded for an infringement by a member of the opposing team, who must stand at least ten yards from where the kick is taken. A goal can be scored by a player taking a direct free kick, whereas an indirect free kick requires that the ball touch another player before entering the goal.

free radical *noun* an atom or group of atoms that is highly reactive owing to the presence of an unpaired electron (NOTE: Because of the effect they have on cells in the body, free radicals are thought to be a contributory cause of medical conditions such as cancer, atherosclerosis and Alzheimer's.)

free riding *noun* a basic style of snowboarding that involves travelling over the snow without performing stunts

freeskiing *noun* the sport of skiing on downhill skis that have curved tips front and back, permitting the skier to execute moves similar to those of snowboarders on slopes and in half-pipes

free-standing *adjective* standing alone, not fixed to a wall, floor or other structure for support

freestyle *adjective* used for describing events in such sports as figure skating, surfing and downhill skiing in which any manoeuvre can be performed, with the contestants judged on their athleticism, technique and artistry

free throw *noun* (*in basketball*) an opportunity to shoot at the basket unhindered by the opposing players, awarded to a player who has been fouled

free-throw line *noun* same as **foul line**

free weight *noun* a weight that is not attached to a weightlifting machine, in the form of, e.g., a barbell or dumbbell. Compare **fixed weight**

frequency *noun* **1.** the number of times something takes place in a given time **2.** the rate of vibration in oscillations

friction *noun* deliberate rubbing of a body part as a way of stimulating blood circulation, warming or relieving pain

friction blister *noun* a blister caused by repeated chafing of the skin, as by sports clothing or footwear

Frisbee a trade name for a plastic disc thrown from person to person in a game

frontenis *noun* a form of Jai Alai played on a smaller court with tennis rackets

frozen shoulder *noun* same as **adhesive capsulitis**

fructose *noun* the sugar found in honey and fruits such as figs

frustration *noun* a feeling of disappointment, exasperation or weariness caused by not getting something expected or desired

full back *noun* (*in sports such as football, rugby and hockey*) a player in a defensive position

full time *noun* (*in football and other sports*) the end of a match

fumble *verb* to fail to catch a ball ■ *noun* an act or instance of fumbling

functional food *noun* food, often containing additives, that is said to be beneficial to health and able to prevent or reduce diseases such as tooth decay and cancer

functional overload *noun* training in a particular sport in which the athlete wears heavier clothes or shoes or carries weights to work the muscles harder

functional short leg *noun* ♦ **short leg**

functional strength training *noun* training that helps to develop strength needed for everyday activities, such as for those who do a lot of lifting in their job

fun run *noun* a noncompetitive run over a moderately long course, organised to promote health and fitness or to raise money for charity

fusiform *adjective* of a muscle, having a fleshy body which tapers towards a single tendon at either end, such as with the biceps brachii

FVC *abbreviation* forced vital capacity

G

GABA *abbreviation* gamma-aminobutryic acid

Gaelic football *noun* a game played in Ireland with 15 players on each side, the aim of which is to punch or kick a ball into or over a goal

gait *noun* a way of walking

gait analysis *noun* biomechanical analysis of a person's walking style, including stride length, pronation, balance and posture

gala *noun* a sporting event, especially a swimming contest, with a variety of different races and competitions

galvanic skin response *noun* increased sweating and blood flow caused by a strong emotion such as fear

galvanise *verb* to stimulate the nerves or muscles of someone's body using an electric current

galvanism *noun* medical treatment that applies low-voltage electricity directly to a muscle or nerve

game *noun* **1.** a sporting or other activity in which players compete against each other by following a fixed set of rules **2.** an occasion when a competitive game is played **3.** in sports such as tennis, a subsection of play that goes towards making up a set or match **4.** the total number of points needed to win a contest

game plan *noun* **1.** a strategy that someone devises to achieve a goal **2.** the strategy that a team or player devises for use during a game

game point *noun* **1.** (*in sports such as tennis and badminton*) a situation in which one player or side has only to win the next point in order to win the game **2.** same as **match point**

games *plural noun* **1.** an event that consists of many different sporting activities and usually lasts for several days **2.** gymnastics, athletics, team sports, and other forms of physical exercise taught to children at school

Games of the Small States of Europe *plural noun* an annual athletic championship for European countries with a population of less than one million, including Andorra, Cyprus, Malta and Iceland. Abbreviation **GSSE**

gamma-aminobutryic acid *noun* a stimulant and secretagogue used by athletes. Abbreviation **GABA**

ganglion *noun* **1.** a mass of nerve cell bodies and synapses usually covered in connective tissue, found along the peripheral nerves with the exception of the basal ganglia **2.**

a cyst of a tendon sheath or joint capsule, usually at the wrist, that results in a painless swelling containing fluid (NOTE: [all senses] The plural is **ganglia**.)

gas analysis *noun* a breakdown of the components of a gas, especially the breath, that can detect any medical abnormalities

gas exchange *noun* the process by which oxygen in the air is exchanged in the lungs for waste carbon dioxide carried by the blood

gastric emptying *noun* the speed with which ingested food is processed and removed from the stomach into the intestines

gastric reflux *noun* the regurgitation of gastric juices into the oesophagus, where the acid causes irritation and the burning sensation commonly referred to as heartburn

gastrocnemius *noun* the largest muscle in the calf of the leg, extending from the thigh bone to the Achilles tendon

gate *noun* **1.** in rowing, a fastening with a hinge that serves to keep an oar in its rowlock **2.** a device for controlling the passage of water or gas through a pipe

Gay Games *plural noun* an international multi-sport event that places an emphasis on gay and lesbian acceptance but is open to all participants, regardless of sexual orientation

gene *noun* a unit of DNA on a chromosome which governs the synthesis of a protein sequence and determines a particular characteristic

gene doping *noun* genetic engineering that allows an athlete to perform better at their sport

general fitness *noun* a non-athlete's fitness for performing everyday tasks, achieved by eating a healthy diet and taking moderate exercise

General Medical Council *noun* in the UK, the official body that licenses qualified doctors to practise medicine. Abbreviation **GMC**

General National Vocational Qualification *noun* in the UK, a qualification designed to provide vocationally orientated skills and knowledge for progression from school to employment or university. Abbreviation **GNVQ**

genetic *adjective* relating to or contained in genes

genetic engineering, genetic manipulation *noun* the combination of genetic material from different sources to produce organisms with altered characteristics

geniculate *adjective* **1.** bent at an angle like a knee **2.** with a joint or joints that can be bent like a knee

genoa *noun* a very large triangular front sail on a sailing boat, especially a racing yacht

Gestalt psychology *noun* a branch of psychology that treats behaviour and perception as an integrated whole and not simply the sum of individual stimuli and responses

Gestalt therapy *noun* a form of psychotherapy in which emphasis is placed on feelings and on the influence on personality development of unresolved personal issues from the past

giant killer *noun* a person or team that defeats a superior or better-known opponent

Gilmore's groin *noun* same as **groin disruption**

ginglymus *noun* movement of a joint in a hinge-like motion, e.g. the motion of the elbow and the knee

ginkgo biloba *noun* a herbal preparation made from the pulverised leaves of the ginkgo tree, used in the treatment of circulatory and cardiovascular disorders

girdle *noun* a set of bones that make a ring or arch

gladiolus *noun* the middle section of the sternum

glance *verb* **1.** to strike something briefly or lightly at an angle **2.** (*in cricket*) to hit a bowled ball with the bat held at an angle so that the ball is deflected to the leg side

gland *noun* an organ in the body containing cells that secrete substances such as hormones, sweat or saliva which act elsewhere

Glasgow coma scale *noun* a system for assessing the severity of brain impairment in someone with a brain injury that uses the sum of scores given for eye-opening, verbal and motor responses

glenohumeral *adjective* relating to both the glenoid cavity and the humerus

glenohumeral joint *noun* the shoulder joint, a ball and socket joint that is the most mobile in the body

glenoid *adjective* shaped like a small shallow cup or socket

glenoid cavity *noun* the socket at the shoulder to which the glenoid labrum is attached

glenoid labrum *noun* a strong band of tissue that connects the ligaments to the socket at the shoulder joint

global strength *noun* the overall muscle strength of a person's body

glossopharyngeal nerve *noun* the ninth cranial nerve which controls the pharynx, the salivary glands and part of the tongue

glove *noun* a padded protective covering for the hand worn in some sports

glow *noun* a brightness or redness in someone's complexion, e.g. as a result of exercise or good health

glucagon *noun* a hormone secreted by the islets of Langerhans in the pancreas, which increases the level of blood sugar by stimulating the breakdown of glycogen

glucocorticoid *noun* a natural steroid hormone that regulates carbohydrate digestion

glucokinase *noun* an enzyme in the liver that plays a key role in carbohydrate metabolism

gluconeogenesis *noun* the production of glucose in the liver from protein or fat reserves

glucosamine *noun* a glucose derivative found in supportive tissues and plant cell walls

glucosamine sulphate *noun* a supplement used by athletes that is thought to help rebuild damaged cartilage

glucose *noun* a simple sugar found in some fruit, but also broken down from white sugar or carbohydrate and absorbed into the body or secreted by the kidneys

glucose intolerance *noun* an inability to metabolise a high dose of glucose, indicative of diabetes

glucose tablet *noun* a supplement of glucose in a solid form, taken for extra energy

glucose tolerance *noun* the ability to metabolise a high dose of glucose, which is a test for diabetes

glucosuria *noun* the presence of glucose in the urine, an indicator of diabetes

glucuronic acid *noun* an acid derived from glucose that is present in cartilage and detoxifies poisons

glutamic acid *noun* an amino acid

glutamine *noun* an amino acid that is also used as a supplement by weightlifters and bodybuilders

gluteal *adjective* relating to the buttocks

gluteals *plural noun* the three gluteus muscles

gluten *noun* a protein found in some cereals that makes the grains form a sticky paste when water is added

gluten-free *adjective* used for describing foods that do not contain gluten

glutes *plural noun* same as **gluteals**

gluteus *noun* one of three muscles in the buttocks, responsible for movements of the hip, the largest being the **gluteus maximus** and the smaller two being the **gluteus medius** and **gluteus minimus**

glycaemia *noun* the level of glucose found in the blood. ◊ **hypoglycaemia, hyperglycaemia**

glycaemic effect *noun* the extent to which a food containing carbohydrate can raise blood sugar levels

glycaemic index *noun* a points rating for different types of food, based on their glycaemic effect. Abbreviation **GI**

glycaemic load *noun* a rating for different types of food based on the amount of carbohydrate that they contain, as well as the extent to which this raises blood sugar levels

glycine *noun* an amino acid

glycogen *noun* a type of starch, converted from glucose by the action of insulin, and stored in the liver as a source of energy

glycogenesis *noun* the synthesis of glycogen from glucose by insulin

glycogenolysis *noun* the breakdown of glycogen into glucose

glycogen storage disease *noun* a condition in which the liver and muscles accumulate excess amounts of glycogen

GMC *abbreviation* General Medical Council

GNVQ *abbreviation* General National Vocational Qualification

goal *noun* **1.** in a game such as football or hockey, the space or opening into which a ball or puck must go to score points, usually a pair of posts with a crossbar and often a net **2.** the score gained by getting the ball or puck into the goal **3.** a successful attempt at hitting, kicking, or throwing a ball or hitting a puck into a goal **4.** something you are striving to do or achieve **5.** a final state reached when a task has been finished or has produced satisfactory results **6.** in Australian Rules football, six points, scored by kicking the ball between the two goal posts

goal area *noun* in football, the rectangular area marked out in front of the goal within which goalkeepers may handle the ball

goalball *noun* a game developed for athletes with visual impairments, played using a ball with bells inside that can be tracked by the sound it makes

goal difference *noun* in football and other sports, the difference between the number of goals scored for and against a team in a specific competition. It is often used as a decider between teams with equal points.

goalkeeper *noun* in games such as football and hockey, a defensive player positioned in or near a goal whose main task is to keep the ball or puck from crossing the goal line into the goal

goal kick *noun* **1.** (*in football*) a free kick taken from the six-yard-line by a defensive player when the ball has been driven out of play over the goal line by an opposing player **2.** (*in rugby*) a free kick by a member of the attacking team, aimed at clearing the defenders' crossbar and designed to convert a five-point try into a seven-point score

goal line *noun* (*in games such as football, rugby and hockey*) the line where goalposts are positioned and over which the ball must pass or be carried to make a score

goalpost *noun* in games such as football and hockey, either of two posts, usually supporting a crossbar between them, that together mark the boundary of the goal

going *noun* the state of the ground as it affects ease and speed of movement, especially for horses in a race

golden goal *noun* formerly in some football competitions, the first goal scored in extra time after a drawn game, which decides the winning team

gold medal *noun* a medal that is made of gold or something representing gold, given as a first prize for excellence or winning a competition

golf *noun* an outdoor game in which an array of special clubs with long shafts are used to hit a small ball from a prescribed starting point into a series of holes. The object of the game is to complete the course in as few strokes as possible.

golf ball *noun* a small hard ball used for playing golf

golfer's elbow *noun* same as **medial epicondylitis**

Golgi organ *noun* a sensory organ at the point where a tendon attaches to skeletal muscle, which measures the degree of tension and inhibits over-stretching

good cholesterol *noun* cholesterol that is transported away from cells and tissue by high density lipoprotein (*informal*)

goofy *adjective* (*in skateboarding, snowboarding and similar sports*) used for describing a stance on the board in which the rider's right foot is nearer the front end (*slang*)

googly *noun* in cricket, a ball that looks like a leg break on delivery and then moves unexpectedly in the opposite direction after it pitches

gout *noun* pain caused by crystallisation of uric acid in the joints

governing body *noun* a group of people appointed to supervise and regulate a field of activity or institution

grade 1 injury *noun* (*in sports medicine*) an injury in which tissue has been stretched or bruised but not seriously damaged

grade 1 sprain *noun* (*in sports medicine*) the mildest form of sprain, in which there is pain but minimal damage to the tissue

grade 2 injury *noun* (*in sports medicine*) an injury in which tissue has been moderately damaged, causing some loss of function

grade 2 sprain *noun* (*in sports medicine*) a form of sprain in which there is a moderate amount of damage to the tissue

grade 3 injury *noun* (*in sports medicine*) an injury in which tissue has been severely damaged, causing total loss of function

grade 3 sprain *noun* (*in sports medicine*) the most severe form of sprain, in which the tissue is very damaged

Graham diet *noun* a dietary plan that is wholly vegetarian and allows fats only in small quantities

grand prix *noun* any of a number of important international annual races for racing cars, held to decide the world motor-racing championship

grand slam *noun* **1.** (*in sports such as tennis and golf*) the winning of all of a series of major competitions by one player or team in one year **2.** (*in sports such as tennis and golf*) a major competition that is part of a series **3.** (*in baseball*) a home run made when the bases are loaded

grandstand *noun* an open structure or platform, usually with a roof, containing rows of seats for spectators at a sports stadium or racecourse

grandstand finish *noun* a finish to a race or competition that is exciting because the outcome is unclear until the very end

grappling *noun* (*in combat sports such as wrestling and martial arts*) the act of holding your opponent to subdue or control them

Gravity Games *plural noun* any of various extreme sports tournaments held around the world

green *noun* the closely mown area at the end of a fairway on a golf course on which the hole for the ball is located

green card *noun* (*in hockey*) a card shown by the referee to a player as a warning for dangerous play or misconduct. ◊ **red card**, **yellow card**

greenstick fracture *noun* a type of fracture, occurring in children, in which a long bone bends but is not completely broken

grey matter *noun* nerve tissue which is of a dark grey colour and forms part of the central nervous system

groin *noun* the area of the body between the tops of the thighs and the abdomen

groin disruption *noun* a tendon strain occurring in the pelvic region of male athletes, usually caused by overuse

groin hernia *noun* same as **inguinal hernia**

groin itch *noun* same as **tinea cruris**

groin strain *noun* a strain of the adductor magnus or sartorius muscles, causing pain in the groin

groin support *noun* a piece of protective clothing that reduces the risk of developing a hernia, used by weightlifters

gross anatomy *noun* the study of the structure of the body that can be seen without the use of a microscope

gross motor skills *plural noun* the use of groups of large muscles to achieve a simple movement, as, e.g., when walking or swinging the arm. Compare **fine motor skills**

ground rule *noun* a sports rule that is specific to a particular place of play

ground substance *noun* the solid, semisolid or liquid material that exists between the cells in connective tissue, cartilage or bone

group aspiration *noun* a goal that all members of a team would like to achieve, working together

growth hormone *noun* same as **somatotrophin**

growth spurt *noun* ♦ **adolescent growth spurt**

grudge match *noun* a match between players or teams who have a long-standing animosity between them or a specific past insult or injury to revenge

GSSE *abbreviation* Games of the Small States of Europe

GTP *abbreviation* guanosine triphosphate

guanosine triphosphate *noun* a nucleotide made of guanosine linked to three phosphate groups. Abbreviation **GTP**

guard *noun* **1.** (*in basketball*) either of the two players who regularly defend the backcourt and initiate attacks **2.** (*in cricket*) a position taken by a batsman when ready to receive a bowled ball **3.** (*in American football*) each of two attackers on each side of the centre

gumshield *noun* a hard plastic cover that fits inside somebody's mouth over the teeth and gums, worn as protection from injury by people involved in contact sports such as boxing and rugby

gun lap *noun* the last lap of an athletics race, signalled by the firing of a gun as the leading runner begins it

guns *plural noun* the biceps (*slang*)

gym *noun* a room or building with equipment for physical exercise of various kinds (*informal*)

gym ball *noun* a piece of gym equipment like a large inflatable ball, used when performing some exercises

gym mat *noun* a soft floor covering used for protecting a gym floor or for comfort when performing exercises on the floor

gymnasium *noun* a hall equipped for physical exercise or physical training of various kinds, e.g. in a school or a private club

gymnast *noun* an athlete who performs gymnastics, especially as a competitive sport

gymnastic *adjective* **1.** relating to or involving gymnastics **2.** involving or demonstrating athleticism and agility

gymnastics *noun* **1.** physical training using equipment such as bars, rings and vaulting horses, designed to develop agility and muscular strength **2.** the competitive sport in which athletes perform a series of exercises on pieces of gymnastic equipment

gym rat *noun* somebody who spends a lot of time exercising or playing a sport at a gymnasium (*informal*)

gym shoe *noun* same as **plimsoll**

gynecomastia *noun* enlarged breasts on a man caused by hormonal imbalance or hormone therapy

H

habit *noun* **1.** an action that is an automatic response to a stimulus **2.** a regular way of doing something

habituation *noun* reduced muscle shivering after prolonged exposure to cold, which can lead to hypothermia

hack *verb* (*in rugby or football*) to commit a foul by kicking the shins of an opposing player

haemarthrosis *noun* pain and swelling caused by blood leaking into a joint

haematinic *adjective* promoting the healthy growth of blood cells in bone marrow

haematocrit *noun* the red blood cell count in the body, which, when high, may indicate use of the banned substance erythropoietin

haematology *noun* the branch of medicine devoted to the study of blood, blood-producing tissues and diseases of the blood

haematoma *noun* a mass of blood under the skin caused by a blow or by the effects of an operation

haematuria *noun* the presence of blood in the urine, as a result of injury to or disease of the kidneys, ureters, bladder or urethra

haem iron *noun* dietary iron found in meat and seafood. Compare **non-haem iron**

haemochromatosis *noun* an excess of iron in the body that can cause tissue damage and discoloration of the skin

haemoglobin *noun* a red pigment in red blood cells that gives blood its red colour and carries oxygen to the tissues. Abbreviation **Hb**

haemorrhage *noun* the loss of blood from a ruptured blood vessel, either internally or externally ▪ *verb* to bleed heavily

haemosiderin *noun* an insoluble protein that contains iron, produced by the action of phagocytes on haematin

haka *noun* a version of a traditional Maori war dance performed by sports teams, especially the New Zealand rugby team

half back *noun* (*in a team sport*) a player who is positioned just in front of the last defensive line

half-marathon *noun* a race on foot over a distance equivalent to half a marathon, 13 miles 352 yards

half-pipe *noun* a structure in the shape of the bottom half of a pipe, built for freestyle snowboarding, in-line skating and skateboarding

half-time *noun* a short break between the halves of a game, during which players rest

half volley *noun* a stroke or shot that makes contact with the ball immediately after it has bounced

half-volley *verb* to strike a ball immediately after it has bounced

hallux rigidus *noun* stiffness of the joint at the big toe, caused by the cartilage wearing away

hallux valgus *noun* a deformity of the big toe in which the joint points outwards and the tip points inwards, often leading to bunions

hamate *noun* a small hook-shaped bone in the wrist, at the base of the third and little fingers

hammer *noun* a heavy metal ball attached to a handle of flexible wire, thrown in an athletics field event

hammer throw *noun* a field event in which competing athletes try to throw a heavy metal ball attached to a handle of flexible wire as far as they can

hammer toe *noun* a toe that has the middle joint permanently bent downwards

hamstring *noun* one of a group of tendons behind the knee that the thigh muscles to the bones in the lower leg

hamstring muscle *noun* a muscle belonging to a group of three at the back of the thigh that control leg movements such as flexing the knee

hamstring stretch *noun* a stretch in which the athlete sits on the floor with one leg extended out in front and pulls the top of the foot back towards the body, extending the hamstring

hamulus *noun* a hook-shaped part at the end of a bone

handball *noun* **1.** (*in football*) a rule infringement committed when a player other than a goalkeeper inside his or her penalty area uses a hand to control the ball **2.** a game for two or four people in which players hit a small hard ball against a wall with their hands **3.** the small hard ball used in the game of handball

hand-eye coordination *noun* the ability to perform tasks that involve coordinating the movement of the hands and eyes, e.g. catching or hitting a ball

hand grip *noun* a resistant piece of equipment used to develop hand strength

handicap *noun* **1.** a contest, especially a horse race, in which individual competitors are given an advantage or disadvantage in an attempt to give every contestant an equal chance **2.** a compensation in strokes given to a golfer on the basis of skill in past performances

handlebar palsy *noun* same as **ulnar neuropathy**

hand plant *noun* (*in skateboarding*) a move in which the board is held to the feet with one hand while the skateboarder performs a handstand on a ramp or obstacle with the other

handspring *noun* a gymnastic movement in which somebody flips the body forwards or backwards and lands briefly on the hands before continuing the flip so as to land on the feet again

hand wrap *noun* a supportive bandage used for protecting the hands from injury during sports

hang-glider *noun* an aircraft with no engine that consists of a rigid frame in the shape of a wing, with the pilot usually suspended in a harness below the wing

hang-gliding *noun* the sport of flying in a hang-glider

hapkido *noun* a Korean martial art that emphasises control of the opponent

harangue *verb* to criticise someone in a forceful angry way that undermines their confidence

hard lenses *plural noun* rigid contact lenses that can cause eye trauma if knocked, as may occur, e.g., in some contact sports

hard set *noun* a set of exercises that are difficult, used after the easy set as an actual muscle workout

Hatha yoga *noun* a low-impact yoga that helps to regulate breathing by exercises consisting of postures and stretches intended to sustain healthy bodily functioning and induce emotional calmness

hat trick *noun* a series of three wins or successes, especially three goals scored by the same player

Haversian canal *noun* a fine canal that runs vertically through the Haversian systems in compact bone, containing blood vessels and lymph ducts

Haversian system *noun* a unit of compact bone built around a Haversian canal, made of a series of bony layers that form a cylinder. Also called **osteon**

Hb *abbreviation* haemoglobin

hCG *abbreviation* human chorionic gonadotrophin

HDL cholesterol *noun* ▸ **high density lipoprotein**

head *verb* to use the head to hit a ball

head blocks *plural noun* a piece of equipment for stabilising the head of an injured person with suspected spinal injuries during transport

head game *noun* the psychological aspect of a competitive endeavour, especially a sport

headstand *noun* a position in gymnastics or yoga in which the body is balanced upside down on the head, usually using the hands for support

heal *verb* **1.** to return to a healthy state **2.** to make someone or something get better

healing *noun* the process of getting better

health *noun* the fact of being well or being free from any illness

healthcare *noun* the provision of medical and related services aimed at maintaining good health, especially through the prevention and treatment of disease

healthcare assistant *noun* someone with no specialised training employed in a hospital or other healthcare facility to perform basic nursing-support tasks

healthcare provider *noun* a professional who offers medical care, e.g. a doctor, physiotherapist or chiropractor

health-conscious *adjective* used for describing someone who is keen to eat healthy and nutritious foods and to look after his or her health in other ways, e.g. by exercising

health counsellor *noun* a general adviser on matters of health, fitness and nutrition in an institution such as a school

health food *noun* food with no additives or natural foods, which are good for your health

health freak *noun* a person who is very keen to be fit and healthy and follows a strict diet and exercise regime (*informal*)

health pack *noun* a dietary supplement consisting of a combination of ingredients, with supposed benefits for a specific aspect of health

health problem *noun* any illness or chronic injury indicating that a person must take precautions when carrying out particular activities

health professional *noun* same as **healthcare provider**

health promoting claim *noun* wording or a logo on food packaging that makes a claim about the nutritional content of the food inside

health risk *noun* a situation in which there is a risk to health caused by something such as not following safety procedures

health trainer *noun* a person who acts as a link between health professionals and the community, giving personal advice and support to people looking to improve their health

health walking *noun* walking as a form of exercise

healthy *adjective* **1.** in good physical condition **2.** helping to maintain or bring about good health

healthy eating *noun* the practice of eating food that is rich in essential nutrients and within recommended dietary guidelines

healthy lifestyle *noun* activities and diet choices that make a person healthy

heart *noun* the main organ in the body, which maintains the circulation of the blood around the body by its pumping action

heart attack *noun* a condition in which the heart has a reduced blood supply because one of the arteries becomes blocked by a blood clot, causing myocardial ischaemia and myocardial infarction (*informal*)

heartbeat *noun* the regular noise made by the heart as it pumps blood

heart block *noun* the slowing of the action of the heart because the impulses from the sinoatrial node to the ventricles are delayed or interrupted (NOTE: There are either longer impulses (**first degree block**) or missing impulses (**second degree block**) or no impulses at all (**complete heart block**), in which case the ventricles continue to beat slowly and independently of the sinoatrial node.)

heart disease *noun* a general term for any disease of the heart

heart murmur *noun* ♦ **murmur**

heart rate *noun* the number of heartbeats that occur within a specific length of time, typically a minute. Abbreviation **HR**

heart rate monitor *noun* a small machine that straps over the chest or onto the wrist to accurately measure a person's heart rate

heart-smart *adjective* used for describing food that is low in fat and cholesterol and therefore reduces the risk of heart disease

hearty *adjective* **1.** showing physical health, strength and vigour **2.** used for describing food that is substantial and gives considerable satisfaction and nourishment

heat *noun* one of several preliminary rounds before a race or contest, especially one in which competitors are eliminated, or one that determines players' starting order for the main event

heat cramps *plural noun* muscle cramps caused by dehydration and lack of salt

heat exhaustion *noun* collapse caused by physical exertion in hot conditions, involving loss of salt and body fluids

heat injury, heat stress *noun* any condition arising from becoming overheated, e.g. dehydration, cramps and heatstroke

heatstroke *noun* a condition in which someone becomes too hot and his or her body temperature rises abnormally, leading to headaches, stomach cramps and sometimes loss of consciousness

heat therapy *noun* the application of heat to an injured part of the body in order to loosen muscles or relieve pains

heavy-duty *adjective* designed for long or hard wear or use

heavyweight *noun* **1.** (*in professional boxing*) the heaviest weight category, for competitors whose weight does not exceed 79.5 kg **2.** (*in amateur boxing*) the heaviest weight category, for competitors whose weight does not exceed 91 kg **3.** a professional or amateur boxer who competes at heavyweight level **4.** a contestant in the heaviest weight class of any contact sport **5.** a person or organisation with considerable power or influence

heelbone *noun* same as **calcaneus**

heel cup *noun* an orthotic shoe insert that covers the heel

heel spur *noun* a soft deposit of calcium on the heel that indicates plantar fasciitis

height *noun* how tall someone or something is

heliskiing *noun* skiing in which skiers are taken to a usually remote ski slope by helicopter

heptathlon *noun* an athletics competition, usually for women, in which the contestants compete in seven different events and are awarded points for each to find the best all-round athlete. The events are the javelin, hurdles, high jump, long jump, shot put, sprint and 800-metre race.

hernia *noun* a condition in which an organ bulges through a hole or weakness in the wall that surrounds it. Also called **rupture**

herniated disc *noun* ♦ displaced intervertebral disc

herniography *noun* a medical examination of the abdomen in order to diagnose a hernia

herpetic infection *noun* a skin infection caused by the herpes virus, able to be passed on in close contact sports such as wrestling

HGH *abbreviation* human growth hormone

HGH booster *noun* same as **secretagogue**

high-arched feet *plural noun* feet in which the arches are unusually high, which may require special support during exercise. Compare **flat feet**

high biological value *noun* the fact of containing large amounts of bioavailable proteins

high blood pressure *noun* same as **hypertension**

high-calorie *adjective* used for describing food that contains a high number of calories from fat or carbohydrates

high density lipoprotein *noun* an aggregate of fat and protein that transports cholesterol away from the arteries, high levels of which are associated with a decreased risk of heart disease. Abbreviation **HDL**

high-energy *adjective* used in marketing to describe foods such as glucose drinks or high-sugar items such as honey that can be broken down easily by the body to provide a rapid supply of energy

high-fibre *adjective* used for describing foods that are rich in dietary fibre and therefore help to maintain a healthy colon

high-impact *adjective* used for describing exercise that puts pressure on the joints by jarring them, as does running on a hard surface

High in Fat, Salt or Sugar *adjective* used for describing calorie-dense snack foods. Abbreviation **HFFS**

high-intensity interval training *noun* interval training in which the bursts of faster exercise are extremely intense, designed to burn fat and build cardiovascular fitness. Abbreviation **HIIT**

high-intensity training *noun* exercise that raises the heart rate and works muscles, giving a tiring workout

high jump *noun* an athletics event in which the contestants run forward to gain momentum and then jump over a horizontal pole using any of a number of jumping styles

Highland Games *plural noun* an outdoor meeting at which there are competitions in various traditional Scottish sports such as tossing the caber, in Scottish dancing, and in piping

high-protein diet *noun* a dietary plan that is high in protein, used for building muscle mass especially while training

high quality protein *noun* protein that is bioavailable and contains high levels of all essential amino acids

HIIT *abbreviation* high-intensity interval training

hinge joint *noun* a joint such as the knee that allows two bones to move in one direction only. ◊ **ginglymus**

hip bone *noun* a set of bones consisting of the ilium, the ischium and the pubis, forming part of the pelvic girdle. Also called **innominate bone**

hip flexor muscles *plural noun* a group of muscles that connect the pelvis to the lower spine and to the knee

hip flexor strain *noun* strain in the upper thigh area caused by repeated kicking movements, often suffered by martial artists

hip girdle *noun* same as **pelvic girdle**

histamine *noun* a substance released in response to allergens. Histamines dilate blood vessels, constrict the cells of smooth muscles and cause an increase in acid secretions in the stomach.

histidine *noun* an amino acid involved in the repair of tissues that is also the precursor of histamine

histo- *prefix* relating to tissue

histology *noun* the study of the anatomy of tissue cells and minute cellular structure

histolysis *noun* the breakdown and disintegration of bodily tissue

histotrophic *adjective* causing the growth or nourishment of tissue

hit *verb* to strike a ball, puck or similar object

hitter *noun* a player of a sport who can hit the ball well

hit the wall *verb* to reach a point at which no more can be done or achieved, e.g. a state of total exhaustion during a marathon run

HMB *abbreviation* beta-hydroxy beta-methylbutyrate

hockey *noun* **1.** an outdoor sport played on grass between two teams of eleven, using wooden sticks with curved ends, the aim being to hit a small hard ball into the opposing goal **2.** *US* same as **ice hockey**

holding *noun* in some sports, the illegal use of the arms to hold or obstruct an opponent

hole *noun* **1.** (*in golf*) a small round cavity or cup on a green into which the ball is hit **2.** a part of a golf course that consists of a tee, a fairway, and a green with a hole and is a basic element in scoring. A golf course usually has 18 holes. ■ *verb* to hit or drive a ball into one of the holes of a golf course

holistic *adjective* used for describing a medical treatment that takes account of someone's mental and personal circumstances, in addition to their physical symptoms

home *noun* in many games, the place or point that must be hit in order to score or reached in order to be safe from attack

home base *noun* same as **home plate**

home exercise programme *noun* a general fitness plan using basic equipment, devised for elderly people or people confined to the home through illness or injury

home game *noun* a match played at the team's own ground

home gym *noun* a set of exercise equipment at a person's house, often comprising an exercise bicycle and rowing machine as well as free weights

homeostasis *noun* the process by which the functions and chemistry of a cell or internal organ are kept stable, even when external conditions vary greatly

home plate *noun* (*in baseball*) a flat slab marking the area over which a pitcher must throw the ball for a strike and on which a base runner must land in order to score. Also called **home base**

home run *noun* (*in baseball*) a hit that allows a player to make a circuit of all four bases and score a run, usually by hitting the ball out of the playing area

homocysteine *noun* an amino acid produced in the body during the metabolism of methionine, an essential amino acid

hook *noun* **1.** (*in boxing*) a short blow to an opponent delivered with a swing and a bent arm **2.** (*in cricket*) a shot with the bat held parallel to the ground that sends the ball towards the leg side **3.** the act of using an ice hockey stick to prevent another player from moving freely ■ *verb* **1.** (*in boxing*) to deliver a sharp curving blow to an opponent, using a curved or bent arm **2.** (*in rugby*) to kick the ball backwards out of a scrum to the scrum half **3.** (*in cricket*) to strike the ball towards the leg side with the bat held parallel to the ground

hooker *noun* (*in rugby*) a front row forward who hooks the ball out of the scrum

hooligan *noun* an aggressive young man, especially one acting as part of a group, who commits acts of vandalism and violence in public places

hooliganism *noun* acts of vandalism and violence in public places, committed especially by youths. Sport has been dogged by incidents of hooliganism, as it attracts large gatherings of young people and inspires strong emotions.

horizontal bar *noun* **1.** a metal bar fixed in a horizontal position and used for gymnastic exercises **2.** a competitive gymnastics event involving feats of skill and strength on the horizontal bar

horizontal flexion *noun* the movement of a joint from side to side

hormonal *adjective* relating to hormones

hormone *noun* a substance that is produced by one part of the body, especially the endocrine glands, and is carried to another part of the body by the bloodstream where it has particular effects or functions

horse *noun* same as **vaulting horse**

horse racing *noun* a sport in which horses ridden by jockeys race against each other, usually with spectators and others betting on the result

horseriding *noun* the practice of riding on horseback for recreation or as a sport

hot pack *noun* a soft, heated package of gel that is applied to the skin to loosen muscles or relieve pains

HR *abbreviation* heart rate

human chorionic gonadotrophin a hormone supplement taken by bodybuilders to counteract testicle shrinkage caused by steroid use. Abbreviation **hCG**

human growth hormone *noun* same as **somatotrophin**

humerus *noun* the top bone in the arm, running from the shoulder to the elbow (NOTE: The plural is **humeri**.)

hurdle *noun* one of a number of light barriers over which runners have to jump in some athletics events ■ *verb* **1.** to run in an athletics event in which hurdles must be jumped **2.** to clear a hurdle in a race

hurdles *noun* an athletics event in which runners have to race to clear a series of light barriers

hurdling *noun* the activity of jumping over hurdles

hurling *noun* an Irish field sport resembling hockey and lacrosse that is played with broad sticks and a leather ball that is passed from player to player through the air

hyaline cartilage *noun* a type of cartilage found in the nose, larynx and joints

hyaluronic acid *noun* a substance that binds connective tissue

hyaluronidase *noun* an enzyme that destroys hyaluronic acid

hydralazine *noun* a drug that lowers blood pressure, usually given with drugs that cause increased urine output

hydrate *verb* to give water to someone so as to re-establish or maintain fluid balance

hydration *noun* the state of having a healthy fluid balance in the body

hydroadenitis *noun* infection of the sweat glands

hydrocolloid strip *noun* a gelatinous waterproof dressing that seals a wound, retaining moisture and protecting from germs and dirt

hydrocortisone *noun* a steroid hormone secreted by the adrenal cortex or produced synthetically, used in the treatment of rheumatoid arthritis and inflammatory and allergic conditions

hydrolyse *verb* to undergo hydrolysis, or make a substance undergo hydrolysis

hydrolysis *noun* a chemical reaction in which a compound reacts with water, causing decomposition and the production of two or more other compounds, e.g. in the conversion of starch to glucose

hydropathy *noun* the treatment of injuries or disease by applying water both internally and externally

hydropoeisis *noun* the production of sweat by the body

hydrotherapy *noun* the treatment of disease by the external use of water, e.g. by exercising weakened limbs in a pool

hydrotic *adjective* used for describing a substance that increases the body's production of sweat

hydroxyproline *noun* an amino acid present in some proteins, especially in collagen

hyperactive *adjective* having hyperactivity

hyperactivity *noun* a condition in which someone is unusually active, restless and lacking the ability to concentrate for any length of time

hyperammonaemia *noun* high levels of ammonia in the blood, caused by inadequate metabolisation of proteins

hyperbaric chamber *noun* a pressurised chamber used for treating decompression sickness in divers

hypercapnia *noun* an unusually high level of carbon dioxide in the blood

hypercholesterolaemia *noun* a higher-than-average presence of cholesterol in the blood

hyperglycaemia *noun* an excess of glucose in the blood

hyperglycaemic *adjective* having hyperglycaemia

hyperhydrosis *noun* excessive sweating

hyperkinesia *noun* a condition in which there is unusually great strength or movement

hyperkinetic *adjective* used for describing a joint that allows too much movement as a result of loose tendons

hyperlipidaemia *noun* large concentrations of lipids in blood plasma

hyperlordosis *noun* excessive forward curvature of the lower part of the spine

hypermobility *noun* excessive mobility at a joint caused by looseness of the ligaments

hyperostosis *noun* excessive growth on the outside surface of a bone, especially the frontal bone

hyperoxemia *noun* a condition in which there is an unusually high concentration of oxygen in the blood and bodily tissues

hyperphosphataemia *noun* a higher-than-average presence of phosphate in the blood

hyperpiesia *noun* same as **hypertension**

hyperpnoea *noun* a test for exercise-induced asthma in the form of an inhaled medicine, which causes temporary bronchial dilation only in sufferers

hyperresponsive *adjective* used for describing the airways of athletes that are quick to respond to different air conditions by dilating or constricting

hypertension *noun* arterial blood pressure that is higher than the usual range for gender and age. Also called **high blood pressure**, **hyperpiesia**. Compare **hypotension**

hyperthermia *noun* unusually high body temperature, especially when induced for therapeutic reasons

hyperthyroidism *noun* a condition in which the thyroid gland is too active and releases unusual amounts of thyroid hormones into the blood, giving rise to a rapid heartbeat, sweating and trembling. Also called **thyrotoxicosis**

hypertonia *noun* an increased rigidity and spasticity of the muscles

hypertonic *adjective* **1.** used for describing a solution that has a higher osmotic pressure than another specified solution **2.** used for describing a muscle that is under unusually high tension

hypertrophy *noun* an increase in the number or size of cells in a tissue

hyperventilate *verb* to breathe unusually deeply or rapidly because of anxiety or disease and in excess of the body's requirements, causing too much loss of carbon dioxide

hypervitaminosis *noun* excessively high intakes of vitamins, which can be toxic in large doses

hyphaemia *noun* a small haemorrhage of blood into the eyeball following an eye trauma such as a blow, temporarily obscuring vision

hypnotherapy *noun* the use of hypnosis in treating illness, e.g. in dealing with physical pain or psychological problems

hypoglossal nerve *noun* the twelfth cranial nerve which governs the muscles of the tongue

hypoglycaemia *noun* a low concentration of glucose in the blood

hypoglycaemic *adjective* having hypoglycaemia

hypokinesis *noun* a decrease in the ability of the heart to contract, usually caused by a heart attack and resulting in sluggish circulation

hyponatraemia *noun* a lack of sodium in the blood caused by excessive sweating, persistent diarrhoea or overuse of diuretic drugs

hypophosphataemia *noun* a lower-than-average presence of phosphate in the blood

hypoproteinaemia *noun* a low concentration of protein in blood plasma

hypotension *noun* a condition in which the pressure of the blood is unusually low. Also called **low blood pressure**

hypotensive resuscitation *noun* the resuscitation of a person suffering from hypovolaemia using fluid infusion to raise blood pressure

hypothalamus *noun* the part of the brain that controls the production of hormones by the pituitary gland and regulates important bodily functions such as hunger, thirst and sleep

hypothyroidism *noun* underactivity of the thyroid gland, causing a decrease in the metabolic rate and corresponding sluggishness and weight gain

hypotonia *noun* the medical condition of low or diminished muscle tone or tension

hypotonic *adjective* **1.** showing hypotonia **2.** used for describing a solution with a lower osmotic pressure than plasma

hypoventilate *verb* to breathe in an unusually slow and shallow way leading to a dangerous build-up of carbon dioxide in the blood

hypovitaminosis *noun* an unhealthily low intake of vitamins

hypovolaemia *noun* a condition in which a person's blood pressure falls owing to excessive fluid loss

hypoxia *noun* a condition in which there is an unusually low concentration of oxygen in the blood and bodily tissues

I

iatrogenic *adjective* caused by medical interference or drug use

iceberg profile *noun* the tendency of elite athletes to suffer from generally increased energy and lower levels of stress, anger and depression than others

ice climbing *noun* the sport of climbing ice formations such as glaciers, using specialist equipment

ice hockey *noun* a game played on ice by two teams of six skaters. Points are scored by hitting a rubber disc (**puck**) into the opposing team's goal with a long flat-bladed stick.

ice pack *noun* an ice-filled cloth or bag held against an injured part of the body to ease pain or reduce swelling

ice rink *noun* an area of frozen water used by ice-skaters, ice-hockey players and curlers, especially an enclosed prepared surface

ice therapy *noun* the application of an ice pack to an injured part of the body to reduce swelling or relieve pains

ideal body weight *noun* a healthy weight for a person based on a formula such as body mass index

IF *abbreviation* information feedback

ileum *noun* the lower part of the small intestine, between the jejunum and the caecum. Compare **ilium**

ileus *noun* obstruction of the intestine, usually distension caused by loss of muscular action in the bowel

iliopsoas *noun* a muscle that lies over the hip joint

iliopsoas bursitis *noun* inflammation of the bursa at the hip joint

iliopsoas tendinitis *noun* inflammation of the tendon connecting the iliopsoas muscle to the ileum, caused by overuse

iliotibial band syndrome *noun* a condition in which a band of thickened tissue over the front of the thigh rubs repeatedly over the bone during exercise, causing irritation. Abbreviation **ITBS**

ilium *noun* the top part of each of the hip bones, which form the pelvis. Compare **ileum** (NOTE: The plural is **ilia**.)

immediate care *noun* medical assistance given at the scene of an injury

immobilise *verb* to rest a joint or keep the parts of a fractured limb fixed in place so that they are unable to move

immoderate *adjective* going beyond what is healthy, moral, appropriate or socially acceptable

immune system *noun* a complex network of cells and cell products that protects the body from disease, including the thymus, spleen, lymph nodes, white blood cells and antibodies

impact *noun* **1.** a collision of one object against another **2.** the effect that something or someone has

impacted fracture *noun* a fracture in which the two pieces of bone are also forced together by the impact that fractured them, causing further tissue damage

impact force *noun* a force that is a result of colliding with another body, e.g. when a runner's foot hits the ground. Compare **active force**

impassible *adjective* not susceptible to or not capable of feeling physical pain or injury

impulse *noun* **1.** a message transmitted by a nerve **2.** a sudden feeling of wanting to act in a specific way

in *adjective* (*in sports such as cricket and rounders*) used for indicating that a sports team or player is batting

inactivity *noun* a lack of activity

inarticulate *adjective* used for describing a bone that has no joints or segments, as do the bones of the skull

incentive *noun* something that encourages or motivates someone to do something

incidence *noun* the number of sports injuries incurred in a sample population, relative to the amount of time exposed to the risk

incline *noun* a slope or slant

incline bench press *noun* a bench press performed with the top end of the bench slightly raised, so that the body is not parallel with the ground

incline chest press *noun* a chest press performed with the top end of the bench slightly raised, so that the body is not parallel with the ground

incline dumbbell bench press *noun* a dumbbell bench press performed with the top end of the bench slightly raised, so that the body is not parallel with the ground

incompetence *noun* the inability to perform a particular action

incompetent *adjective* lacking the skills, qualities or ability to do something

incomplete fracture *noun* a fracture that does not go all the way through a bone

incoordination *noun* an inability to control voluntary muscular movements

incretion *noun* secretion of a substance into the bloodstream, particularly of a hormone from the endocrine gland

independent sampling officer *noun* an official who oversees the collection of samples from athletes for drug testing. Abbreviation **ISO**

indirect free kick *noun* ♦ **free kick**

indispensable amino acids *plural noun* same as **essential amino acids**

individual medley *noun* a swimming race divided into three or four equal parts, in each of which the swimmers must use a particular stroke

individual skill *noun* a skill that is performed without interacting with others or the environment, e.g. throwing a javelin

indolent *adjective* used for describing a disease or condition that is slow to develop or be healed, and causes no pain

ineffective anticipation *noun* reaction to an anticipated stimulus before it is actually given, resulting in a mistake or violation of game rules

inertia *noun* a lack of activity in the body or mind

infarct *noun* an area of tissue that has recently died as a result of the sudden loss of its blood supply, e.g. following blockage of an artery by a blood clot

inferior *adjective* used for describing a body part that is situated in the lower half of the body

infertility *noun* the physical inability of a person to have children

inflame *verb* to become, or make body tissue become, red and swollen in response to injury or infection

inflamed *adjective* sore, red and swollen

inflammation *noun* the fact of having become sore, red and swollen as a reaction to an infection, an irritation or a blow

information feedback *noun* feedback given by a coach on a sporting performance that gives the player information about what to do to improve. Abbreviation **IF**

infringement *noun* a failure to obey a regulation or rule

ingrowing *adjective* growing or appearing to grow inwards

ingrown toenail *noun* a painful condition in which the toenail grows into the surrounding skin, caused by routinely wearing shoes which are too tight

inguinal hernia *noun* a hernia of the intestine through the muscles of the lower abdomen, often caused by lifting heavy objects

inguinal ligament *noun* a tight ligament in the abdomen, with weak spots that can lead to the formation of a hernia

inhalation *noun* **1.** the act of breathing in. Opposite **exhalation 2.** the action of breathing in a medicinal substance as part of a treatment

inhale *verb* **1.** to breathe in, or breathe something in **2.** to breathe in a medicinal substance as part of a treatment. Opposite **exhale**

inhaled beta agonist *noun* a medicine in the form of a fine mist that is used for treating asthma by dilating the bronchioles

inhaled drug *noun* medicine in the form of a fine spray that is inhaled, as are some asthma medications

inhibition *noun* the slowing down or prevention of a chemical reaction

inhibitor *noun* a molecule that attaches to an enzyme and make it less active, widely used in drugs

injure *verb* to hurt someone or a part of the body

injury *noun* damage or a wound caused to a person's body

injury management *noun* medical treatment and rehabilitation provided for a sports injury

injury mechanism *noun* the way in which a casualty sustained his or her injury, e.g. in a fall or collision, which may help with diagnosis and treatment decisions

injury time *noun* extra time allowed at the end of some matches, especially football and rugby, to compensate for time spent attending to injured players during the game

inline skating *noun* same as **rollerblading**

innervate *verb* to cause a muscle, organ or other part of the body to act

innerve *verb* to provide a person or object with nervous energy or something resembling such energy

inning *noun* each of the divisions of a game of baseball or softball during which each team bats until it makes three outs. Nine innings are standard for baseball and seven for softball, but extra innings are played if the score remains tied.

innings *noun* **1.** (*in cricket*) a team's or batsman's turn at batting **2.** (*in cricket*) the runs scored by a player or team during a turn at batting

innominate bone *noun* same as **hip bone**

inosine *noun* an organic compound involved in the formation of purines and energy metabolism, used in sports supplements

inotropic *adjective* having an effect on the force of muscular contraction

insertion *noun* **1.** the point at which a muscle is attached to a bone **2.** the point at which an organ is attached to its support

in shape *adjective* having a healthy and attractive physique

inside *adjective* (*in football, hockey and other sports*) used for describing a position nearer to the centre of the field than another position of the same name

insoluble fibre *noun* the fibre in bread and cereals that is not digested but swells inside the intestine

inspiration *noun* the act of process of breathing in

inspire *verb* same as **inhale**

Institute for Optimum Nutrition *noun* an independent educational body that specialises in clinical and therapeutic nutrition. Abbreviation **ION**

instructor *noun* a person who gives information or training

insulin *noun* a hormone produced in the pancreas that regulates the body's metabolism of carbohydrates and has widespread effects on the body

insulinaemic index *noun* the rise in blood sugar measured after consumption of a particular carbohydrate

insulin resistance *noun* a medical condition in which bodily or injected insulin has a reduced effect in metabolising glucose, a possible cause of metabolic syndrome

insulin sensitivity *noun* the effect that insulin has on metabolising glucose in an individual

insulin shock *noun* a severe drop in blood sugar resulting from an excess of insulin and marked by sweating, dizziness, trembling and eventual coma

insult *noun* an injury or trauma to the body, or something that causes such harm

integrated *adjective* bringing together processes or functions that are normally separate

intellectual disability *noun* (*in disabled sport events such as the Paralympics*) a category for athletes with long-term mental impairment, usually classified as having an IQ below 70

intensity *noun* the strength of something, e.g. pain

intensive care *noun* the monitoring, care and treatment in hospital of patients who are seriously ill or injured, especially by the use of specialist equipment such as that aiding breathing

interactive skill *noun* a skill that is performed by interacting with the environment, e.g. hitting a golf ball

intercept *verb* to stop or interrupt the intended path of something

intercostal *adjective* between the ribs

intercostal muscles *plural noun* muscles between the ribs that control inhalation and exhalation

interdigital neuroma *noun* inflammation of a nerve in the foot caused by wearing ill-fitting footwear, causing a burning pain in the balls of the feet

interdisciplinary *adjective* combining two or more different areas or disciplines

intermittent claudication *noun* a condition of the arteries causing severe pain in the legs that makes the person limp after having walked a short distance

intermural *adjective* involving participants from two or more educational institutions, athletic clubs, or other groups

intermuscular *adjective* between muscles

internal *adjective* **1.** located within or affecting the inside of something, especially the inside of the body **2.** between the members of a team

internaliser *noun* a personality type in which individuals believe that they have a high degree of control over what happens to them. Compare **externaliser**

internal obliques *plural noun* a pair of abdominal muscles that run diagonally outwards from the inner ribs to the pelvis

internal rotation *noun* movement of a ball-and-socket joint so that the limb turns inwards

internal secretion *noun* a secretion, especially a hormone, that is absorbed into the blood directly after production

internal state *noun* the various internal factors that act on an athlete and affect performance, including mood, mental alertness and level of skill acquisition

international *noun* **1.** a sports contest between teams or players from two or more countries **2.** a member of a team representing his or her country in an international event

International Olympic Committee *noun* the body that oversees the organisation of the Summer and Winter Olympic Games. Abbreviation **IOC**

interoceptor *noun* a nerve cell that reacts to a change taking place inside the body

interpersonal *adjective* concerning or involving relationships between people

interpersonal anxiety *noun* fear of how other people will see and judge you, sometimes a factor in athletic performance

interval training *noun* training consisting of bursts of intense exercise, with periods of slower, easier exercise in between to give the body time to recover

intervertebral disc *noun* one of the flexible plates of cartilage connecting adjacent vertebrae of the backbone that impart flexibility and act as shock absorbers to protect the spinal cord from impact, e.g. when running

intolerant *adjective* unable to eat or drink a particular food, ingredient or substance, or to take a particular drug without having an allergic reaction or becoming ill

intra-articular *adjective* inside a joint

intramuscular *adjective* inside a muscle

intravenous nutrition *noun* same as **parenteral nutrition**

intrinsic motivation *noun* motivation to achieve a goal for reasons of pride, enjoyment and self-worth

introverted *adjective* referring to someone who thinks only about himself or herself

inversion *noun* the fact of being turned towards the inside

invertebral disc *noun* same as **intervertebral disc**

inverted U theory *noun* (*in performance theory*) a model of arousal levels and their effect on performance, which is optimal when stimulation is of a medium intensity and decreases when arousal is very low or very high

involucrum *noun* a covering of new bone that forms over diseased bone

IOC *abbreviation* International Olympic Committee

iodine *noun* a chemical element that is essential to the body, especially to the functioning of the thyroid gland (NOTE: The chemical symbol is I.)

ipsative *adjective* using yourself as the norm against which to measure something, e.g. your present performance against your past performance rather than the performance of others

iron *noun* a chemical element essential to the body, present in foods such as liver and eggs

iron man *noun* **1.** a male athlete with great endurance who takes part in a triathlon or iron man competition **2.** a male bodybuilder

iron man competition *noun* a triathlon for men and women that includes competitions in endurance events, usually cycling, swimming and running

iron woman *noun* **1.** a female athlete with great endurance who takes part in a triathlon or iron woman competition **2.** a female bodybuilder

iron woman competition *noun* an athletic competition for women that includes a variety of sports, e.g. surfing, canoeing, swimming and running

irrational *adjective* lacking the normal ability to think clearly, especially because of shock or injury to the brain

irregular *adjective* of a heartbeat, not reliably occurring at regular intervals, leading to potential complications

ischaemia *noun* insufficient blood supply to an organ

ischaemic heart disease *noun* a disease of the heart caused by a failure in the blood supply, as in coronary thrombosis. Abbreviation **IHD**

ischium *noun* the lower part of the hip bone in the pelvis (NOTE: The plural is **ischia**.)

Island Games *plural noun* a multi-sport event, held every two years, in which only athletes from 25 small islands around the world, including Rhodes, Guernsey, Bermuda and Menorca, are invited to take part

islets of Langerhans *plural noun* clusters of endocrine cells found in the pancreas that secrete insulin and glucagon

ISO *abbreviation* independent sampling officer

isokinetic training *noun* weight training in which the muscle contracts at a constant speed, requiring specialised equipment

isolation training *noun* targeted training of a specific muscle or muscle group in order to remedy a weakness

isometric *adjective* **1.** involving equal measurement **2.** used for describing muscle contraction in which tension occurs with very little shortening of muscle fibres **3.** used for describing exercises in which the muscles are put under tension but not contracted

isometrics *noun* a form of exercise in which the muscles are pushed against something fixed or against other muscles to strengthen them

isometric stretching *noun* a form of static stretching in which the muscles are tensed in resistance against a force but do not move

isometric training *noun* weight training in which the muscle fibres contract but the muscle does not shorten, developing static strength

isoprenaline *noun* a drug that dilates the bronchial tubes, used in the treatment of asthma

isotonic *adjective* used for describing a solution, e.g. a saline drip, that has the same osmotic pressure as blood serum and can therefore be passed directly into the body. Compare **hypertonic**, **hypotonic**

isotonic drink *noun* a liquid supplement that has nutrients in the same proportions in which they are normally found in the body

ITBS *abbreviation* iliotibial band syndrome

J

j *abbreviation* joule

jab *verb* to make a short fast punch at an opponent, e.g. in boxing

Jai Alai *noun* a version of the game pelota, for two or four players

javelin *noun* **1.** a long thin piece of wood, plastic or metal with a pointed end, thrown in field competitions **2.** an athletics event in which the contestants compete to throw a javelin as far as possible

jaw thrust *noun* the act of manually stabilising a patient's jaw to open the airway without aggravating potential spinal injuries

jerk *noun* **1.** a sudden movement of part of the body which indicates that the local reflex arc is intact **2.** ⟡ **clean and jerk**

jerks *plural noun* ⟡ **physical jerks**

Jeux de la Francophonie *plural noun* a multi-sport event, held every four years, in which only athletes from French-speaking countries around the world, e.g. France, Canada and parts of Africa, are invited to take part

jockey *noun* a rider of racehorses, especially professionally

jock itch *noun* same as **tinea cruris**

jockstrap *noun* an elasticated belt with a pouch at the front, worn by sportsmen to support their genitals or to keep a protective cup in place

jog *verb* to run at a slow steady pace as a fitness exercise ■ *noun* a spell of slow steady running for exercise

jogger *noun* somebody who runs at a moderate pace, often over long distances, for exercise ■ *plural noun* **joggers** loose-fitting trousers with an elasticated waist and ankles, used for jogging

jogger's nephritis *noun* the presence of blood and protein in a person's urine caused by jarring to the kidneys during strenuous activity such as running

jogging *noun* a fitness or recreational activity that involves running at a moderate pace, often over long distances

joint *noun* a part of the body where two bones meet

joint capsule *noun* white fibrous tissue that surrounds and holds a joint together

joint cavity *noun* the space between the ends of two bones that is usually filled with cartilage and cushioning fluid and is surrounded by the joint capsule

Jones fracture *noun* a bone fracture caused by stress and overuse

joule *noun* the SI unit of measurement of work or energy. Abbreviation **J** (NOTE: 4.184 joules equals one calorie.)

judo *noun* a Japanese martial art in which opponents use balance and body weight, with minimal physical effort, to throw each other or hold each other in a lock

jugal *adjective* same as **zygomatic**

juice *noun* the liquid inside a fruit or vegetable

juice drink *noun* a flavoured drink containing between 6% and 30% fruit juice, water, sugar and flavourings

jujitsu *noun* a Japanese system of unarmed fighting devised by the samurai, or the martial art based on it

jumper's knee *noun* same as **patellar tendinitis**

jump jockey *noun* a jockey specially trained to jump horses over fences and ride in steeplechases

jump mat *noun* a type of force platform designed specifically for testing jumps

jump rope *noun US* same as **skipping rope**

jump shot *noun* in basketball, a shot made with one or both hands by a player who is at the highest point of a jump

junk food *noun* food of little nutritional value, e.g. high-fat processed snacks, eaten between or instead of meals

K

kabaddi *noun* a team sport in which players must capture members of the opposing team while holding their breath, popular in South Asia

kallikrein *noun* an enzyme present in blood, urine and body tissue that, when activated, dilates blood vessels

karate *noun* a traditional Japanese form of unarmed combat, now widely popular as a sport, in which fast blows and kicks are used

kata *noun* a sequence of movements in some martial arts such as karate, used either for training or to demonstrate technique

kayak *noun* a lightweight fibreglass canoe propelled by a double-bladed paddle, used for leisure and in competitive sport

kayaking *noun* the sport of racing or travelling in a kayak

keep-fit *noun* a programme of physical exercises designed to keep the body in good condition

kempo *noun* a martial art that combines karate with elements of Chinese fighting styles

kendo *noun* a Japanese martial art in which people fence using bamboo sticks instead of swords

Keshan disease *noun* selenium deficiency that causes damage to the heart

ketone *noun* an organic compound containing a carbon atom connected to an oxygen atom by a double bond and to two carbon atoms

ketosis *noun* the metabolisation of ketone bodies to provide the brain with energy when sufficient glucose is not available through the diet

kettle bell *noun* a hand-held weight with a loose ball that moves during exercise, forcing the lifter to constantly adjust and compensate

Khmer boxing *noun* a form of kickboxing, originating in Cambodia, in which blows with the knees and elbows are used in addition to punches and kicks

kick *verb* **1.** to strike a ball with the foot **2.** to strike something or somebody with the foot, e.g. in martial arts **3.** to make a thrashing movement with the legs, e.g. when fighting or swimming **4.** (*in cricket*) to bounce up high and quickly ■ *noun* **1.** a blow with the foot, e.g. in martial arts **2.** a thrashing movement with the leg when swimming **3.** the striking of a ball with the foot

kickabout *noun* an informal game of football

kickboard *noun US* a small buoyant board held by a swimmer in order to stay afloat while practising kicking techniques

kickboxing *noun* a form of boxing that involves kicking as well as punching

kick-off *noun* **1.** (*in football*) the place kick from the centre spot that begins the match **2.** the time at which a football match is due to start

kill *verb* **1.** (*in football*) to bring a fast-moving ball under instant control **2.** (*in racket games*) to hit the ball so hard, with such skill or in such a direction that your opponent has no chance of returning it **3.** to hit a ball very hard

killer instinct *noun* an overpowering drive to overcome an opponent

kilocalorie *noun* a unit of measurement of heat equal to 1000 calories. Abbreviation **kcal** (NOTE: In scientific use, the SI unit **joule** is now more usual. 1 calorie equals 4.186 joules.)

kilogram *noun* an SI unit of measurement of weight equal to 1000 grams. Abbreviation **kg**

kilojoule *noun* an SI unit of measurement of energy or heat equal to 1000 joules. Abbreviation **kJ**

kilometre *noun* a measure of length equal to 1000 metres or 0.621 miles. Abbreviation **km** (NOTE: The US spelling is **kilometer**.)

kinaesthesia *noun* the fact of being aware of the movement and position of parts of the body

kinematics *noun* the scientific study of motion

kinesin *noun* a protein that uses chemical energy from ATP to create movement within cells, e.g. separating chromosomes during division and transporting neurotransmitters inside nerve cells

kinesiology *noun* the study of human movements, particularly with regard to their use in treatment

kinetic energy *noun* the energy that a body or system has because of its motion. Symbol T, E_k

kinin *noun* a polypeptide that makes blood vessels widen and smooth muscles contract

kit *noun* a set of items used for a specific purpose

kite surfing, kiteboarding *noun* a water sport in which the participants ride on surfboards with a kite attached to their bodies to give propulsion and lift

kloofing *noun* the extreme sport of following the course of a river through a gorge by climbing, swimming and jumping

knead *verb* to press and rub someone's muscles hard during massage

knee bend *noun* an exercise in which a person squats and raises himself or herself again repeatedly

kneecap *noun* same as **patella**

knee jerk *noun* same as **patellar reflex**

knee pad *noun* a piece of padding attached to straps, used for protecting the knees from injury during sports

knee support, knee wrap *noun* a supportive bandage used for protecting the knees from injury during sports

knockabout *noun* an informal ball game (*informal*)

knock out *verb* **1.** (*in boxing and some other full-contact sports*) to knock an opponent down for a count of ten, thus winning the match **2.** to eliminate an opponent or team from a competition by winning a match or game

knockout *noun* **1.** (*in boxing*) a punch that knocks an opponent down for a count of ten and so wins a contest **2.** a sports competition in which a person or team beaten in one game or match is eliminated from the entire competition

knock up *verb* **1.** (*in racket sports*) to hit the ball back and forth in practice with an opponent, especially before beginning a match **2.** (*in cricket*) to score a particular number of runs

knockup *noun* (*in racket games*) a practice period with an opponent, especially before the beginning of a match

KO *noun* a knockout, especially in boxing

korfball *noun* a game similar to basketball that is played by two teams of twelve players, each team having six men or boys and six women or girls

krav maga *noun* a martial art from Israel, used for self-defence and by the military, that emphasises attack and techniques for causing injury

Krebs cycle *noun* an important series of reactions in which the intermediate products of fats, carbohydrates and amino acid metabolism are converted to carbon dioxide and water in the mitochondria. Also called **citric acid cycle**

kyphosis *noun* an excessive backward curvature of the top part of the spine (NOTE: The plural is **kyphoses**.)

kyu *noun* a level of proficiency in some martial arts

L

labral tear *noun* damage caused to the labrum during an arm or shoulder injury

labrum *noun* a ring of cartilage in the shoulder and hip joints

lab testing *noun* testing for something such as biomechanical analysis that is carried out in a controlled private environment. Compare **field testing**

laceration *noun* a deep and jagged cut in the flesh

lacrosse *noun* a sport in which two teams of ten players use sticks with a net pouch (**crosse**) at one end to throw and catch a small hard rubber ball. The aim is to score a goal by throwing the ball into the opposing team's goal net. Lacrosse was originated by Native North Americans.

lactalbumin *noun* a milk protein that contains all the essential amino acids

lactase *noun* an enzyme, secreted in the small intestine, that converts milk sugar into glucose and galactose

lactate *noun* a chemical compound that is formed by the breakdown of lactic acid, used as a fuel by the body

lactate threshold *noun* the point at which the breakdown of lactic acid for fuel results in a high enough concentration of hydrogen in the body to cause fatigue

lacteal *noun* a lymphatic vessel in the small intestine that absorbs fats

lactic acid *noun* a sugar that forms in cells and tissue, and also in sour milk, cheese and yoghurt

lactic testing *noun* testing the level in lactic acid present in muscles at various stages during an activity

lactic threshold *noun* same as **onset of blood lactate accumulation**

lacto-ovo-vegetarian *adjective* involving a diet that includes no animal flesh, poultry or fish but does include eggs and milk products. ◊ **vegetarian, vegan**

lactose *noun* a type of sugar found in milk

lactose intolerance *noun* a condition in which a person cannot digest lactose because lactase is absent in the intestine or because of an allergy to milk, causing diarrhoea

lacuna *noun* a small hollow or cavity (NOTE: The plural is **lacunae**.)

lacunar *adjective* used for describing hollows or cavities in tissue such as in bone or cartilage, especially ones that are unusual

ladder tournament *noun* a tournament based on a list of ranked players in a game or sport, in which each player may challenge any other player who is ranked one or two positions higher

lamella *noun* **1.** a thin sheet of tissue **2.** a thin medicated disc placed under the eyelid in order to apply the medicine to the eye (NOTE: [all senses] The plural is **lamellae**.)

lamina *noun* a side part of the bony arch in a vertebra

laminectomy *noun* a surgical operation to cut through the lamina of a vertebra in the spine to get to the spinal cord. Also called **rachiotomy** (NOTE: The plural is **laminectomies**.)

land training *noun* exercises on land for athletes, usually swimmers, who usually train in water

lane *noun* a section of track assigned to a competitive runner on a racing track or a swimmer in a swimming pool

langlauf *noun* same as **cross-country skiing**

lap *noun* a single circuit of a racetrack or running track or one length of a swimming pool ■ *verb* to overtake a competitor on a racetrack or running track after having completed at least one circuit more than he or she has

lap of honour *noun* an extra lap round a racetrack or running track run by the winner of a race or game to acknowledge the presence and applause of spectators

larynx *noun* the organ in the throat which produces sounds. Also called **voice box** (NOTE: The plural is **larynges** or **larynxes**.)

last *noun* the foot shape around which a training shoe is built, with a greater or lesser inward curve for different types of runner

latent learning *noun* learning that is not apparent when it occurs but can be inferred later from improved performance

lateral *adjective* **1.** further away from the midline of the body **2.** referring to one side of the body

lateral collateral tendon sprain *noun* a sprain of the tendon connecting the thigh bone to the fibula, caused by receiving a violent twist to the knee

lateral epicondylitis *noun* pain in the elbow joint caused by repeatedly moving the forearms, as in some racket sports, which strains the tendons at their point of attachment

lateral flexion *noun* sideways movement of the spine, as occurs when the neck moves towards the shoulder

lateral plane *noun* same as **sagittal plane**

lateral raises *plural noun* exercises performed using weights held in either hand, in which the arms hang down and are raised to a horizontal position at the sides of the body

late tackle *noun* in a game such as football, a foul resulting from an attempt to tackle an opposing player after the ball has been passed. This can be a bookable offence, especially if the player making the tackle comes into physical contact with the player who had possession of the ball.

latissimus dorsi *noun* a large flat triangular muscle covering the lumbar region and the lower part of the chest

lat pulldown *noun* same as **pulldown**

lats *plural noun* ♦ **latissimus dorsi**

layered eating *noun* a weight-management plan in which low-calorie, high-bulk foods are eaten first to reduce the appetite for the higher-calorie foods

lay up *verb* to prevent someone from leading a normal active life, usually temporarily because of injury or illness

LBM *abbreviation* lean body mass

LDL cholesterol *noun* ♦ low density lipoprotein

lead *verb* **1.** to be ahead in a race or competition **2.** (*in baseball*) to leave a base as a runner before a pitch **3.** to aim something such as a ball at a point in front of a moving player to allow for the time of flight

league *noun* **1.** an association of sports clubs or teams that compete with each other **2.** a level of performance or skill

league table *noun* a list of teams or players that ranks them according to performance in a league

lean *adjective* used for describing meat with little fat

lean body mass *noun* same as **fat-free mass**

lean muscle *noun* muscle definition that is not obscured by subcutaneous fat

learning curve *noun* a graphical description of how someone can acquire knowledge over time

learning disability *noun* a condition that either prevents or significantly hinders someone from learning basic skills or information at the same rate as most people of the same age

left-footed *adjective* **1.** having a natural tendency to lead with or use the left foot, especially in playing sports such as football **2.** performed using the left foot

left-footer *noun* a left-footed sportsperson

left-handed *adjective* **1.** having a natural tendency to use the left hand, especially in playing sports such as tennis **2.** performed using the left hand

left-hander *noun* **1.** a left-handed sportsperson **2.** a blow delivered with the left hand

left wing *noun* **1.** the side of a playing field that is to the left of a player facing the opponent's goal **2.** a player whose position in a team is on the left wing

leg *noun* **1.** a part of the body with which a person or animal walks and stands **2.** one of the parts of a relay race that a single athlete completes **3.** one of several stages, events or games that is part of a larger competition but is treated independently of the other parts and has its own winner **4.** either of two games in a competition played between two football teams, one game being played at home, the other away. The aggregate score of the two games determines the overall winner of the round. **5.** the part of a cricket field that lies on the left of and behind a right-handed batsman as he or she stands in position to hit the ball

leg before wicket *adjective* (*in cricket*) the dismissal of a batsman whose leg has obstructed a ball that the umpire adjudges would otherwise have hit the wicket

leg-break *noun* (*in cricket*) a ball with a bounce that spins from the leg side to the off side

leg curl *noun* same as **leg extension**

leg extension *noun* **1.** a backwards or downwards movement of the leg from the hip joint **2.** a curl performed sitting down with a weight over the lower legs, or a machine that simulates this

leg flexion *noun* a forwards or upwards movement of the leg from the hip joint

leg press *noun* an exercise in which the legs are brought together against resistance provided by a machine

leisure centre *noun* a building where people can exercise, with equipment usually including exercise machines, swimming pool and space for sports such as badminton, as well as changing and refreshment facilities

lemniscus *noun* a bundle of fibres, especially a bundle of nerve fibres

leotard *noun* a tight-fitting one-piece elastic garment that covers the torso and is worn especially by dancers, gymnasts, and acrobats

les autres *plural noun* (*in disabled sport*) a classification for those athletes who do not fit into the established categories, e.g. athletes with multiple sclerosis or restricted growth

lesion *noun* a wound, sore or damage to the body (NOTE: Used to refer to any damage to the body, from the fracture of a bone to a cut on the skin.)

let *noun* in games such as tennis and squash, a service in which the ball is obstructed and the shot has to be played again

leucine *noun* the most common amino acid found in proteins, essential for growth in infancy

leukocyte *noun* a white blood cell that contains a nucleus but has no haemoglobin

levator *noun* **1.** a surgical instrument for lifting pieces of fractured bone **2.** a muscle that lifts a limb or a part of the body

LH *abbreviation* luteinising hormone

libero *noun* (*in sports such as volleyball and ice hockey*) a defensive player who operates freely across the whole playing area

life-saving *noun* the activity of saving people from drowning in a swimming pool or the sea

lifestyle *noun* the way in which a person or group of people live their daily lives, including habits, diet and activities

lifestyle change *noun* a change to a person's daily routine caused by starting one or more new activities, e.g. taking more daily exercise

ligament *noun* a thick band of fibrous tissue that connects the bones at a joint and forms the joint capsule

light flyweight *noun* (*in amateur boxing*) a weight category for competitors whose weight does not exceed 48 kg or 106 lb

light heavyweight *noun* (*in professional boxing*) a weight category for competitors who weigh between 72.5 and 79.5 kg or 160 and 175 lb

light middleweight *noun* (*in amateur boxing*) a weight category for competitors who weigh between 67 and 71 kg or 148 and 156 lb

lightweight *noun* (*in professional boxing*) a weight category for competitors who weigh between 59 and 61 kg or 130 and 135 lb

light welterweight *noun* (*in amateur boxing*) a weight category for competitors who weigh between 60 and 63.5 kg or 132 and 139 lb

limber up *verb* to do gentle physical exercises to loosen and warm the muscles prior to taking part in more strenuous physical activity

limiting amino acid *noun* the amino acid that is present in the smallest amount in a particular foodstuff, limiting the amount of protein that can be absorbed

limp *verb* to walk with an uneven step because of an injury or disability ■ *noun* a way of walking or running that involves a degree of motion impairment, usually as a result of injury

line *noun* **1.** a long narrow mark that shows the boundary of any of the divisions of a playing area or race track **2.** (*in American football*) either of the two rows of opposing players facing each other on either side of the line of scrimmage

line judge *noun* (*in sports such as tennis*) an official who assists the umpire by signalling when the ball is out of play, and sometimes when it is in play at times of uncertainty

lineman *noun* (*in American football*) a player on the forward line

line of scrimmage *noun* (*in American football*) an imaginary line across the field at which the ball rests and where the players of the opposing teams form up facing each other for a play

line-out *noun* (*in rugby union*) a restart of play in which the ball is thrown from the touchline for two lines of opposing forwards to jump and catch

linesman *noun* **1.** same as **line judge 2.** (*in American football*) an official who watches for infringements, marks the downs and places the ball in position **3.** (*in football*) an assistant referee positioned along a touchline (*dated*)

linesperson *noun* in sports such as tennis, football, and American football, an official who assists the referee or umpire, e.g. by signalling that a ball is out of play

lineswoman *noun* in sports such as tennis, football, and American football, a woman official who assists the referee or umpire, e.g. by signalling that a ball is out of play

line-up *noun* a list of players in a team together with the positions they play in

liniment *noun* an oily liquid rubbed on the skin to ease the pain or stiffness of a sprain or bruise by acting as a vasodilator or counterirritant. Also called **embrocation**

liparia *noun* same as **obesity**

lipectomy *noun* the surgical removal of fatty tissue from beneath the skin

lipid *noun* any organic compound that is insoluble in water, e.g. fat, oil or wax

lipidaema *noun* subcutaneous fat deposits that form in the lower extremities of the body

lipodology *noun* the study of fat and its effects on the body

lipodystrophy *noun* any condition in which fat is ineffectively metabolised

lipolysis *noun* the breakdown of fatty acids in the body

lipoprotein *noun* a protein that combines with lipids and carries them in the bloodstream and lymph system (NOTE: Lipoproteins are classified according to the percentage of protein they carry.)

lisinopril *noun* an oral drug used in the treatment of hypertension

live *adjective* **1.** of an event, appearing, performing, or performed in front of an audience or in person, rather than recorded or filmed **2.** in sports such as baseball or football, used to describe a ball that remains in play because officials have not halted action

living food diet *noun* same as **raw food diet**

load *noun* **1.** a weight or mass which is supported **2.** the force that a body part or structure is subjected to when it resists externally applied forces **3.** the amount of something, usually weight, that a body part can deal with at one time

loading dose *noun* a dose of a dietary supplement that is very high and delivers the maximum amount of the substance to the body in a short space of time

lob *verb* to hit or throw a ball in a high curving trajectory ■ *noun* a ball that travels over the head of a tennis player

locker *noun* a small lockable cupboard or compartment where personal belongings can be left, e.g. at a swimming pool or in a gym

locker room *noun* a room containing lockers, where people change their clothes for sports or swimming

log roll *noun* a technique for moving an injured person that does not risk aggravating any potential spinal injury, in which the body is rolled sideways, e.g. onto a spinal board

long bone *noun* any long limb bone that contains marrow and ends in a part that forms a joint with another bone

long-chain fatty acids *plural noun* fatty acids with more than six carbon bonds

long jump *noun* an athletics event in which the contestants jump for distance, usually from a running start into a sand pit

long shot *noun* a player or team that is unlikely to win a race or competition

Long-Term Athlete Development, Long-Term Player Development *noun* a model that explains sport-specific best practice for a serious athlete at each stage of skills learning. Abbreviation **LTAD, LTPD**

long-term goal *noun* something that a person wants to achieve in the future, which they are working towards

long-term memory *noun* the part of the mind that retains information permanently or nearly so

longwinded *adjective* capable of doing physical exercise for a relatively long period of time without getting short of breath

loose-jointed *adjective* **1.** agile and supple in movement **2.** having joints that are very mobile

loosen up *verb* to do exercises, or exercise muscles or joints, in order to become more limber, prior to strenuous activity

lordosis *noun* excessive forward curvature of the lower part of the spine. ◊ **kyphosis**

love *noun* a score of zero in some sports and games, e.g. tennis and squash

love game *noun* a game in tennis and some other sports in which the loser scores no points

low biological value *noun* the fact of containing a relatively low amount of bioavailable proteins

low blood pressure *noun* same as **hypotension**

low-calorie *adjective* used for describing foods and drinks with a low energy value, in the EU generally less than 40 kcal per 100g

low density lipoprotein *noun* the lipoprotein that carries cholesterol to cells and tissue. Abbreviation **LDL**

lower abs *plural noun* the abdominal muscles that are below the navel

lower oesophageal sphincter *noun* a ring of muscle at the lower end of the oesophagus that prevents stomach contents from refluxing. Abbreviation **LOS**

lower-reference nutrient intake *noun* an amount of a nutrient that is sufficient for people with low nutrition requirements, but not for the majority of people. Abbreviation **LRNI**

low-fat *adjective* containing very little fat

low-impact *adjective* used for describing exercise that involves little compression of the joints

low-sugar *adjective* containing very little sugar

LRNI *abbreviation* lower-reference nutrient intake

LTAD *abbreviation* Long-Term Athlete Development

LTPD *abbreviation* Long-Term Player Development

lucid *adjective* rational and mentally clear, especially in circumstances in which someone might be expected to exhibit opposite behaviour, e.g. because of a head injury

luge *noun* a racing toboggan on which the riders lie on their backs with their feet pointing forwards

lumbar *adjective* relating to the lower back

lumbar stenosis *noun* narrowing of the spinal canal, through which the spine and attached nerves pass, in the lower part of the back, causing pain and interruption to the nerve functions

lumen *noun* **1.** the inside width of a passage in the body or of an instrument such as an endoscope **2.** a hole at the end of an instrument such as an endoscope

lunate bone *noun* a bone of the wrist that articulates with the bones of the forearm

lung *noun* one of two organs of respiration in the body into which air is sucked when a person breathes

lung capacity *noun* the volume of oxygen that a person can hold in their lungs

lung disease *noun* medical conditions affecting the lungs, including asthma, emphysema and bronchitis

lunge *noun* **1.** an exercise in which a person steps forward with one leg and moves the bulk of their body downwards, supporting it on the front leg **2.** (*in fencing*) a sudden thrust made at an opponent

lupus erythematosus *noun* an inflammatory disease of connective tissue, the more serious form of which affects the heart, joints and blood vessels. Abbreviation **LE**

luteinising hormone *noun* a hormone, secreted by the pituitary gland, that regulates testosterone production, the action of which is affected by steroid use. Abbreviation **LH**

luxate *verb* to displace the bones of a joint (*technical*)

luxation *noun* same as **dislocation**

Lycra a trade name for a lightweight stretchy polyurethane fibre, or a fabric made from this, used for making sportswear

lymph *noun* a fluid containing white cells that is drained from tissue spaces by the vessels of the lymphatic system

lymphatic *adjective* relating to lymph or the lymphatic system

lymphatic flow *noun* the flow of substances transported by the lymphatic system

lymphatic system *noun* a network of vessels that transport fluid, fats, proteins and lymphocytes to the bloodstream as lymph, and remove microorganisms and other debris from tissues

lymph gland, lymph node *noun* an oval body in the lymphatic system that produces and houses lymphocytes and filters microorganisms and other particles from lymph, thus reducing the risk of infection

lymphocyte *noun* an important cell class in the immune system that produces antibodies to attack infected and cancerous cells, and is responsible for rejecting foreign tissue

lysine *noun* an essential amino acid

M

Maccabiah Games *plural noun* an international athletics event for Jewish athletes, held every four years in Israel, the year following the Olympic Games

machine weight *noun* same as **fixed weight**

macrobiotic *adjective* relating to macrobiotics

macrobiotics *noun* a dietary system based on vegetarian foods without artificial additives or preservatives, especially organically grown whole grains, fruit and vegetables

macrocycle *noun* a training cycle that typically lasts for a year

macronutrient *noun* a substance that an organism needs in large amounts for normal growth and development, e.g. nitrogen, carbon or potassium. Compare **micronutrient**

macronutrient cycling *noun* same as **food combining**

Maddocks' questions *plural noun* a set of questions, used in a sports concussion assessment tool alongside the AVPU ratings, that assess what the player can remember about the game and their recent history

madison *noun* a cycling event in which competitors ride as teams, each rider relieving the other in turn

magnesium *noun* a chemical element found in green vegetables, essential for the correct functioning of muscles (NOTE: The chemical symbol is **Mg**.)

magnesium deficiency *noun* a condition that can cause heart arrhythmia and electrolyte disturbances

magnetic resonance image scan *noun* full form of **MRI scan**

maiden *noun* (*in cricket*) an over in which no runs are scored

maintenance dose *noun* a dose of a dietary supplement which is moderate and help to maintain a constant level of the substance in the body

maintenance training *noun* training that maintains an already-attained level of fitness, rather than increasing it

maize protein *noun* the protein found in corn

major league *noun* **1.** either of the two main professional baseball leagues in the United States **2.** a top league of professional football, ice hockey or basketball teams in the United States

major muscle *noun* a large muscle that exerts a lot of force

malabsorption *noun* a situation in which the intestines are unable to absorb the fluids and nutrients in food properly

malabsorption syndrome *noun* a set of symptoms caused by not taking in enough of a particular nutrient

malassimilation *noun* the poor or inadequate incorporation of food constituents such as proteins and minerals into bones, muscles and other body structures

malnourished *adjective* not having enough to eat or having only poor-quality food, and therefore ill

malnutrition *noun* **1.** a lack of food or of good-quality food, leading to ill-health **2.** the state of not having enough to eat

manage *verb* **1.** to be in charge or control of something **2.** to guide the career and control the business affairs of somebody such as a professional entertainer or athlete (NOTE: **managing – managed**)

manager *noun* someone who organises and controls the training of an athlete or a sports team

manikin *noun* an anatomical model of the human body, used in teaching anatomy

manipulate *verb* to rub or move parts of the body with the hands to treat a joint, a slipped disc or a hernia

manipulation *noun* a form of treatment that involves moving or rubbing parts of the body with the hands, e.g. to treat a disorder of a joint

man-to-man *adjective* in sports such as football, hockey, or basketball, having each defender of one team mark a corresponding attacker of the other team

manual therapy *noun* treatment for an injury involving massage and physical contact

MAO B *abbreviation* monoamine oxidase B

marathon *noun* **1.** a long-distance footrace run over a distance of 42.195 km/26 mi. 385 yds **2.** a test of endurance, especially in a competition

mark *verb* in games such as football and hockey, to stay close to an attacking player in the opposing team to prevent the player from receiving the ball or scoring

marker *noun* **1.** in games such as football and hockey, a player who stays close to an attacking player in the opposing team to prevent him or her from receiving the ball or scoring **2.** a substance which reveals the use of a banned substance, found in drugs testing

marks *plural noun* a runner's individual starting position for a race

marrow *noun* soft red or yellow fatty tissue that fills the central cavities of bones

marrow bone *noun* any large hollow bone that contains bone marrow, soft spongy tissue in which new blood cells are produced

martial arts *plural noun* any of various systems of combat and self-defence, e.g. judo or karate, developed especially in Japan and Korea and now usually practised as a sport

masking agent *noun* an agent that disguises the signs of banned substance use so that an athlete can pass drugs tests, e.g. albumin solution

mass *noun* **1.** a large quantity, e.g. a large number of people **2.** a body of matter with no clear shape **3.** a mixture for making pills **4.** the main solid part of bone

massage *noun* a treatment for muscular conditions which involves rubbing, stroking or pressing the body with the hands

masseur *noun* a man who gives massages professionally

masseuse *noun* a woman who gives massages professionally

massotherapy *noun* the use of massage as a medical treatment

mast *noun* a vertical spar that supports sails, rigging or flags on a ship

mast cell *noun* a large cell in connective tissue that carries histamine and reacts to allergens

master *verb* to become highly competent in a skill or acquire a complete understanding of some process

mastitis *noun* an inflammation of the breast, which can occur in female athletes not wearing a supportive sports bra

match *noun* 1. a contest between opponents, especially a sporting contest 2. somebody or something capable of competing equally with another person or thing

match-fit *adjective* used for describing a sportsperson who is ready to perform in competition, having recovered from an injury

match point *noun* the final point needed to win a match, especially in tennis and other racket sports

matkot *noun* a sport played in Israel on the beach using a small ball and wooden bats

matrix *noun* the substance that exists between cells and from which tissue such as cartilage and bone develops

maul *noun* (*in rugby*) a loose scrum that members of both teams form around the player holding the ball or trying to run with the ball

maximal oxygen consumption *noun* same as **VO2Max**

maximum heart rate *noun* the number of heartbeats per minute that an athlete should work at for maximum efficiency, usually expressed as 220 minus the age of athlete. Abbreviation **MHR**

ME *noun* a complex disorder with symptoms of profound fatigue and any of a range of other symptoms, including pain, muscle weakness, loss of brain function, hypersensitivity, digestive disturbances and depression. Full form **myalgic encephalopathy**

meal replacement product *noun* a bodybuilding supplement containing concentrated proteins, vitamins and minerals, usually powdered and taken mixed with water or milk. Abbreviation **MRP**

meat alternative, **meat replacement** *noun* a vegetarian food product that provides protein and takes the place of meat

mechanical *adjective* related to mechanics

mechanical ileus *noun* an ileus caused by a physical obstruction in the bowel

mechanical injury *noun* an injury inflicted by a piece of equipment used in a sport, e.g. a blister caused by running shoes

mechanical sport *noun* any sport in which a machine or vehicle is used, e.g. motor racing

mechanical traction *noun* treatment for an injury which uses traction to separate or properly align the skeleton

mechanics *noun* the study of the forces acting on moving parts or systems, e.g. the human body

mechanoreceptor *noun* a sensory receptor of a nerve that responds to pressure, vibration, or another mechanical stimulus

mechanotherapy *noun* the treatment of injuries through mechanical means such as massage and exercise machines

medal *noun* a small flat piece of metal, usually shaped like a coin and stamped with an inscription or design, awarded to the winners of a sporting competition ■ *verb* to win a medal in a competition

medial *adjective* nearer to the central midline of the body or to the centre of an organ. Compare **lateral**

medial collateral tendon sprain *noun* a sprain of the tendon connecting the thighbone to the shinbone, caused by receiving a violent twist to the knee

medial epicondylitis *noun* pain in the elbow joint caused by repeatedly moving the hand and wrist, which strains the tendons at their point of attachment

medial stress syndrome *noun* a condition in which a set of muscles in the lower leg are inflamed, causing shin pain

median nerve *noun* one of the main nerves of the forearm and hand

median plane *noun* same as **sagittal plane**

medic *noun* a doctor or medical student

medical food *noun* food specially processed or formulated to be given, under medical supervision, to patients who require a special diet

medicine ball *noun* a large heavy ball that people throw to each other as a strength-building exercise

medicolegal *adjective* relating to the possible legal implications of giving medical care, especially when this is faulty or negligent

meditation *noun* the emptying of the mind of thoughts, or the concentration of the mind on one thing, in order to aid mental or spiritual development, contemplation, or relaxation

Mediterranean diet *noun* a diet high in fibre and monounsaturated fat from fish, vegetables, grains and olive oil

medium-term goal *noun* something that a person wants to achieve over a period of a few months or years, which they are working towards

medley *noun* a swimming race between individual swimmers or relay teams in which sections are swum using different strokes

medley relay *noun* a relay swimming race between teams of four swimmers, each of whom uses a different stroke

medulla *noun* **1.** the soft inner part of an organ, as opposed to the outer cortex **2.** bone marrow **3.** any structure similar to bone marrow

medullary cavity *noun* a hollow centre of a long bone, containing bone marrow

megadose *noun* a large dose of something such as a vitamin

megajoule *noun* a unit of measurement of energy equal to one million joules. Abbreviation **MJ**

megavitamin *noun* a dose of a vitamin or vitamins that is much higher than the usual dose

membrane *noun* a thin layer of tissue that lines or covers an organ

membrane bone *noun* a bone that develops from tissue and not from cartilage

meniscectomy *noun* the surgical removal of a cartilage from the knee

meniscus *noun* a cartilage pad inside the knee which can become damaged if the knee is twisted forcefully

mental attitude *noun* whether a person is optimistic or pessimistic about their chances of success

mental health *noun* the condition of someone's mind

mentor *noun* somebody who advises and guides a younger, less experienced person

mesocycle *noun* a training cycle that typically lasts for a few weeks

mesomorph *noun* a body type that is muscular and powerful

MET *abbreviation* metabolic equivalent

metabolic equivalent *noun* a unit used for expressing the resting metabolic rate. Abbreviation **MET**

metabolic fuels *plural noun* reserves of energy which the body draws upon, primarily muscle glycogen and free fatty acids

metabolic nitrogen *noun* nitrogen in the body that comes from internal sources and not the diet, e.g. from intestinal bacteria

metabolic pathway *noun* a series of chemical reactions in the body, controlled by enzymes

metabolic rate *noun* a measure of how fast the chemical reactions in living cells happen

metabolic syndrome *noun* a medical condition characterised by symptoms such as obesity, diabetes, hypertension and high cholesterol

metabolic waste *noun* a substance produced by metabolism, e.g. carbon dioxide, which is not needed by the organism which produces it

metabolic waste products *plural noun* substances which build up in the body as a result of metabolism, e.g. lactic acid in muscles

metabolisation *noun* the act of metabolising food

metabolise *verb* when the body metabolises food, it converts food into new or repaired cell material and tissues and energy after it has been broken down in the gut and transported in the blood to the cells of the body

metabolism *noun* the chemical processes that are continually taking place in the human body and are essential to life, especially the processes that convert food into energy

metabolite *noun* a substance produced by metabolism, or a substance taken into the body in food and then metabolised

metacarpal *noun* any bone in the human hand between the wrist and digits

metacarpus *noun* the five bones in the hand between the fingers and the wrist

metacognitive *adjective* relating to the activity of monitoring and revising one's own performance

metatarsal *noun* any of the five bones in the metatarsus

metatarsalgia *noun* pain in the metatarsals caused by excessive weight-bearing activity or poor-fitting shoes

metatarsus *noun* the five long bones in the foot between the toes and the tarsus (NOTE: The plural is **metatarsi**.)

methanedienone *noun* a steroid supplement, taken orally by bodybuilders, that is thought to increase aerobic glycosis and also helps maintain bone mass

MHR *abbreviation* maximum heart rate

microcycle *noun* a training cycle that typically lasts for one week

microfibre *noun* a wrinkle-resistant washable fabric made of fine synthetic fibres

micronutrient *noun* a substance that an organism needs for normal growth and development, but only in very small quantities, e.g. a vitamin or mineral. Compare **macronutrient**

microtear *noun* a minute tear in muscle-fibre tissue, seen in competitive cyclists and other distance athletes

middle scalene *noun* a pair of muscles involved in tilting the neck

middleweight *noun* **1.** in professional boxing, a weight category for competitors who weigh between 66.5 and 72.5 kg/147 and 160 lb **2.** in amateur boxing, a weight category for competitors who weigh between 71 and 75 kg/157 and 165 lb **3.** a professional or amateur boxer who competes at middleweight level **4.** in various sports such as wrestling, a contestant of approximately the same weight as a middleweight boxer

midfield *noun* **1.** the middle portion of a sports pitch, especially the area midway between the two penalty areas **2.** the group of players who contest control of the central area of the pitch between the two penalty areas

midfielder *noun* a member of a football team active in the central area of the playing field, often both in attack and defence

midline *noun* an imaginary line drawn down the middle of the body from the head through the navel to the point between the feet

midsection *noun* the middle part of something, especially the area of the human body between the chest and waist

mid-shaft fracture *noun* a bone fracture caused by severe trauma to the limb

mile *noun* an imperial measurement of distance, equal to 1.609 km

mileometer *noun* a device that records distance travelled, e.g. one fitted to a racing cycle

military press *noun* an exercise in which a barbell is lifted from the chest to over the head

milk protein *noun* the protein found in milk, which is highly bioavailable and often used in protein supplements

mind-body-spirit *adjective* same as **holistic**

mindfulness *noun* the act of concentrating or being deliberately attentive

mindfulness training *noun* a programme designed to reduce the psychological and physical effects of stress that involves meditation, yoga and other relaxation methods

mindset *noun* a set of beliefs or a way of thinking that determine somebody's behaviour and outlook

mineral *noun* an inorganic substance with a characteristic chemical composition that occurs naturally and is an essential part of the human diet

mineralisation *noun* ♦ bone mineralisation

mineral salt *noun* a crystalline compound formed from the neutralisation of an acid solution containing a mineral

mineral water *noun* water that comes naturally from the ground and is sold in bottles

miner's cramp *noun* a cramping of the muscles due to salt loss through excess sweating

mini-stepper *noun* a small home exercise machine with two foot pads that are pushed up and down against some resistance to work the leg muscles

mini-stroke *noun* same as **transient ischaemic attack**

minute ventilation *noun* a test for respiratory capacity that measures the volume of air expired in one minute

mishit *verb* to hit something badly, e.g. a ball or puck, so that it does not go in the desired direction or has insufficient force behind it

miskick *verb* to fail to kick a ball in the right or intended way

misplay *verb* to play or move something such as a ball or game piece badly or carelessly ■ *noun* a bad or unintended play in sport or a game

misthrow *verb* to throw something such as dice or a ball in a wrong or invalid way

misuse *noun* of an addictive substance

mitochondrion *noun* a small round or rod-shaped body that is found in the cytoplasm of most cells and produces enzymes for the metabolic conversion of food to energy

mitral valve *noun* a valve in the heart which allows blood to flow from the left atrium to the left ventricle but not in the opposite direction. Also called **bicuspid valve**

mobile *adjective* able to move freely or easily

mobilisation *noun* the act of helping something such as a stiff joint to move freely again

mobilised *adjective* used for describing teeth that have been loosened by an impact

mobility *noun* the ability to move about

mobility training *noun* exercises that increase the range of movement of the joints

modern pentathlon *noun* an athletics competition in which the contestants compete in five different events and are awarded points for each to find the best all-round athlete. The events are swimming, horse riding, cross-country running, fencing and pistol shooting.

molybdenum *noun* a metallic trace element (NOTE: The chemical symbol is **Mo**.)

monitor *noun* a screen on a computer

monoamine *noun* an amine compound that contains one amino group, especially the neurotransmitters adrenaline and serotonin

monoamine oxidase B *noun* an enzyme which inhibits the action of dopamine, high levels of which have been implicated in cases of depression and neurological disorders such as Parkinsonism. Abbreviation **MAO B**

monoaminergic *adjective* caused or mediated by monoamines

monolift *noun* a machine which holds a weightlifter's barbell in place until they are ready to lift

mononucleosis *noun* a infectious disease, caused by a virus, that causes fatigue and fever-like symptoms and increases the chances of splenic rupture

monoplegia *noun* the paralysis of one part of the body only, i.e. one muscle or one limb

monosaccharide *noun* a simple sugar of the type that includes glucose, fructose and galactose

monounsaturated fat *noun* a fat or oil containing a single double bond in the chain of carbon atoms that make up the fatty acid part (NOTE: Olive oil is the commonest example.)

Montignac diet *noun* a dietary plan that advises that carbohydrates and proteins or fats should not be eaten at the same time

mood swing *noun* a sudden and extreme change in someone's mood, possibly as a result of their diet

morbidity *noun* how prevalent a disease or condition is in a population

morbid obesity *noun* severe obesity, as much as twice the ideal body weight of a person

morphine *noun* a powerful painkilling drug the use of which is banned for athletes

Morton's toe *noun* a disorder of the foot in which the second toe is longer than the big toe, causing gait problems and a tendency to overpronate

motion control *noun* same as **stability control**

motivate *verb* to make somebody feel enthusiastic, interested and committed to a goal, or to give them a reason or incentive to perform

motivation *noun* **1.** the act of giving somebody a reason or incentive to do something **2.** a feeling of enthusiasm, interest, or commitment that makes somebody want to do something, or something that causes such a feeling **3.** the biological, emotional, cognitive, or social forces that activate and direct behaviour

motocross *noun* a motorcycle race, or the sport of racing motorcycles, over a rough course with steep hills, wet or muddy areas, and turns of varying difficulty. Abbreviation **MX**

motor *adjective* relating to muscle activity, especially voluntary muscle activity, and the consequent body movements

motorbike *noun* same as **motorcycle**

motorbike racing *noun* the sport of racing on motorcycles

motor cortex *noun* the region of the outer surface of the brain where nervous impulses controlling voluntary muscle activity are initiated

motorcycle *noun* a two-wheeled road vehicle powered by an engine

motor dysfunction *noun* the incorrect function of motor neurons, causing an inability to control muscle movements

motoric *adjective* relating to voluntary muscle movement

motor nerve *noun* a nerve which carries impulses from the brain and spinal cord to muscles and causes movements. Also called **efferent nerve**

motor neuron, motor neurone *noun* a neuron that is part of a nerve pathway transmitting impulses from the brain to a muscle or gland

motor neuron disease *noun* a progressive degenerative disease involving the motor neurons and causing weakness and wasting of the muscles

motor output *noun* the movement made by a person in response to nerve impulses

motor protein *noun* any of a group of cell proteins that use chemical energy from ATP to create movement within cells, e.g. by separating chromosomes during cell division and transporting neurotransmitters inside nerve cells

motor skill learning *noun* the acquisition of new motor skills, either as a child or as part of sports training

motor skills *plural noun* the ability of a person to make movements to achieve a goal, with stages including processing the information in the brain, transmitting neural signals and coordinating the relevant muscles to achieve the desired effect

motorsport *noun* a sport in which participants race motor vehicles, usually around a track

motor unit *noun* a motor neuron and the muscle fibres it acts on

mountain bike *noun* a bicycle built for rough terrain with wide thick tyres, straight handlebars, a strong frame, and more gears than a standard bicycle

mountain board *noun* a board similar to a skateboard but with bigger wheels, used for travelling over rough ground as an extreme sport

mountainboarding *noun* the sport of travelling down hillsides on a board similar to a skateboard but with bigger wheels

mountaineering *noun* the sport or pastime of climbing mountains

mouthguard *noun* a moulded piece of plastic that fits over the teeth, used for protecting them during heavy contact sports such as boxing

MRI scan *noun* an imaging technique that uses electromagnetic radiation to obtain images of the body's soft tissues, e.g. the brain and spinal cord. Full form **magnetic resonance image scan**

MRP *abbreviation* meal replacement product

Muay Thai *noun* a martial art that is a form of kickboxing, practised in Thailand and across Southeast Asia

mucous membrane *noun* a wet membrane that lines internal passages in the body, e.g. the nose, mouth, stomach and throat, and secretes mucus

mucus *noun* a slippery liquid secreted by mucous membranes inside the body in order to protect them

multidisciplinary *adjective* studying or using several specialised subjects or skills

multi-event *noun* an athletic contest, e.g. the pentathlon or decathlon, that includes several different events

multifidus *noun* a collection of bundles of muscle fibres that help to stabilise the spine

multigym *noun* an exercise apparatus with a range of weights, used for muscle toning

multipennate *adjective* used for describing a muscle with tendons leading to several points of attachment, e.g. the pectoralis muscles

multiple sclerosis *noun* a serious progressive disease of the central nervous system that leads to the loss of myelin in the brain or spinal cord and causes muscle weakness, poor eyesight, slow speech and some inability to move. Abbreviation **MS**

multiracialism *noun* the principle or practice of ensuring that people of various races are fully integrated into a society

multisport event *noun* a large sporting competition, e.g. the Olympic Games, in which more than one sport is practised over a period of several days or weeks

multi-task attention *noun* the skill of concentrating on several tasks at once, as employed in complex performances

multivitamin *noun* a preparation containing several vitamins and sometimes minerals, used as a dietary supplement

murderball *noun* same as **quad rugby**

murmur *noun* a soft blowing or fluttering sound, caused by turbulent blood flow, that originates from the heart, lungs or arteries and may indicate disease or structural concerns

muscle *noun* **1.** an organ in the body that contracts to make part of the body move **2.** same as **muscle tissue**

muscle-bound *adjective* having muscles that are so bulky that they restrict movement

muscle building *noun* developing the muscles by training with weights and having a diet rich in protein

muscle candy *noun* US a dietary supplement used by athletes to enhance bursts of high performance (*slang*)

muscle cell *noun* a long contractile cell of the kind that forms the muscles of the body

muscle confusion *noun* the act of using several different exercises for a single muscle so that it cannot adapt to a predictable workout and is therefore forced to work harder

muscle endurance *noun* the capacity of muscles to sustain prolonged aerobic activity

muscle failure *noun* the inability of muscles to produce enough energy to sustain further activity

muscle fatigue *noun* tiredness in the muscles after strenuous exercise

muscle fibre *noun* a component fibre of muscles (NOTE: There are two types of fibre, one forming striated muscles and one forming smooth muscles.)

muscle function *noun* the smooth expansion or contraction of muscles in the body to create movement

muscle group *noun* same as **compartment**

muscle insertion *noun* the point of attachment of a muscle to a bone

muscle man *noun* a very strong man with highly developed muscles

muscle relaxant *noun* a drug that reduces contractions in the muscles

muscle spasm *noun* a sudden uncontrolled contraction of a muscle

muscle spindle *noun* any of the sensory receptors that lie along striated muscle fibres

muscle tissue *noun* the specialised type of tissue that forms the muscles and can contract and expand

muscle tone *noun* same as **tone**

muscle wasting *noun* a condition in which the muscles lose weight and become thin

muscular *adjective* relating to muscle

muscular branch *noun* a branch of a nerve to a muscle carrying efferent impulses to produce contraction

muscular defence *noun* a rigidity of muscles associated with inflammation such as peritonitis

muscular disorder *noun* a disorder which affects the muscles, e.g. cramp or strain

muscular fatigue *noun* same as **muscle fatigue**

muscular system *noun* the muscles in the body, usually applied only to striated muscles

muscular tissue *noun* same as **muscle tissue**

musculature *noun* the way that the muscles are arranged in a body or body part

musculo- *prefix* relating to or affecting muscle

musculocutaneous nerve *noun* a nerve in the brachial plexus which supplies the muscles in the arm

musculoskeletal *adjective* relating to muscle and bone

musculoskeletal screening *noun* medical screening of an athlete designed to identify weak areas where injury might occur, so that it can be prevented

myalgia *noun* a muscle pain

myalgic encephalopathy *noun* full form of **ME**

myasthenia *noun* an autoimmune disease involving extreme weakness of some muscles, caused by the blocking of the receptors for acetylcholine, the neurotransmitter that causes muscular contraction

mycoprotein *noun* a food, especially a meat substitute, made by fermenting a fungus and heating, draining and texturing the resultant product

mydriasis *noun* excessive dilation of the pupils of the eye, usually caused by prolonged drug therapy, coma or injury to the eye

myelin *noun* the substance of the cell membrane of Schwann cells that coils into a protective covering (**myelin sheath**) around nerve fibres

myelinated *adjective* used for describing nerve fibre that are covered by a myelin sheath

myelin sheath *noun* a layer of myelin that insulates some nerve cells and speeds the conduction of nerve impulses

myelitis *noun* **1.** inflammation of the spinal cord **2.** inflammation of bone marrow

myelo- *prefix* relating to spinal cord or bone marrow

myelogenous *adjective* originating in or produced by the bone marrow

myeloid *adjective* **1.** relating to bone marrow, or produced by bone marrow **2.** relating to the spinal cord

myo- *prefix* referring to muscle

myocardial *adjective* referring to the myocardium

myocardial infarction *noun* the death of part of the heart muscle after coronary thrombosis. Abbreviation **MI**

myocardial ischaemia *noun* insufficient blood supply to the heart

myocardiograph *noun* an instrument that records the contractions of the heart muscle

myocardium *noun* the middle layer of the wall of the heart, formed of heart muscle

myocele *noun* a condition in which a muscle pushes through a gap in the surrounding membrane

myocete *noun* a cell that can contract, especially a muscle cell

myoclonus *noun* a sudden muscular contraction, or a series of these, that usually indicates a disorder of the nervous system if experienced persistently

myocyte *noun* a muscle cell

myoelectric *adjective* **1.** relating to or involving the electrical properties of muscle **2.** using the detection of electrical impulses in muscle to activate a bionic part such as an artificial limb

myoelectrical *adjective* relating to or involving the electrical properties of muscle

myofascial release *noun* a form of gentle massage involving the stretching and manipulation of the tough connective tissue that surrounds the body

myofibril *noun* a long thread of striated muscle fibre

myofilament *noun* one of the filaments that make up a myofibril, either the thicker filaments composed of the protein myosin or the thinner filaments composed of the proteins actin or troponin

myogenic *adjective* used for describing movement that comes from an involuntary muscle

myoglobin *noun* muscle haemoglobin, which takes oxygen from blood and passes it to the muscle

myokymia *noun* twitching of a particular muscle

myology *noun* the study of muscles and their associated structures and diseases

myoneural *adjective* relating to or involving both the muscles and the nerves

myoneural junction *noun* same as **neuromuscular junction**

myopathy *noun* a disease of a muscle, especially one in which the muscle wastes away

myoplasty *noun* a form of plastic surgery to repair a muscle

myosarcoma *noun* a malignant tumour occurring in muscle

myosin *noun* a protein in muscles that helps them contract

myositis *noun* inflammation and degeneration of a muscle

myotome *noun* **1.** a cell in early embryos that gives rise to muscle in the body **2.** a muscle that is supplied by a nerve of the spine

myotonia *noun* difficulty in relaxing a muscle after exercise

myotonic *adjective* referring to tone in a muscle

myotonus *noun* muscle tone

N

NAD *noun* a supplement used for fighting the symptoms of fatigue. Full form **nicotinamide adenine dinucleotide**

nandrolone *noun* an anabolic steroid that builds muscle (NOTE: Its use is banned by the International Amateur Athletics Federation.)

nap *noun* (*in horse racing*) a tip for a horse that is very likely to win

naprapathy *noun* a system of therapy that combines diet with manipulation of joints, ligaments and muscles to assist the body's natural regenerative ability

narcotic *noun* any typically addictive drug, especially one derived from opium, e.g. cocaine, that may produce effects ranging from pain relief and sleep to stupor, coma and convulsions

narcotic analgesic *noun* a painkiller sometimes misused by athletes to allow them to continue to train despite injury

nares *plural noun* the nostrils (NOTE: The singular is **naris**.)

nasopharynx *noun* the top part of the pharynx that connects with the nose

nationals *plural noun* a sports or games competition in which participants from all parts of a nation are involved

national sport *noun* a sport that is very popular in a country and is considered to be part of its culture

natriuresis *noun* the loss of excessive amounts of sodium in urine

natural additive *noun* a food additive that is a natural extract of a raw material, rather than a synthesised chemical

nature cure *noun* a holistic approach to medicine that only uses natural substances and remedies in order to allow the body's own natural powers of healing and protection to treat illness or disease

nature-identical *adjective* referring to a synthesised additive that is chemically identical to one naturally occurring in food

Nautilus a trade name for a manufacturer of professional exercise equipment

nebulin *noun* a molecule in muscle tissue that binds actin

neck *noun* a part of the body that connects the head to the shoulders

necrosis *noun* the death of a part of the body such as a bone, tissue or an organ as a result of disease or injury

necrotic *adjective* referring to, or affected with, necrosis

negative *noun* an exercise in which a weight is lowered slowly against gravity

negative attitude *noun* a pessimistic mental attitude towards an activity that may decrease the chance of succeeding

negative energy balance *noun* a situation in which a person is using more energy on a day-to-day basis than he or she consumes, leading to weight loss

negative thinking *noun* a way of thinking that is pessimistic and focusing only on bad things that may happen

neoprene *noun* a type of plastic used for making sports injury braces and supports and for making wetsuits

nerve *noun* **1.** a bundle of fibres that can transmit electrochemical impulses and that forms part of the network that connects the brain and spinal cord to the body's organs **2.** the sensitive tissue in the root of a tooth

nerve block *noun* the act of stopping the function of a nerve by injecting an anaesthetic

nerve cell *noun* same as **neuron**

nerve centre *noun* the point at which nerves come together

nerve ending *noun* same as **sensory receptor**

nerve fibre *noun* a thin structure leading from a nerve cell and carrying nerve impulses, e.g. an axon

nerve impulse *noun* an electrochemical impulse that is transmitted by nerve cells

nerve regeneration *noun* the growth of new nerve tissue after damage has occurred

nerve root *noun* the first part of a nerve as it leaves or joins the spinal column

nerve tissue *noun* tissue which forms nerves, and which is able to transmit the nerve impulses

nervous system *noun* the nervous tissues of the body, including the peripheral nerves, spinal cord, ganglia and nerve centres

nervous tic *noun* an involuntary twitch of a muscle, especially of the face, that is sometimes a symptom of nervousness or a nervous disease

net *noun* **1.** in some sports such as tennis and volleyball, a strip of meshwork material that divides a court into halves and over which the players must hit a ball or shuttlecock **2.** in some sports such as football and water polo, a goal with a backing made of meshwork material **3.** (*in cricket*) an indoor or outdoor practice pitch surrounded on three sides by nets that contain the ball after it has been hit ■ *verb* **1.** in games such as football and hockey, to hit the ball into the net so as to score **2.** in games such as tennis and volleyball, to hit the ball into the net so as to lose a serve, and sometimes a point

netball *noun* an indoor or outdoor game usually played by girls or women in which goals are scored by throwing a ball through a raised net. Players can hand or throw the ball to each other but not run with it.

net cord *noun* a tennis shot, especially a serve, that touches the net before landing on the opponent's side. In the case of a serve, the server retakes the shot.

net dietary protein energy ratio *noun* the protein content of a food, expressed as the amount of protein contained and the quality of it. Abbreviation **NDpE**

net protein retention *noun* a measure of protein quality, comparing its protein efficiency ratio with the weight loss of a test group fed no protein. Abbreviation **NPR**

net protein utilisation *noun* a measure of protein quality, taking into account both its biological value and its digestibility. Abbreviation **NPU**

nettle tea *noun* an infusion of nettle leaves, traditionally used for cleansing and detoxifying the body

neural *adjective* relating to a nerve or the nervous system

neural arch *noun* a curved part of a vertebra, which forms the space through which the spinal cord passes

neuralgia *noun* a spasm of pain that runs along a nerve

neuralgic *adjective* relating to pain felt in the nerves

neural network *noun* an interconnecting system of nerve cells, e.g. the system that makes the brain function

neurasthenia *noun* a type of neurosis in which a person is mentally and physically irritable and extremely fatigued

neurectomy *noun* a surgical operation to remove all or part of a nerve (NOTE: The plural is **neurectomies**.)

neuritis *noun* inflammation of a nerve, giving a constant pain

neuroactive *adjective* having an effect on neural tissue or the nervous system

neuroanatomy *noun* the scientific study of the structure of the nervous system

neurobiology *noun* same as **neuroscience**

neurochemistry *noun* the study of the chemical composition of and reactions within the nervous system

neurodegenerative *adjective* sued for describing a disorder such as Alzheimer's disease or Parkinson's disease that causes damage to the nerves

neuroendocrinology *noun* the study of the interrelationships between the nervous system, the endocrine system, and hormones

neurogenic *adjective* **1.** coming from the nervous system **2.** relating to the growth of nerve tissue

neurohormone *noun* a hormone produced in some nerve cells and secreted from the nerve endings

neuroleptic *noun* an anti-psychotic drug that calms a person and stops him or her from worrying, e.g. chlorpromazine hydrochloride

neurological *adjective* relating to neurology

neurology *noun* the scientific study of the nervous system and its diseases

neuromuscular *adjective* referring to both nerves and muscles

neuromuscular junction *noun* the point where a motor neuron joins muscle fibre. Also called **myoneural junction**

neuron, neurone *noun* a cell in the nervous system that transmits nerve impulses

neuropathy *noun* any disease involving destruction of the tissues of the nervous system (NOTE: The plural is **neuropathies**.)

neuropeptide Y *noun* a neurotransmitter that has a role in controlling feeding behaviour and appetite

neurophysiology *noun* the study of the physiology of nerves

neuroscience *noun* the scientific study of the molecular and cellular levels of the nervous system, of systems within the brain such as vision and hearing, and of behaviour produced by the brain. Also called **neurobiology**

neurosecretion *noun* **1.** a substance secreted by a nerve cell **2.** the process of secretion of an active substance by nerve cells

neurotoxic *adjective* harmful or poisonous to nerve cells

neurotoxicity *noun* the extent to which a substance damages, destroys or impairs the functioning of nerve tissue

neurotoxin *noun* a substance that damages, destroys or impairs the functioning of nerve tissue

neurotransmission *noun* communication of electrical impulses between nerve cells or between a nerve cell and a muscle

neurotransmitter *noun* a chemical substance that transmits nerve impulses from one neuron to another

neurotripsy *noun* surgical bruising or crushing of a nerve

neurotrophic *adjective* relating to the nutrition and maintenance of tissue of the nervous system

neurovascular *adjective* in or involving the nerves and blood vessels

neutral spine *noun* a position for the spine in which no joint is flexed and force is distributed equally

neutral zone *noun* (*in sport*) the space between the areas of two competing teams, especially the area between the linemen of American football teams or the middle area of an ice hockey rink between the two blue lines

niacin *noun* a vitamin of the vitamin B complex found in milk, meat, liver, kidney, yeast, beans, peas and bread, lack of which can cause mental disorders and pellagra. Also called **nicotinic acid**

nicotinamide adenine dinucleotide *noun* full form of **NAD**

ninjitsu *noun* a Japanese martial art that emphasises stealth in movement and camouflage

nitrate *noun* a chemical compound containing the nitrate ion, e.g. sodium nitrate

nitric oxide *noun* a sports supplement that promotes vasodilation, causing an increased blood flow to the muscles. Abbreviation **NO**

nitrogen-free extract *noun* the portion of a foodstuff when analysed that comprises only sugars and starches. Abbreviation **NFE**

nitrogen narcosis *noun* light-headedness, confusion or exhilaration caused by increased nitrogen in the blood. This occurs in deep-sea divers exposed to pressures several times that of the atmosphere.

nitrox *noun* a mixture of nitrogen and oxygen used for recreational diving

NO *abbreviation* nitric oxide

no ball *noun* in cricket, a ball that has been bowled in a way not permitted by the rules of the game

noci receptor *noun* a sensory nerve that carries pain to the brain

nollie *noun* (*in skateboarding*) a leap into the air on the board performed by pushing down on the front end of the board

non-aerobic exercise *noun* exercise in which there is little or no increase of respiration and heart rate, e.g. stretching

non-competitive *adjective* used for describing a sport or activity that does not involve any element of competition

non-dietary polysaccharides *noun* same as **dietary fibre**

non-displaced fracture *noun* a fractured bone in which the pieces of bone remain in alignment with each other

non-energy-dependent *adjective* used for describing a sport that involves skill more than movement and so does not require a large amount of energy metabolism, e.g. golf

non-essential *adjective* manufactured by the body and therefore not essential in the diet

non-essential amino acids *plural noun* amino acids that can be synthesised in the body and so do not need to be obtained in the diet. ◊ **essential amino acids**

non-fat *adjective* without fat solids, or with the fat content removed

non-fattening *adjective* not likely to cause a gain in weight

non-haem iron *noun* dietary iron found in plants. Compare **haem iron**

non-nutrient *adjective* used for describing a foodstuff that contains no nutrients

non-prescription drug *noun* a drug that can be bought without a doctor's prescription

non-sporting *adjective* not relating to, used in sports activities

non-steroid anti-inflammatory drug *noun* an anti-inflammatory drug that does not contain a steroid substance. Abbreviation **NSAID**

non-team *adjective* used for describing an athlete who does not take part in team sports

non-therapeutic *adjective* not used in the treatment of diseases or disorders or for maintaining health

non-title *adjective* used for describing a match or competition in which a sports title or championship is not at stake

non-weight-bearing *adjective* used for describing exercise that does not carrying any weight and so encourages the strengthening of bone fibres

non-zero-sum competition *noun* a competition in which the losing players still may achieve something, e.g. a position on a league table

noradrenaline *noun* a hormone secreted by the medulla of the adrenal glands that acts as a vasoconstrictor and is used for maintaining blood pressure in shock, haemorrhage or hypotension

noradrenergic *adjective* releasing or involving noradrenaline in the transmission of nerve impulses

norandrostenedione *noun* a sports supplement that converts to nandrolone in the body

Nordic *adjective* used for describing any skiing activity or event in which the boots are fitted to the skis at the toe only

Nordic Walking *noun* a form of health walking in which the upper body is worked out, using poles for balance

norethisterone *noun* a drug used for treating amenorrhoea and menstrual disorders suffered by female athletes

norming *noun* the third stage of team development according to the Tuckman model, in which the members of the team agree on basic principles and each brings his or her behaviour into line with that of the others

nosebleed *noun* an incident of bleeding from the nose, usually caused by a blow or by sneezing, by blowing the nose hard or by high blood pressure (*informal*) Also called **epistaxis**

nourish *verb* to give food or nutrients to a person

nourishing *adjective* providing the substances that people need to allow them to grow and be healthy

nourishment *noun* food or the valuable substances in food that help people to grow and be healthy

NSAID *abbreviation* non-steroid anti-inflammatory drug

numb *adjective* used for describing a part of the body that has no feeling

nutraceutical food *noun* same as **functional food**

nutrient *noun* a substance in food that is necessary to provide energy or to help the body grow, e.g. a protein, a fat or a vitamin

nutrient-dense *adjective* used for describing food that is rich in vitamins and minerals and comparatively low in calories

nutrification *noun* the enriching of foods with added nutrients so as to make a significant difference to the diet

nutrigenomics *noun* the study of the way in which genetic and environmental influences act together on a human or an animal, and how this information can be used to boost productivity and health

nutrition *noun* **1.** the way in which food affects health **2.** the study of food

nutritional disorder *noun* any disorder or disease caused by poor nutrition

nutritional guidelines *plural noun* public advice about healthy eating given by an authority

nutritional information *noun* additional information about the nutritional value of a food product, often used on food labelling in the UK

nutritional programme *noun* a dietary plan that is designed to achieve a particular aim, e.g. muscle building, weight loss or recovery from illness

nutritional status *noun* the balance of nutritional needs against intake and absorption

nutritional supplement *noun* ⏵ **supplement**

nutritional therapist *noun* a person who works with patients to devise a dietary plan for optimum health or to identify any intolerances

nutritional therapy *noun* the alleviation of symptoms by dietary changes, sometimes using vitamin and mineral pills

nutritional value *noun* the nutrient content of a food

nutrition claim *noun* wording or a logo on food packaging that makes a claim about the nutritional content of the food inside

nutrition consultant *noun* a professional who offers advice on a suitable diet to support a particular lifestyle

nutrition insecurity *noun* the state of having a restricted or deficient diet that makes it difficult to get all essential nutrients

nutritionist *noun* a person who specialises in the study of nutrition and advises on diets

nutrition security *noun* the state of having a varied diet that will provide all essential nutrients

nutritious *adjective* providing a fairly high level of nourishment

nutritive *adjective* relating to nourishment

nutritive value *noun* the degree to which a food is valuable in promoting health

O

O *noun* a human blood type of the ABO system containing the O antigen. Someone with this type of blood can donate to all other types in the group but can receive only type O blood.

obdurator nerve *noun* a large nerve in the pelvis that may be touched on by inflammation in the region

obese *adjective* so overweight as to be at risk of several serious illnesses, including diabetes and heart disease

obesity *noun* the condition of being seriously overweight

obesity rates *plural noun* the proportion of a country's population who are more than 20% overweight

obesogenic *adjective* promoting or causing obesity

object ball *noun* in billiards, pool or snooker, the ball that a player intends to hit with the cue ball

OBLA *abbreviation* onset of blood lactate accumulation

obliques *plural noun* two pairs of muscles in the abdomen that run diagonally from the ribs to the pelvis

observational learning *noun* skills learning that emphasises immersion in the situation so as to learn by seeing others perform

obstruction *noun* **1.** something that blocks a passage or a blood vessel **2.** the blocking of a passage or blood vessel

occupational activity levels *plural noun* the extent to which a person is active in their job, affecting their dietary energy requirements

octopush *noun* a sport rather like hockey that is played underwater with fins and a mask

oculomotor nerve *noun* the third cranial nerve which controls the eyeballs and eyelids

odds *plural noun* **1.** a ratio of probability given to people placing a bet, usually the likelihood of something happening, or of a competitor, team or animal winning **2.** an advantage or handicap given to a person, animal or team in a sporting contest, to equalise competitors' chances of winning **3.** a perceived advantage or disadvantage, especially one that one person is believed to have over another in a competition

odometer *noun US* same as **mileometer**

oedema *noun* the swelling of part of the body caused by accumulation of fluid in the intercellular tissue spaces

oestrogen *noun* any steroid hormone that stimulates the development of secondary sexual characteristics in females at puberty

oestrogen inhibitor *noun* a substance or drug that reduces or blocks the action of oestrogen, used as a sports supplement and in the treatment of breast cancer

oestrogen replacement *noun* treatment recommended in the case of female athlete triad, which regulates the monthly cycle and slows bone loss

off *noun* the side of the cricket field facing the batsman taking strike

off-break *noun* in cricket, a ball with a bounce that spins from the off side to the leg side

offence *noun* the players in a team whose role is to attack, especially in American-based sports

offensive *adjective* used, or designed to be used, when attacking

officiate *verb* to act as a referee at a sports event

off-piste *adjective* relating to or taking place on fresh trackless snow that is away from the regular skiing runs

off season *noun* a period after the end of one annual sports season and before the beginning of the next

off-side *adjective* illegally beyond or in advance of a ball or puck during play

off-side trap *noun* (*in football*) a tactic in which defenders coordinate their collective movement upfield in order to catch attacking players offside

000 *noun* **1.** (*in golf*) a small wooden or plastic peg with one pointed and one cupped end, inserted in the ground to hold a ball **2.** an area on a golf course where play for a new hole begins **3.** a plastic device that supports a football or rugby ball on the ground in a position for kicking **4.** a mark aimed at in curling, quoits and some other games

olecranon *noun* the upper end of the ulna bone that extends beyond the joint of the elbow to form the elbow's hard projecting point

olecranon bursitis *noun* bursitis at the elbow joint

olfactory nerve *noun* the first cranial nerve which controls the sense of smell

olighydria *noun* inefficient bodily production of sweat

oligoallergenic diet *noun* a restricted diet used for diagnosing the effects that particular foods have on a person

oligodipsia *noun* a reduced sense of thirst

oligotrophic *adjective* used for describing foods that do not contain sufficient nutrients

ollie *noun* (*in skateboarding*) a leap into the air on the board performed by pushing down on the rear end of the board

Olympic Games, Olympics *plural noun* a large-scale international sports contest intended to promote international goodwill, held every four years since 1896 in different cities around the world

Olympic Movement *noun* all the international sporting federations who abide by the rules of the Olympic Charter

omega-3 fatty acid *noun* a polyunsaturated fatty acid found in fish oils, seeds and whole grains, used in the prevention of such conditions as high cholesterol, heart disease and arthritis

omega-6 fatty acid *noun* a polyunsaturated fatty acid, deficiency of which can cause skin problems and hormonal imbalances

one rep max *noun* full form of **1RM**

1RM *noun* the maximum weight that a person can lift for a single rep of any given exercise. Full form **one rep max**

onion skin *noun* very dehydrated skin showing muscle definition

onset of blood lactate accumulation *noun* the stage in exercising where there is no longer enough oxygen being supplied to the muscle, leading to a build-up of lactic acid causing pain and tiredness. Abbreviation **OBLA**

on-side *adjective* (*in sports such as soccer and hockey*) in a position that is allowed within the rules of the game

open fracture *noun* same as **compound fracture**

open skill *noun* a skill that the athlete must adapt to the rapidly-changing circumstances in which it is performed, as in team ball games. Compare **closed skill**

ophthalmologist *noun* a doctor qualified to diagnose and treat eye injuries and diseases

opiate *noun* a sedative which is prepared from opium, e.g. morphine or codeine

opponent *noun* **1.** someone who plays, fights or competes against you in a contest **2.** any muscle that counteracts the motion of another

opponent sports *plural noun* same as **martial arts**

oppose *verb* to be in competition with another player or team

opposition *noun* **1.** the person or team that you or another player or team have to play against **2.** a movement of the hand muscles in which the tip of the thumb is made to touch the tip of another finger so as to hold something

opsonin *noun* a protein that promotes the destruction of antigens by white blood cells

optimal *adjective* most desirable or favourable

ORAC *abbreviation* oxygen radical absorbance capacity

oral rehydration salts *plural noun* same as **rehydration salts**

orexigenic *adjective* stimulating the appetite

oreximania *noun* an unusually large appetite

organic food *noun* food grown or reared without synthetic or chemically produced fertilisers, pesticides and herbicides on land that itself has been organic for two years

organotrophic *adjective* nourishing bodily organs

orienteering *noun* a sport that combines map-reading and cross-country running. Competitors make their way through unfamiliar terrain using a compass and a topographical map.

ornithine *noun* an amino acid produced by the liver that forms part of urea and is therefore involved in the disposal of excess nitrogen

ornithine alpha-ketoglutarate *noun* a compound of ornithine and glutamine used as a sports supplement to build muscle. Abbreviation **OKG**

oropharyngeal airway *noun* a tube inserted into an unconscious patient's airway to maintain airway patency

oropharynx *noun* a part of the pharynx below the soft palate at the back of the mouth (NOTE: The plural is **oropharynxes** or **oropharynges**.)

orotic acid *noun* a chemical produced by the body when there is a block in the flow of urea, used as a sports supplement

orthopaedic *adjective* **1.** used for describing treatment that corrects badly formed bones or joints **2.** referring to or used in orthopaedics

orthopaedics *noun* the branch of medicine concerned with the nature and correction of disorders of the bones, joints, ligaments or muscles

orthopaedic surgeon *noun* a doctor who specialises in the surgical correction of disorders of the bones, joints, ligaments and muscles

orthorexia *noun* an obsession with eating only the right things, which may lead to extreme weight loss as so many foods are rejected

orthoses *plural noun* same as **orthotics**

orthotics *noun* the branch of medical engineering concerned with the design and fitting of devices such as braces in the treatment of orthopaedic disorders ■ *plural noun* supports for the arch of the foot, worn inside the shoe during exercise

Osgood-Schlatter disease *noun* a condition in which the shinbone develops a painful bump below the knee, caused by excessive sporting activity putting strain on the area during the teenage growth spurt

osmolality *noun* the concentration of particles in a fluid such as blood serum

osmosis *noun* the movement of a solvent from one part of the body through a semi-permeable membrane to another part where there is a higher concentration of molecules

osmotic pressure *noun* the pressure that must be applied to a solution to stop osmosis

osseous *adjective* relating to or resembling bone

ossification *noun* the formation of bone. Also called **osteogenesis**

ossify *verb* to change soft tissue such as cartilage into bone as a result of impregnation with calcium salts, or be changed in this way

osteitis *noun* inflammation of a bone owing to injury or infection

osteitis pubis *noun* painful inflammation in the pelvis where the pubic bones meet, caused by repetitive activity such as running or jumping

osteoarthritis *noun* a degenerative disease of middle-aged and elderly people characterised by inflamed joints which become stiff and painful

osteochondrosis *noun* a defect in the growth plate of a bone, possibly caused by poor circulation, which can lead to pain and a tendency to suffer overuse injuries

osteoclasis *noun* the process of disintegration and assimilation of bony tissue that occurs during normal growth of bone or as part of healing at a fracture site

osteoclast *noun* **1.** a cell which destroys bone **2.** a surgical instrument for breaking bones

osteogenesis *noun* same as **ossification**

osteology *noun* the study of bones and their structure

osteomalacia *noun* a softening and bending of the bones resulting from an inability to absorb calcium caused by a vitamin D deficiency

osteomyelitis *noun* inflammation of the interior of bone, especially the marrow spaces

osteomyositis ossificans *noun* a hard lump in a muscle caused by the calcification of blood from a haematoma

osteon *noun* same as **Haversian system**

osteopath *noun* a doctor who practises osteopathy

osteopathy *noun* **1.** the treatment of disorders by massage and manipulation of joints **2.** any disease of bone (NOTE: The plural is **osteopathies**.)

osteopenia *noun* same as **bone loss**

osteoplastic *adjective* relating to or typical of bone surgery or bone development

osteoplasty *noun* plastic surgery on bones

osteoporosis *noun* a condition in which the bones become thin, porous and brittle owing to low levels of oestrogen, lack of calcium and lack of physical exercise. Also called **brittle bone disease**

osteotomy *noun* a surgical operation to cut a bone, especially to relieve pain in a joint (NOTE: The plural is **osteotomies**.)

-ostosis *suffix* referring to the formation of bone

otitis externa *noun* a condition often suffered by swimmers in which the ear canal becomes infected from exposure to dirty water

out *adjective* **1.** unable to take part any longer in a game or sport **2.** (*in baseball*) retired from attacking play ■ *noun* in baseball, a play that retires a batter or base runner

outfield *noun* the outer areas of slightly longer grass on a cricket pitch, away from the shorter grass of the square and the wicket

out of shape *adjective* unhealthy or unused to exercise

outside *adjective* (*in football, hockey and other sports*) used for describing a position further from the centre of the field than another position of the same name

over *noun* (*in cricket*) a series of six correctly bowled balls, or the play that takes place during this

over-achieve *verb* to be excessively or unhealthily dedicated to achieving success

overarm *adjective* **1.** beginning a stroke in swimming with the arm raised above the shoulder and rotating forward **2.** thrown or done with the arm raised above the shoulder and rotating forward

overdevelop *verb* to develop something, e.g. muscles, to excess

overeat *verb* to eat too much food, especially habitually

overhit *verb* to hit a ball too hard, or put too much force into a stroke

overhydration *noun* a condition in which the body contains more water than it needs, leading to excessive excretion of sodium in the urine

overload *verb* to give a part of the body too much weight to bear

overload principle *noun* the training principle of taking on slightly more than you are comfortably capable of, in order to force your body to improve and adapt

overnutrition *noun* the act of taking in too much of a particular nutrient, causing a condition such as obesity or hypervitaminosis

overpitch *verb* to bowl a ball in cricket so that it lands too close to the batsman, making a shot easy

overplay *verb* **1.** to exaggerate the importance or strength of something **2.** to hit or kick a ball too hard or too far

overpronate *verb* to roll the foot inwards excessively while running. Compare **supinate**

overpronation *noun* excessive inward rolling of the foot while running. Compare **supination**

overreaching *noun* the fact of overburdening the body which too much training, which can lead to unexplained underperformance syndrome

overshoot *verb* to shoot a projectile beyond the target that was being aimed at

overstrain *verb* to try to force someone, yourself or your body to perform beyond capacity, especially with the result that damage, injury or breakdown occurs

overstretch *verb* to stretch something such as a muscle too much, so as to cause injury or damage

overthinking *noun* (*in performance theory*) the state of being too conscious about the elements of a particular skill, with the result that performance is impaired

overthrow *verb* to throw a ball too far so that it goes beyond the player or target it was intended to reach

overtrain *verb* to train or exercise, or make somebody train or exercise, excessively, especially before a competition, with a resulting decrease in effectiveness

overtraining syndrome *noun* same as **unexplained underperformance syndrome**

overuse *noun* the excessive use of something

overuse injury *noun* an injury caused by repeated stress on a particular part of the body

overweight *adjective* having a body weight greater than that considered ideal or healthy

own goal *noun* (*in a sport such as football or hockey*) a goal scored by mistake for the opposing team, usually as a result of a miskick, mishit or deflection off another player. Abbreviation **o.g.**

oxidase *noun* an enzyme that encourages oxidation by removing hydrogen

oxidative capacity *noun* the amount of oxygen that a muscle is capable of using during an aerobic workout

oxidative stress *noun* damage to cells caused by free radicals produced in aerobic metabolisation

oxycalorimeter *noun* an instrument that measures the amount of oxygen consumed and carbon dioxide produced when a food is burned

oxygen *noun* a common colourless gas that is present in the air and essential to human life (NOTE: The chemical symbol is **O**.)

oxygenate *verb* to combine blood with oxygen

oxygen consumption *noun* the body's ability to take in oxygen through the respiratory system and use it for the aerobic breakdown of glucose

oxygen debt *noun* the amount of oxygen needed to replenish the body's oxygen stores after they become depleted by exercise such as running

oxygen-depleted *adjective* lacking oxygen because of excessive use

oxygen radical absorbance capacity *noun* a way of measuring the antioxidant properties of different foodstuffs. Abbreviation **ORAC**

oxygen toxicity *noun* damage caused to body tissues by an excessive intake of oxygen at a high pressure, as may occur when scuba diving

oxyhaemoglobinometer *noun* a device for measuring the levels of oxygen in the blood

oxymetazoline *noun* a vasoconstrictive nasal spray that can cause tissue damage and addiction if overused

oxypathy *noun* a disorder in which the body cannot expel unoxidisable acids, which damage tissues

ozone *noun* a harmful gas formed by the reaction of industrial pollutants with sunlight, especially in large cites, that can damage bodily tissues and reduce a person's VO2Max over time

P

pace *noun* the speed at which someone or something moves, especially when walking or running

pacemaker *noun* **1.** (*in long-distance running*) a clearly marked athlete who runs at a set pace to help other runners set their pace **2.** a battery-operated electrical device inserted into the body to deliver small regular shocks that stimulate the heart to beat in a normal rhythm

pacer *noun* same as **pacemaker** 1

pack *noun* **1.** the main body of competitors in a race or competition **2.** the forwards playing for a rugby team, or the forwards from both teams in a match, especially when involved in a scrum or maul

pad *noun* a cushioned target used in boxing and martial arts

paddock *noun* an area near the pits on a motor-racing track where cars are worked on before a race

Paget's disease *noun* a disease that gradually softens and thickens the bones in the spine, skull and legs, with the result that they become curved

pain *noun* the feeling of severe discomfort that a person has when hurt (NOTE: Pain can be used in the plural to show that it recurs: *She has pains in her left leg.*)

pain barrier *noun* the point at which pain reaches its peak and begins to diminish, especially as experienced by an athlete

Pan Arab Games *plural noun* a multi-sport event, held every four years, that is open to participants from all Arabic-speaking countries

pancreas *noun* a gland on the back of the body between the kidneys that produces digestive enzymes and important hormones, including insulin

pangamic acid *noun* a supplement that is claimed to be an antioxidant and to ease tiredness, sometimes called vitamin B15

Panner's disease *noun* osteochondrosis of the capitellum, usually seen in children and teenagers who participate in a lot of sports

pantothenic acid *noun* a vitamin of the vitamin B complex, found in liver, yeast and eggs

par *noun* the standard score assigned to each hole on a golf course, or to the sum total of these holes

para-amino benzoic acid *noun* part of the folic acid molecule, without which folic acid cannot be synthesised. Abbreviation **PABA**

paraben *noun* a chemical that mimics the hormone oestrogen (NOTE: Evidence suggests that parabens can play a role in the development of breast tumours.)

paraesthesia *noun* an unusual or unexplained tingling, pricking or burning sensation on the skin

paragliding *noun* a sport in which someone jumps from an aircraft or a high place wearing a rectangular parachute that allows control of direction in the descent to the ground

parallel bars *plural noun* **1.** a piece of gymnastic equipment consisting of two horizontal bars parallel to each other and supported on vertical posts **2.** an event in a gymnastics competition that uses the parallel bars

Paralympian *noun* an athlete who competes in the Paralympics

Paralympic Games, **Paralympics** *plural noun* an international sports competition for athletes with disabilities, held every four years in the same year as the Olympic Games

paralyse *verb* to make a part of the body unable to carry out voluntary movements by weakening or damaging muscles or nerves so that they cannot function, or by using a drug (NOTE: The US spelling is **paralyze**.)

paralysis *noun* a condition in which part of the body cannot be moved because the motor nerves have been damaged or the muscles have been weakened

parapente *noun* a modified parachute used for paraskiing and paragliding, with a framework of inflatable tubes that give it a semirigid structure, allowing it to be steered like a hang-glider

parapenting *noun* same as **paragliding**

paraplegia *adjective* total inability to move both legs and usually the lower part of the trunk, often as a result of disease or injury of the spine

paraplegic *noun* someone who has paraplegia ▪ *adjective* paralysed in the lower part of the body and legs

parasailing *noun* a sport in which somebody wearing a parachute rises high into the air from a platform at the back of a moving motorboat or from the water behind the boat and is towed along

parascending *noun* a sport in which somebody wearing an open parachute is towed along by a speedboat or land vehicle, rises into the air, and descends independently using the parachute

paraskiiing *noun* the sport of skiing off high mountains and descending through the air using a parapente made of inflatable tubes of fabric

paraskiing *noun* the sport of skiing off high mountains and descending through the air using a light steerable parachute (**parapente**) made of inflatable tubes of fabric

parasympathetic *adjective* relating to the parasympathetic nervous system

parasympathetic nervous system *noun* one of two parts of the autonomic nervous system. Its messages reach the organs of the body through the cranial and sacral nerves to the eyes, the gastrointestinal system and other organs. ◊ **sympathetic nervous system**

parathyroid hormone *noun* one of four small glands which are situated in or near the wall of the thyroid gland and secrete a hormone which controls the way in which calcium and phosphorus are deposited in bones

parenteral nutrition *noun* administration of nutrients directly into the veins, either as a supplement or as a complete source of nutrition for a patient

paresis *noun* muscular weakness or partial inability to move caused by disease of the nervous system

Parkinsonism *noun* a nervous disorder marked by symptoms of trembling limbs and muscular rigidity

participate *verb* to take part in an event or activity

participation *noun* the act of taking part in an activity

partner drill *noun* a series of warm-up exercises performed with a partner's help

pass *verb* to throw, kick or hit a ball or other object to another player during a game ■ *noun* an act of throwing, kicking or hitting a ball or other object to another player in a sport

pass back *verb* (*in games such as football and hockey*) to pass the ball to a member of your own team who is closer to your own goal than you are

passenger *noun* someone in a team who does not do his or her fair share of the work

passing shot *noun* in racket games such as tennis, a winning shot that passes beyond the reach of an opponent at the net

passive stretch *noun* a muscle stretch that is performed with the aid of equipment or a partner to hold the limb in place. Compare **active stretch**

patella *noun* the small bone in front of the knee joint. Also called **kneecap**

patellar reflex *noun* the jerk made as a reflex action by the knee, when the legs are crossed and the patellar tendon is tapped sharply

patellar subluxation *noun* dislocation of the kneecap, caused by overdevelopment of the inner or outer thigh muscles

patellar tendinitis, patellar tendinopathy *noun* inflammation of the tendon that connects the kneecap to the shin bone, caused by repeated jumping as in some sporting activities

patellar tendon *noun* a tendon just below the kneecap

pathological fracture *noun* a fractured bone that has been weakened by previous damage or disease, with the result that it breaks easily

pathology *noun* the scientific study of the nature, origin, progress and cause of disease

patterning *noun* a type of physical therapy in which the patient performs exercises designed to strengthen specific muscles and nerves

PBM *abbreviation* peak bone mass

PCSA *abbreviation* physiological cross-sectional area

PE *abbreviation* physical education

peak *noun* the highest point, e.g. of achievement or fitness

peak bone mass *noun* the amount of bone tissue present in the body at full maturation of the skeleton. Abbreviation **PBM**

peak fitness *noun* the maximum fitness level for an athlete, the product of a stringent and injury-free period of training

peak-flow meter *noun* a device that measures lung capacity

pear shaped *adjective* used for describing a person with a body shape in which most of the subcutaneous fat deposits are carried around the hips and bottom

pecs *plural noun* same as **pectorals**

pectoral girdle *noun* the shoulder bones, the scapulae and clavicles, to which the upper arm bones are attached. Also called **shoulder girdle**

pectoralis major *noun* a large chest muscle that pulls the arm forward or rotates it

pectoralis minor *noun* a small chest muscle that allows the shoulder to be depressed

pectorals, pectoral muscles *plural noun* the muscles of the chest

pedometer *noun* an instrument that measures the distance covered by a walker by recording the number of steps taken

pellagra *noun* a disease caused by a deficiency of nicotinic acid, riboflavin and pyridoxine from the vitamin B complex, where patches of skin become inflamed and the person has anorexia, nausea and diarrhoea

pelota, pelota basque *noun* a sport, similar to squash, in which ball is hit against a wall with the racket, wooden bat or the hand, or launched against it using a basket-like device strapped to the wrist

pelvic floor *noun* the lower part of the space beneath the pelvic girdle, formed of muscle

pelvic girdle *noun* the ring formed by the two hip bones to which the thigh bones are attached. Also called **hip girdle**

pelvis *noun* **1.** the strong basin-shaped ring of bone near the bottom of the spine, formed of the hip bones at the front and sides and the sacrum and coccyx at the back **2.** the internal space inside this

penalise *verb* to punish a team or player for breaking a rule by giving an advantage to the opposing team or player

penalty *noun* **1.** a disadvantage imposed on a player or team for breaking a rule in a sport or game, e.g. a free shot at the goal awarded to the opposing side. Also called **penalty shot 2.** (*in football and some other sports*) a goal scored from a penalty kick

penalty area *noun* a rectangular area in front of a football goal within which the goalkeeper is allowed to handle the ball

penalty kick, penalty *noun* **1.** (*in football*) a free kick from the penalty spot at the opposing team's goal, defended only by its goalkeeper, awarded for some types of foul within the penalty area **2.** (*in rugby*) a kick worth three points that can be aimed at the goal after a serious foul by a member of the opposing side

pendulum stretch *noun* a stretch in which the body is bent forward with the arms falling loosely in front, holding a weighted ball, and the arms swung in a rotating movement allowing momentum to stretch the muscles

penicillin *noun* any of a group of antibiotics used in the treatment of bacterial infection

pennant *noun* US **1.** in some sports, especially baseball, a flag that symbolises a championship **2.** a championship that is symbolised by a pennant

pentathlete *noun* an athlete who takes part in a pentathlon

pentathlon *noun* **1.** same as **modern pentathlon 2.** an athletics competition in which the contestants compete in five different events, usually sprint, hurdles, long jump, discus and javelin. ◊ **triathlon, heptathlon, decathlon**

pep talk *noun* a short speech designed to give advice and generate enthusiasm, e.g. in a sports team (*informal*)

peptide *noun* a compound formed of two or more amino acids

peptide hormone *noun* a supplement sometimes misused by athletes to increase size, strength and muscle growth

perceived exertion scale *noun* a sliding scale on which the intensity of exercise is rated, according to the exerciser's subjective judgement

perception *noun* the process of using the senses to acquire information about the surrounding environment or situation

perfectionism *noun* rigorous rejection of any performance or level of competence that is less than perfect

perfectionist *noun* someone who demands or seeks to achieve nothing less than perfection

perfluorocarbon *noun* a substance that enhances oxygen transfer in the circulatory system, used in the manufacture of blood substitutes

perforated eardrum *noun* a hole or tear in the membrane of the inner ear, which can be caused by a heavy blow or by pressure inequalities as when diving

performance *noun* the level at which a player or athlete is carrying out their activity, either in relation to others or in relation to personal goals or standards

performance accomplishment *noun* something that an athlete has previously achieved, e.g. a victory or personal record, which gives him or her feelings of confidence about a forthcoming competition

performance assessment *noun* a biomechanical analysis of an athlete's performance by a professional

performance decline *adjective* a measurable worsening of performance in sport caused by fatigue, stress or overthinking

performance diminuation *noun* same as **performance decline**

performance enhancer *noun* a dietary supplement used by athletes to enhance bursts of high performance

performance last *noun* a last that is curved slightly inwards, suitable for runners with high arches. Compare **straight last**, **standard last**

performance theory *noun* the study of what motivates people to perform actions, both in the short and long term

performing *noun* the final stage of team development according to the Tuckman model, in which the team is a tight unit, able to perform its duties without conflict

perfuse *verb* to introduce a liquid into tissue or an organ, especially by circulating it through blood vessels

perfusion *noun* the process in which a liquid passes through vessels, an organ or tissue, e.g. the flow of blood into lung tissue

pericardium *noun* a membrane which surrounds and supports the heart

perichondrial haematoma *noun* deformation of the outer ear as a result of repeated traumas that cause the formation of blood clots in the connective tissue

perichondrium *noun* the fibrous membrane that covers the surface of cartilage except at joints

perimysium *noun* a sheath which surrounds a bundle of muscle fibres

periodisation *noun* the act of planning a long-term training schedule for professional athletes, working around competitions

periorbital contusion *noun* same as **black eye**

periosteum *noun* a dense layer of connective tissue around a bone

periostitis *noun* same as **shin splints**

peripheral heart action *noun* a style of training, suitable for deconditioned exercisers, in which separate groups of muscles are worked in turn to stimulate the circulation. Abbreviation **PHA**

peripheral nerves *plural noun* the parts of motor and sensory nerves which branch from the brain and spinal cord

peripheral nervous system *noun* all the nerves in different parts of the body that are linked and governed by the central nervous system. Abbreviation **PNS**

peripheral vascular disease *noun* a disease affecting the blood vessels which supply the arms and legs

peristalsis *noun* the movement, like waves, produced by alternate contraction and relaxation of muscles along an organ such as the intestine or oesophagus, which pushes the contents of the organ along it. Compare **antiperistalsis**

peritendinitis *noun* same as **tenosynovitis**

pernicious anaemia *noun* anaemia caused by a deficiency of vitamin B12

peroneal muscles *plural noun* two muscles that run along the outside of the lower leg and support the ankle

peroxisome *noun* a tiny part within a cell containing enzymes that oxidise toxic substances such as alcohol and prevent them from doing any harm

persistence *noun* the existence of a medical condition for a considerable time

persistent *adjective* used for describing a medical condition that has continued for some considerable time

personal best *noun* the best time or score that an individual has achieved in an activity

personal fitness plan *noun* same as **fitness program**

personalised nutrition *noun* an approach to nutrition that meets the needs of the individual, taking into account considerations such as state of health, lifestyle, age and gender

personal trainer *noun* a professional who helps others to devise a training regime and stick to it

perspiration *noun* sweat or the action of sweating

perspire *verb* to produce moisture through the sweat glands

pes anserine bursitis *noun* ♦ **anserine bursitis**

pes anserinus *noun* a point in the knee at which several tendons meet

pethidine *noun* an analgesic that is a banned substance for athletes, although it is widely used in childbirth

petrisage *noun* a stage of sports massage in which kneading movements are used with the palms and fingertips

PHA *abbreviation* peripheral heart action

phagotherapy *noun* the treatment of illness by changes in diet

phagotrophy *noun* the act of obtaining nourishment by ingesting food

phalanx *noun* a bone in a finger or toe

pharmaceutical *adjective* involved in or related to the manufacture, preparation, dispensing or sale of drugs used in medicine

pharmacokinetics *noun* the study of how the body reacts to drugs over a period of time, including their absorption, metabolism and elimination

pharmacological *adjective* relating to pharmacology

pharmacology *noun* the science or study of drugs, especially of the ways in which they react biologically at receptor sites in the body

pharmafood *noun* same as **functional food**

pharynx *noun* a muscular passage leading from the back of the mouth to the oesophagus (NOTE: The plural is **pharynges** or **pharynxes**.)

phaseolamin *noun* a substance that inhibits alpha amylase, allowing less sugar to be absorbed by the digestive tract, sold as a diet aid

phenolic acid *noun* a plant metabolite with antioxidant properties

phenylalanine *noun* an essential amino acid found in many proteins and converted to a non-essential amino acid by the body

phenylephrine *noun* a substance used as a decongestant and for increasing blood pressure in cases of hypotension

phenylpropanolamine *noun* a vasoconstrictive drug taken orally, used as a decongestant and appetite suppressant

phlegm *noun* same as **sputum**

phosphate *noun* a salt of phosphoric acid, stored in muscles as a source of quick energy

phosphaturia *noun* cloudy urine caused by a high concentration of phosphate salts, indicating possible formation of kidney stones

phosphocreatine *noun* a phosphate of creatine found in muscles, providing energy for muscle contraction

phosphoglucomutase *noun* an enzyme that catalyses the breakdown and synthesis of glycogen, providing energy that can be used or stored

phosphoglyceraldehyde *noun* an intermediate product in carbohydrate metabolism

phosphoprotein *noun* a protein that contains an enzymatically bound phosphate group

phosphorylase *noun* an enzyme that aids the process of carbohydrate metabolism

photo finish *noun* the end of a race in which two or more contestants are so close that the result must be determined from a photograph taken as they cross the finish line

photophobia *noun* aversion to light, sometimes an indication of concussion in head injuries

phrenic nerve *noun* a pair of nerves which controls the muscles in the diaphragm

physeal plate *noun* a growth plate on a bone, prone to injury in young athletes

physical *adjective* relating to the body, as opposed to the mind

physical activity *noun* exercise and general movement that a person carries out as part of their day

physical activity level *noun* the amount of physical activity that a person undertakes each day, which is used in calculating their daily calorie requirements. Abbreviation **PAL**

physical challenge, physical disability *noun* a medically diagnosed condition that makes it difficult to engage in the activities of daily life

physical conditioning *noun* same as **conditioning**

physical education *noun* gymnastics, athletics, team sports and other forms of physical exercise taught to children at school. Abbreviation **PE**

physical examination *noun* an examination of someone's body to see if he or she is healthy

physical jerks *plural noun* physical exercises of the kind done regularly to keep fit, e.g. press-ups (*dated informal*)

physically challenged *adjective* used for describing someone with a condition that makes it difficult to perform some or all of the basic tasks of daily life

physical medicine *noun* the branch of medicine concerned with the diagnosis of injuries or physical disabilities and their treatment by external means, including heat, massage or exercise, rather than by medication or surgery

physical therapist *noun* a healthcare provider who specialises in physical therapy

physical therapy *noun* the treatment of disorders by heat, by massage, by exercise and other physical means

physical training *noun* same as **physical education**

physiological *adjective* relating to physiology

physiological cross-sectional area *noun* the average cross-sectional area of an individual muscle, measured by dividing its volume by its length. Abbreviation **PCSA**

physiological psychology *noun* a branch of psychology that studies the interactions between physical or chemical processes in the body and mental states or behaviour

physiologist *noun* a scientist who specialises in the study of the functions of living organisms

physiology *noun* the regular functions of the body, or the subject of study that deals with them

physiotherapist *noun* a trained specialist who gives physiotherapy

physiotherapy *noun* the treatment of a disorder or condition by exercise, massage, heat treatment, infrared lamps or other external means, e.g. to restore strength or function after a disease or injury

pibic symphysitis *noun* ♦ osteitis pubis

pigment *noun* a substance that gives colour to parts of the body such as blood, the skin and hair

pike *noun* a diving or gymnastic position in which the body is bent at the hips with the head tucked under and the hands touching the toes or behind the knees

Pilates *noun* a holistic form of exercise and postural therapy that emphasises the development of the deep abdominal muscles to control body movement and protect the back

pinched nerve *noun* a condition in which a nerve becomes trapped under a joint that maintains a steady pressure on it, causing a painful tingling sensation and possibly a temporary loss of mobility

Ping-Pong a trade name for table tennis

pington *noun* a sport like badminton that is played with wooden paddles instead of stringed rackets

piriformis muscle *noun* a muscle in the buttock that allows the thigh to rotate outwards

piriformis syndrome *noun* inflammation of the sciatic nerve caused by friction against the piriformis muscle

piste *noun* a downhill track or area of densely packed snow that provides good skiing conditions

pitch *noun* **1.** a playing area for a team ball game **2.** (*in cricket*) the area between the two sets of stumps **3.** (*in baseball*) the act of throwing the ball to the batter **4.** a particular way or manner of throwing something, especially a ball ■ *verb* to throw or hurl a ball, particularly as part of a game or sport

pitcher *noun* (*in baseball*) the player on the mound who throws the ball to the batter

pits *plural noun* the area off the side of a motor-racing track where vehicles can get fuel, fresh tyres and repairs

pit stop *noun* a stop in the pits to allow a racing car to be refuelled and serviced during a race

pituitary gland *noun* the main endocrine gland in the body that secretes hormones that stimulate other glands

placebo *noun* a tablet that appears to be a drug but has no medicinal substance in it, used in tests and trials

placebo effect *noun* the apparently beneficial effect of telling someone that he or she is having a treatment, even if this is not true, caused by the hope that the treatment will be effective

placement *noun* **1.** a player's skill in accurately playing the ball, puck or similar object **2.** *US* (*in American football*) a place kick for a field goal or point after a touchdown, or the positioning of the ball for such a kick

plane *noun* a flat surface, especially that of the body seen from a specific angle

plank hold *noun* an exercise in which a person assumes a press-up position, resting the upper body on the forearms, and holds the position for as long as possible with the body perfectly straight

plantar *adjective* referring to the sole of the foot

plantar fasciitis *noun* pain in the arch of the foot suffered by runners, caused by stretching tendons that are not properly warmed up

plantar flexion *noun* the bending of the toes downwards

plasma *noun* **1.** a yellow watery liquid which makes up the main part of blood **2.** lymph with no corpuscles **3.** cytoplasm

plasma expander *noun* a masking agent that temporarily lowers the red blood cell count in athletes who have artificially raised it with erythropoietin, allowing them to pass drug tests

plaster cast *noun* a rigid covering of plaster of Paris moulded round a broken limb to immobilise the fracture site during healing

plastic surgery *noun* the branch of surgery that is concerned with repairing especially external damage to the body, remedying impairments, or improving a person's appearance

plate *noun* **1.** a flat sheet of bone **2.** a flat piece of metal attached to a fractured bone to hold the broken parts together **3.** same as **home plate**

plateau *noun* a phase in athletic development where a person's fitness level becomes stable and it is difficult to make further improvement (NOTE: The plural form is **plateaux**.) ■ *verb* to reach a point in athletic development where it is difficult to make further improvements

platelet *noun* a small blood cell which releases thromboplastin and which multiplies rapidly after an injury, encouraging the coagulation of blood. Also called **thrombocyte**

plates *plural noun* the flat weights attached to the end of a dumbbell

play *verb* **1.** to take part in an enjoyable activity, especially a game, simply for the sake of amusement **2.** to take part in a game or a sporting activity **3.** to compete against someone in a game or sporting event **4.** to assign a player to a particular position on the field, or be assigned such a position **5.** to hit or kick an object such as a ball, puck or shuttlecock in a particular direction **6.** to make a shot or stroke in a sporting event ■ *noun* **1.** the action during a game or series of games **2.** *US* an action or move in a game

play-by-play *adjective US* **1.** consisting of a description of each event as it happens, especially in a sports contest **2.** same as **commentary**

player *noun* someone taking part in a sport or game

playing field *noun* an area of level ground used for organised sporting activities

playmaker *noun* in team games, a player who initiates moves that create scoring opportunities

pleura *plural noun* one of two membranes lining the chest cavity and covering each lung

pleural membrane *noun* same as **pleura**

plexus *noun* a network of nerves, blood vessels or lymphatics

plica *noun* a fold

plimsoll *noun* a light canvas shoe with a rubber sole

plyometrics *noun* a free body movement exercise system that uses no weights or machines and emphasises callisthenics and repeated movements such as jumping high off the ground

PMR *abbreviation* progressive muscular relaxation

PNF *abbreviation* proprioceptive neuromuscular facilitation

PNF stretching *noun* ♦ **proprioceptive neuromuscular facilitation**

poach *verb* to play a shot that properly should be handled by a partner in badminton, tennis, squash or handball

podiatry *noun US* the study of minor diseases and disorders of the feet

point *noun* **1.** a sharp end **2.** the dot used to show the division between whole numbers and parts of numbers (NOTE: **3.256**: say 'three point two five six'; **his temperature was 38.7**: say 'thirty-eight point seven'.) **3.** a mark or score **4.** (*in cricket*) a fielding position on the off side, level with the batsman's wicket and at a distance from it that varies between three or four yards (*silly point*) and about thirty yards (*deep point*), or the player in that position **5.** (*in basketball*) the position in front court taken by the guard who directs the offensive

pointless *adjective* in which no points are scored

poise *noun* a graceful controlled way of standing, moving or performing an action

pole vault *noun* **1.** an athletics event in which the competitors use a long flexible pole to swing themselves up and over a very high crossbar **2.** a jump in the pole vault

polo *noun* **1.** a game played by teams on horseback, with players using long-handled mallets to drive a wooden ball into a goal **2.** a game similar to polo, e.g. one in which the participants are mounted on bicycles rather than horses

polyavitaminosis *noun* an illness caused by a deficiency of more than one vitamin

polydextrose *noun* a bulking agent used in reduced-calorie and low-calorie foods

polydipsia *noun* an unusually intense thirst

polyneuritis *noun* inflammation of many nerves

polyneuropathy *noun* serious nerve damage caused by dietary deficiencies or alcoholism

polypeptide *noun* a type of protein formed of linked amino acids

polysynaptic *adjective* describes a reflex in the central nervous system that uses two or more synapses

polyunsaturated fat *noun* a type of fat with more than one double atom bond, typical of vegetable and fish oils. Compare **saturated fat, unsaturated fat**

polyuria *noun* excessive production of urine

pommel horse *noun* 1. a padded oblong piece of gymnastics apparatus that is raised off the floor and has two curved handles on the top 2. the men's gymnastics event that involves balancing and manoeuvring on a pommel horse

POMS *abbreviation* Profile of Mood States

ponderal index *noun* the cube root of a person's body weight divided by height, a measure of how fat a person is

ponderocrescive *adjective* used for describing foods that stimulate weight gain

ponderoperditive *adjective* used for describing foods that stimulate weight loss

pool *noun* 1. an artificial area of water in which swimming events take place 2. a game played with a cue, a white ball and 15 balls on a felt-covered table with six pockets

popping crease *noun* the line at which a cricket batsman stands when facing the bowler. It runs parallel to the wicket and lies 1.2 m/4 ft in front of it.

porphyria *noun* a hereditary disease affecting the metabolism of porphyrin pigments

porphyrin *noun* a substance that develops into haem when acted upon by enzymes, necessary for the health of the blood and bone marrow

portion *noun* a small quantity, especially enough food for one person

portion control *noun* a method of controlling your daily food intake by serving small portions at mealtimes and not snacking between meals

portion size *noun* the weight or number of each item in one serving

position *noun* 1. the place where a player is standing or playing 2. the way in which a person's body is arranged

positive energy balance *noun* a situation in which a person is consuming more energy on a day-to-day basis than he or she uses, leading to weight gain

positive thinking *noun* a way of thinking that is confident, optimistic and focusing only on good things that may happen

possession *noun* (*in various sports*) control of the ball or puck by a player or team

post *verb* 1. to score something, e.g. points, in a game or sport 2. in horseriding, to bob up and down in the saddle in time with a horse's trot

post cava *noun* a large vein that returns blood from the lower half of the body to the heart

post-concussive syndrome *noun* symptoms including dizziness, headache and confusion that may be experienced for some time after a mild head trauma

posterior *adjective* used for describing a body part that is situated in the rear of the body

posterior cruciate ligament *noun* a ligament in the knee that connects the shin bone to the thigh bone, often torn in sports injuries

posterior dislocation *noun* dislocation of the shoulder joint in which the ball moves behind the socket

posterior scalene *noun* a pair of muscles involved in rotating the neck

posterior tibial tendonitis *noun* pain in the tendons along the inside of the leg, usually caused by overpronation while running

postsynaptic *adjective* used for describing a nerve cell, muscle cell or region of cell membrane that receives signals transmitted across a synapse from another nerve cell

postural *adjective* relating to posture

postural sway *noun* changes in the exact weight distribution of a person, caused by muscle contractions involved in maintaining proper posture

posture *noun* the position in which a body is arranged, or the way a person usually holds his or her body when standing

potassium *noun* a metallic element that exists naturally in seawater and in several minerals (NOTE: The chemical symbol is **K**.)

potential energy *noun* the energy that a body or system has stored because of its position in an electric, magnetic, or gravitational field, or because of its configuration. Symbol V, E_p

Pott's fracture *noun* a fracture of the lower end of the fibula together with displacement of the ankle and foot outwards

pound *noun* an imperial unit of weight equal to 453.6 g, divided into 16 ounces

power *noun* **1.** physical force or strength **2.** the ability, strength, and capacity to do something

powerbag *noun* a piece of equipment used like a medicine ball in resistance training

powerboat *noun* a small motorboat with a powerful outboard or inboard motor

powerboating *noun* the sport of driving or racing powerboats

power lift *noun* a weightlifting exercise which works several muscle groups at the same time, such as the pullover ■ *verb* to perform a power lift

powerlifting *noun* a weightlifting sport that consists of the three events of the squat, the bench press and the deadlift

power play *noun* **1.** (*in cricket*) on of several periods of time during one-day international matches where restrictions are placed on the positioning of fielders **2.** a tactic of concentrating players in one area, especially an attack in American football that involves extra blockers preceding the person carrying the ball **3.** a situation or period of time in ice hockey during which one team has a numerical advantage because the other team has one or more players in the penalty box

power snatch *noun* a snatch performed with very little movement of the knees or feet

power training *noun* intense training that emphasises proper form

power transfer *noun* the transfer of energy between muscle groups as a movement is performed

power walking *noun* a form of exercise involving energetic walking in which the arms are swung backwards and forwards, sometimes using weights, in order to increase the heart rate

practice *noun* **1.** the process of repeating something such as an exercise many times in order to improve performance **2.** the fact of doing something, as opposed to thinking or talking about it

pradal seray *noun* same as **Khmer boxing**

prebiotic *noun* a dietary supplement in the form of non-digestible carbohydrate that promotes the growth of desirable microflora in the large bowel. ◊ **probiotic**

pre-competition *adjective* used for describing a regime or a set of activities that are done immediately before competing, e.g. carb loading

precursor *noun* a substance or cell from which another substance or cell is developed

pre-game *adjective* used for describing activities that are done immediately before competing in a team game, e.g. reviewing tactics and receiving a pep talk

prejudice *noun* an unfounded hatred, fear or mistrust of a person or group, especially one of a particular religion, ethnicity, nationality, sexual preference or social status

preliminary *noun* **1.** a sporting contest held before the main event, especially in boxing or wrestling **2.** an eliminatory contest staged to select the finalists in a sporting competition

premiership *noun* a championship in some sports, or the competition held to decide this

preparatory arousal *noun* the act of mentally preparing oneself for a performance using visualisation or a pep talk

prepatellar bursitis *noun* inflammation of the bursa covering the kneecap, commonly suffered by wrestlers and volleyball players who regularly fall onto their knees

prescription drug *noun* a drug that can only be obtained by someone who has a legally valid prescription

prescriptive zone *noun* the optimum temperature for an athlete to perform in, typically between 5 and 25 degrees centigrade

press *noun* (*in weightlifting*) a lift in which the weight is raised to shoulder height and then to above the head without moving the legs

pressor *adjective* relating to or bringing about an increase in blood pressure

press-up *noun* a physical exercise in which, from a position of lying flat on the front with the hands under the shoulders, the body is pushed off the floor until the arms are straight

pressure point *noun* a place where an artery crosses over a bone, allowing the blood to be cut off by pressing with the finger

pre-stretch *verb* to stretch a muscle before exercising it

prevalence *noun* the average proportion of a sample population, e.g. a sports team, that is injured at any given time

preventive *adjective* used for describing an action taken to stop something happening, especially to stop a disease or infection from spreading

primary curve *noun* in scoliosis, the unusual curve of the spine that throws it out of alignment

primary protein energy malnutrition *noun* malnutrition caused by a severe lack of protein and energy in the diet

prime mover *noun* same as **agonist**

prize fight *noun* a boxing match in which the winner receives a cash prize

prize ring *noun* the sport or business of professional boxing

pro-am *adjective* involving or composed of professional and amateur sports players ■ *noun* a competition in which professional players compete against amateurs, or in which professionals and amateurs compete together

proanthocyanidin *noun* any one of a class of flavonoids found in many plants that can be used as a dietary supplement to enhance immunity and to strengthen connective tissue

probiotic *noun* a substance containing live microorganisms that claims to be beneficial to humans and animals, e.g. by restoring the balance of microflora in the digestive tract. ◊ **prebiotic**

procyanidin *noun* a polyphenol extracted from apples that stimulates human hair growth

proenzyme *noun* a biologically inactive substance that is the precursor of an enzyme

professional *adjective* engaged in an occupation as a paid job rather than as a hobby ■ *noun* an expert player of a sport who is paid to teach other players in a club

professional foul *noun* a deliberate foul in football, usually committed in order to prevent the opposing team gaining a potentially crucial advantage in field position or goal-scoring opportunity

proficient *adjective* having a high degree of skill in something

Profile of Mood States *noun* a questionnaire designed to assess the emotional state of an athlete and diagnose burnout or other factors that may hold back performance. Abbreviation **POMS**

prognosis *noun* a medical opinion as to the likely course and outcome of a disease or injury

prognostic *adjective* relating to or acting as a prognosis of a disease

progress *noun* development, usually of a gradual kind, towards achieving a goal or reaching a higher standard ■ *verb* to move to the next round of a competition

progression *noun* a gradual change or advancement from one state to another

progressive muscular relaxation *noun* a method of deep relaxation in which each muscle is tensed and relaxed in turn. Abbreviation **PMR**

progressive overload, progressive resistance training *noun* to exercise within your comfort zone and progressively build up to a stronger intensity

Prohibited List *noun* a list of the substances banned under the World Anti-Doping Code, published yearly

prohormone *noun* a substance that is the precursor of a hormone, used as a bodybuilding supplement as an attempt to boost the body's natural supply of that hormone

prolapse *noun* a slippage or sinking of a body organ or part such as a valve of the heart from its usual position

promote *verb* to help something to take place, e.g. by advertising it

promoter *noun* **1.** a substance that increases the activity of a catalyst **2.** somebody who tries to make an athlete more widely known or more successful, e.g. to secure sponsorship deals

promotion *noun* advance by a sports team or player into a higher division of a league

pronate *verb* **1.** to lie face downwards **2.** to turn the hand so that the palm faces downwards

pronation *noun* the tendency of the feet to roll slightly inwards while running, cushioning the foot from impact

pronator *noun* a muscle that makes the hand turn face downwards

prone *adjective* **1.** lying face downwards. Opposite **supine 2.** used for describing the position of the arm with the palm facing downwards

prop *noun* (*in rugby*) a forward at either end of the front row of a scrum

propanolol *noun* a drug that slows heart rate and heart output

prophylactic *noun* a drug or agent that prevents the development of disease

prophylactic brace *noun* a supportive brace that is designed to reduce the risk of injuries occurring, rather than to aid recovery

proprioception *noun* awareness of the positions of the parts of the body in relation to each other, or of your own body in relation to the position of others

proprioceptive neuromuscular facilitation *noun* a technique for assisted stretching that is thought to increase the range of motion of the joints by applying resistance during the stretch that is then relaxed. Abbreviation **PNF**

proprioceptor *noun* the end of a sensory nerve that reacts to stimuli from muscles and tendons as they move

prostaglandin *noun* any of a class of unsaturated fatty acids found in all mammals that control smooth muscle contraction, inflammation and body temperature, are associated with the sensation of pain and have an effect on the nervous system, blood pressure and in particular the uterus at menstruation

prosthesis *noun* an artificial limb fitted to patients who have lost a limb through amputation

protein *noun* a compound that is an essential part of living cells and is one of the elements in food that is necessary to keep the human body working properly

protein efficiency ratio *noun* a measure of protein quality, expressed as the amount of weight gained per gram of protein ingested. Abbreviation **PER**

protein energy malnutrition *noun* a severe lack of protein and calories in a person's diet, or their inability to absorb them from food, leading to wasting and general deterioration of health. Abbreviation **PEM**

protein intolerance *noun* an allergic reaction to a particular protein

protein powder *noun* a bodybuilding supplement of concentrated egg or milk proteins, made into a drink

protein retention *noun* the percentage of dietary protein that is absorbed and used by the body

protein retention efficiency *noun* net protein retention shown on a percentage scale. Abbreviation **PRE**

protein score *noun* a measure of protein quality, expressed as its content of certain amino acids as compared to egg protein. Also called **amino acid score**

protein shake *noun* a drink made with protein powder, used as a bodybuilding aid

protein supplement *noun* a supplement food or drink that contains concentrated protein, usually from milk, used by bodybuilders

proteolysis *noun* the breaking down of proteins in food by digestive enzymes

protopathic *adjective* **1.** used for describing nerves that are able to sense only strong sensations **2.** used for describing a first symptom or lesion **3.** used for describing the first sign of partially restored function in an injured nerve ▸ compare **epicritic**

protractor *noun* a muscle with the function of extending a body part

provocation test *noun* a test carried out to diagnose the exact nature of an injury, in which various movements are performed to see which of them cause pain

proximal *adjective* used for describing a body part that is close to the main trunk of the body

psoas *noun* either of two pairs of muscles in the groin, psoas major and psoas minor, which help to move the hip joint

psyche up *verb* to prepare yourself mentally for a competition using positive self-talk and visualisation

psychology *noun* the study of the mind and mental processes

psychomotor *adjective* relating to bodily movement triggered by mental activity, especially voluntary muscle action

psychosocial *adjective* relating to both the psychological and the social aspects of something

PT *noun* in the US, gymnastics, athletics, team sports, and other forms of physical exercise taught to children at school. Full form **physical training**

ptomaine *noun* a nitrogenous compound produced when protein is broken down by bacteria

puberty *noun* the physical and psychological changes that take place when childhood ends and adolescence and sexual maturity begin and the sex glands become active

public health *noun* the study of illness, health and disease in the community. ◊ **community medicine**

puck *noun* a small disc of hard rubber that the players hit in ice hockey

pugilism *noun* the practice, sport, or profession of boxing

pull *verb* **1.** to make a muscle move in a wrong direction **2.** to hit a ball farther left for a right-handed player or farther right for a left-handed player than intended

pull away *verb* to start to win something such as a competition or race by widening the margin over an opponent

pulldown *noun* an exercise in which a weight is suspended in a pulley system on a fixed machine and the exerciser makes it rise towards the ceiling by pulling cables downwards

pullover *noun* an exercise in which the exerciser lies face-up on a bench and lifts a weight from behind the head to over the chest, keeping the arms straight

pull-up *noun* UK a physical exercise in which the hands are placed on an overhead horizontal bar, and the body is lifted by pulling upwards with the arms. Also called **chin**, **chin-up**

pulmonary *adjective* relating to the lungs

pulmonary artery *noun* either of two arteries that carry blood in need of oxygen from the right side of the heart to the lungs, the only arteries that carry deoxygenated blood

pulmonary circulation *noun* the circulation of blood from the heart through the pulmonary arteries to the lungs for oxygenation and back to the heart through the pulmonary veins

pulmonary oedema *noun* the accumulation of fluid in the lungs, causing severe impairment of respiratory function

pulmonary valve *noun* a valve at the opening of the pulmonary artery

pulmonary vein *noun* one of the four veins that carry oxygen-rich blood from the lungs to the left side of the heart

pulse *noun* the regular expansion and contraction of an artery, caused by the heart pumping blood through the body

pump *verb* to force liquid or air along a tube

pumped *adjective* with large muscles achieved through bodybuilding

pump up *verb* to increase the mass of a muscle by bodybuilding techniques (*informal*)

punch *verb* to strike someone or something with the fist, e.g. in boxing or martial arts

punchbag *noun UK* a large heavy bag, usually suspended from a rope, used by boxers to improve their punching skills (NOTE: The US term is **punching bag**.)

punchball *noun* a large heavy ball on a stand, used for training or exercise, especially by boxers

punt *noun* a kick in which a player drops a ball and kicks it before it hits the ground

pupillary response *noun* the contraction or otherwise of the pupils when exposed to light following a head injury, indicative of concussion or eye trauma

purgative *noun* a drug or other substance that causes evacuation of the bowels, sometimes abused in order to lose weight

purge *verb* to induce evacuation of the bowels

purine *noun* a chemical compound which is metabolised into uric acid, excessive quantities of which can cause gout

push press *noun* an exercise in which a barbell is raised from the chest to over the head, using a small jump to create momentum

push-up *noun US* same as **press-up**

pyramiding *noun* (*in weightlifting*) the practice of increasing the weight for each set while decreasing the number of reps performed

pyruvate *noun* a sports supplement that increases metabolism

pyruvic acid *noun* a chemical formed in living cells when carbohydrates and proteins are metabolised

Q

Q angle *noun* the angle of the quadriceps in relation to the patella, which represents the relationship and alignment between the pelvis, leg and foot

quad *noun* same as **quadriceps femoris**

quadrathlon *noun* four tests for measuring improvements in an athlete's explosive power, consisting of a standing long jump, a triple jump, a 30-metre sprint and an overheard shot put

quadratus *noun* any of various muscles with four sides, more or less square in shape

quadratus insertion strain *noun* pain in the tendon connecting the quadriceps muscle to the kneecap, caused by overuse

quadratus lumborum *noun* a deep-level muscle in the lower back, connecting the pelvis to the lowest rib

quadriceps *noun* a large four-part muscle at the front of the thigh that acts to extend the leg

quadriceps femoris *noun* a large four-part muscle at the front of the thigh that acts to extend the leg

quadriplegia *noun* a physical disability in which the movement of all four limbs is impaired to some extent

quadriplegic *noun* a person suffering from quadriplegia

quad rugby *noun* a form of rugby played in wheelchairs, designed for people suffering from quadriplegia

qualifier *noun* **1.** a person or team that is successful in the preliminary part of a competition and earns the right to take part in the next stage **2.** a preliminary round of a competition

quality *noun* a feature of someone's personality such as perfectionism, dedication or single-mindedness

quantitative digital radiography *noun* the use of digital X-ray scans to find out whether a person has a bone disease such as osteoporosis

Queensbury rules *plural noun* a code of practice for boxing matches that sets out such rules as the size of the ring, the length of the rounds and the principle of counting to 10 to determine a knockout

Quetlet index *noun* same as **body mass index**

R

rabbit *noun* a long-distance runner who sets a fast pace for a stronger teammate in the early part of a race

race *noun* a contest to decide who is the fastest ∎ *verb* **1.** to compete with someone in a contest of speed **2.** when your heart races, it beats much faster than usual, e.g. because of nervousness or excitement

racewalk *verb* to compete in the sport of race walking

racewalking *noun* the sport of racing at a fast walking pace, with rules that require walkers to keep at least one foot on the ground at all times

rachiotomy *noun* same as **laminectomy**

racing *noun* the sport of taking part in races, e.g. as a runner, on a horse, or in a sports car

racism *noun* the belief that people of different races have different qualities and abilities, and that some races are inherently superior or inferior

racist *adjective* prejudiced against all people who belong to other races

racket, racquet *noun* a lightweight bat with a network of strings, used in tennis, badminton, squash and similar games. The frame is usually made of wood, aluminium or graphite and the strings of gut or nylon.

racket abuse *noun* (*in tennis*) the act of throwing a racket to the ground in anger, which can be penalised

racket sport *noun* any of various sports that use a racket and ball or shuttlecock, e.g. tennis, badminton or squash

racquetball *noun* a game played on a four-walled indoor court by two, three or four players using short-handled rackets and a ball larger than the ball used in squash or racquets

racquets *noun* a fast game similar to squash played by two or four people on a four-walled indoor court using long-handled racquets and a small hard ball

radial nerve *noun* the main motor nerve in the arm, running down the back of the upper arm and the outer side of the forearm

radial pulse *noun* the main pulse in the wrist, taken near the outer edge of the forearm just above the wrist

radioactive tracer *noun* a mildly radioactive liquid that is injected into an injury site during scintigraphy

radiography *noun* the work of examining the internal parts of the body by taking x-ray photographs

radius *noun* the shorter and outer of the two bones in the forearm between the elbow and the wrist (NOTE: The plural is **radii**. The other bone in the forearm is the **ulna**.)

rally *noun* in tennis and other racket sports, an exchange of several shots between two opponents or sides before a point is scored

rallycross *noun* motor racing on a circuit partly on roads and partly across country

random practice *noun* practice of several different skills in rotation, not mastering one before moving on to the next but coming back to it later

random skill *noun* a skill that is called upon at a moment's notice, as when a person reacts to an unexpected stimulus

range of motion *noun* the direction in which, and distance for which, a joint can be moved comfortably. Abbreviation **ROM**

rapid-adaptation training *noun* training that switches regularly between strength training, flexibility exercises and cardiovascular work in order to confuse the body

rappel *verb* same as **abseil**

rash vest *noun* a thin, synthetic, elasticated, short- or long-sleeved shirt worn by surfers under a wet suit to prevent skin irritation or by swimmers on its own to provide sun protection

rate of perceived exertion *noun* the intensity of an exercise according to the exerciser's subjective judgement, from very light to very heavy. Abbreviation **RPE**

rationale-motive behaviour therapy *noun* a form of cognitive-behavioural therapy in which someone is encouraged to examine and change irrational thought patterns and beliefs in order to reduce dysfunctional behaviour

raw food diet *noun* a diet in which only raw, unprocessed foods may be consumed

RBC *abbreviation* red blood cell

RDA *abbreviation* Recommended Daily Allowance

RDI *abbreviation* Recommended Daily Intake

reaction drill *noun* a repetitive exercise in which a person responds to stimuli, e.g. catching a ball thrown by a partner

reaction time *noun* the interval of time between the application of a stimulus and the first indication of a response

reactive arthritis *noun* arthritis caused by a reaction to something such as a virus

realign *verb* to readjust or manipulate something so that it is in a straight line or is correctly oriented

real tennis *noun* a form of tennis played on an indoor court with a sloping roof against which the ball can be hit

rebound *noun* **1.** a ball that bounces back, particularly off a backboard or rim of the basket in basketball or off the goalkeeper or goalpost in hockey, football or a similar sport **2.** an upward movement or a recovery, especially after a setback

rebounder *noun* a mini trampoline used for exercise

receptor *noun* same as **adrenoceptor**

reciprocal inhibition *noun* the contraction of an agonist muscle, which thereby prevents its antagonist muscle from doing the same as it is forced to lengthen

recombinent *adjective* used for describing a hormone supplement that is produced synthetically

Recommended Daily Allowance, Recommended Daily Intake *noun* the amounts of vitamins, minerals and other nutrients that the government recommends people take in their food or otherwise every day to avoid ill health. Abbreviation **RDA, RDI**

reconstruction *noun* the process of surgically rebuilding torn tissues such as ligaments in the body using grafts from other tissues

reconstructive surgery *noun* surgery that rebuilds a damaged part of the body. ◊ **plastic surgery**

record *noun* something that represents the greatest attainment so far, especially in sports

recovery *noun* **1.** in swimming or rowing, the bringing forward of the arm to make another stroke **2.** the process of returning to health after being ill or injured

recovery diet *noun* a nourishing diet that rebuilds body tissues and restores energy levels after the rigours of competition

recovery time *noun* the time it takes for a the heart rate to return to rest after exertion, used as a measure of physical fitness

recreation *noun* an activity that a person takes part in for pleasure or relaxation rather than as work

recreational *adjective* done or used for pleasure or relaxation rather than work

recreational fitness *noun* exercise undertaken to maintain general fitness and well-being, rather than to train for professional competition

rectilinear *adjective* moving in a straight line

rectus femoris *noun* a flexor muscle in the front of the thigh, one of the four parts of the quadriceps femoris. ◊ **medial**

recumbent bike *noun* same as **exercise bike**

recurrent ankle sprain *noun* a chronic condition in which the ankle ligaments are loose, causing repeated injuries

red blood cell *noun* a blood cell which contains haemoglobin and carries oxygen to the tissues and takes carbon dioxide from them. Abbreviation **RBC**

red card *noun* (*in some team sports*) a red card displayed by the referee when dismissing a player from the field for a serious infringement of the rules. ◊ **green card, yellow card** (NOTE: In some sports, a player who has been shown a red card may also be banned from later games.)

reduced-fat *adjective* same as **low-fat**

ref (*informal*) *noun* a sports referee ■ *verb* to referee a sport or game

referee *noun* an official who oversees the play in a sport or game, judges whether the rules are being followed, and penalises fouls or infringements ■ *verb* to act as a referee in a sport or game

reference nutrient intake *noun* same as **dietary reference value**

reference protein *noun* a standard or test protein against which the quality of others is measured, commonly egg protein

referred pain *noun* pain that is felt in a different body part to the site of injury

reflection *noun* careful thought, especially the process of reconsidering previous actions, events or decisions

reflex *noun* a rapid automatic reaction to a stimulus

reflex action *noun* an automatic reaction to a stimulus, e.g. a knee jerk

reflex arc *noun* the basic system of a reflex action, in which a receptor is linked to a motor neurone that in turn is linked to an effector muscle

reflexology *noun* a form of massage in which pressure is applied to parts of the feet and hands in order to promote relaxation and healing elsewhere in the body

reflex sympathetic dystrophy *noun* a disorder of the sympathetic nervous system that causes stiffness and burning pain in the hands

reflex trainer *noun* a ball that has an unusual centre of gravity and bounces in an unpredictable way, used for training players to have quick reactions

refractory period *noun* a short space of time after the ventricles of the heart have contracted, when they cannot contract again

regatta *noun* a sports event consisting of a series of boat or yacht races

regeneration *noun* regrowth of an organ, limb or other tissue that has been injured or shed

regenerative medicine *noun* the branch of medicine that deals with repairing or replacing tissues and organs by using advanced materials and methodologies such as cloning

regime *noun* a general pattern or system

regimen *noun* a fixed course of treatment, e.g. a course of drugs or a special diet

regular *adjective* (*in skateboarding and similar sports*) used for describing a stance on the board in which the rider's left foot is nearer the front end

regulatory body *noun* an independent organisation, usually established by a government, that makes rules and sets standards for an industry and oversees the activities of companies within it

rehab *noun US* the period or process of rehabilitation, e.g. for someone addicted to a chemical substance (*informal*)

rehabilitate *verb* to make someone fit to work or to lead their usual life

rehabilitation *noun* the process of making someone fit to work or to lead an ordinary life again

rehabilitation exercises *plural noun* gentle exercises designed to maintain flexibility and overall fitness while recovering from an injury

rehydrate *verb* to restore body fluids to a healthy level, or to cause this to occur

rehydration salts *plural noun* minerals mixed with water to make a rehydration solution

rehydration solution *noun* a drink that contains substances such as minerals and electrolytes, used for treatment when a person is dehydrated, e.g. because of illness or strenuous exercise

reigning *adjective* currently holding the champion's title in a particular sport or for a particular sporting event

reiki *noun* (*in alternative medicine*) a treatment in which healing energy is channelled from the practitioner to the patient to enhance energy and reduce stress, pain and fatigue

reinforcement *noun* **1.** the act of strengthening something **2.** a strengthened structure

relative density *noun* same as **specific gravity**

relative protein value *noun* a measure of protein quality, expressed as its ability to support nitrogen balance in the body. Abbreviation **RPV**

relay *noun* a section or lap of a relay race, run or swum by an individual athlete

relay race *noun* a race between teams of competitors in which each member of a team runs or swims only part of the total distance to be covered. In a running race, the current runner must pass a baton to the person running the next section.

release drill *noun* the process of learning to relax fully before playing a sport, in order to improve performance

relegate *verb* to transfer a sports team from a higher to a lower division in a competition, usually because it is one of the least successful teams in the higher division

relegation *noun* the act of moving a sports team into a lower group, or the fact or state of being moved into a lower group

remedial *adjective* intended to cure or relieve the symptoms of someone who is ill or has a physical disability

remedial massage *noun* massage intended to cure or relieve the symptoms of somebody who is ill or injured

repair *verb* to make something that is damaged good again

repetitions *plural noun* same as **reps**

repetitive strain injury *noun* full form of **RSI**

repolarisation *noun* the restoration of the normal electrical polarity of a nerve or muscle cell membrane following depolarisation during passage of a nerve impulse or muscle contraction

reps *plural noun* movements that are repeated exactly, usually a particular number of times. Also called **repetitions**

rerun *verb* to run a race again, or cause a race to be run again, after the result on the first occasion has been disallowed because of an infringement

reserve clause *noun* formerly, a clause in the contract of a professional sportsperson stating that the club, not the sportsperson, has the exclusive right to renew the contract

residual volume *noun* the amount of air left in the lungs after the maximum possible exhalation

resistance *noun* **1.** the ability of a person not to get a disease **2.** the ability of a bacterium or virus to remain unaffected by a drug **3.** opposition to a force

resistance band *noun* a type of extensor

resistance training *noun* training that increases muscle strength by working against resistance such as a weighted dumbbell or barbell

resistance tube *noun* a flexible bar that provides resistance when performing various exercises

resistin *noun* a hormone that increases the resistance of cells to insulin, thereby causing levels of sugar in the bloodstream to rise

resistive boots *plural noun* foam devices worn on the feet to provide extra buoyancy when performing water aerobics

resistive cuffs *plural noun* foam devices worn around the wrist to provide extra buoyancy when performing water aerobics

respect *noun* **1.** a feeling or attitude of admiration and deference towards someone **2.** consideration or thoughtfulness

respiration *noun* the act of taking air into the lungs and blowing it out again through the mouth or nose. Also called **breathing**

respiratory acidosis *noun* same as **acidosis**

respiratory alkalosis *noun* same as **alkalosis**

respiratory dead space *noun* the portion of the respiratory system that does not completely empty on expiration and so cannot receive new air

respiratory quotient *noun* the ratio of the volume of carbon dioxide released to the volume of oxygen absorbed by an organism, cell or tissue over a given time period

respiratory system *noun* a series of organs and passages that take air into the lungs and exchange oxygen for carbon dioxide

respiratory tract *noun* the parts of the body that are responsible for breathing, including the lungs, trachea, mouth and nose

respire *verb* to breathe air in and out

respirometer *noun* an instrument for measuring and studying the process in which oxygen is taken into the body, delivered to tissues and cells, and used by them

response time *noun* the time that it takes for someone to respond to a stimulus

rest *noun* a period of time spent relaxing or sleeping ■ *verb* to restore your energy by means of relaxation or sleep

rest, ice, compression, elevation *noun* a strategy for treating a muscle or joint injury, by not putting any further pressure on it, applying an ice pack, wrapping an elastic bandage to control tissue swelling, and elevating the injured part to drain excess fluid. Abbreviation **RICE**

resting *noun* the practice of taking a short break in between exercises to give the body time to recover

resting energy expenditure *noun* the number of calories needed to maintain the body's normal function while at rest

resting heart rate *noun* the heart rate of a person at rest. Abbreviation **RHR**

resting metabolic rate *noun* the metabolic rate of a person at rest. Abbreviation **RMR**

rest pause training *noun* training in which a short pause is taken between each rep, allowing the exerciser to perform more than the normal set number without stopping to rest

result *noun* the outcome of a game or match

resuscitate *verb* to revive someone from unconsciousness or apparent death after an injury

resuscitation *noun* the revival of someone who is unconscious or near death, especially by cardiac massage and artificial respiration

resynthesis *noun* the synthesis of fresh energy from the breakdown of lactic acid

retake *verb* to take a shot in a game again because of an infringement of the rules during the first attempt

retina *noun* the inside layer of the eye which is sensitive to light

retinol *noun* a vitamin found in liver, vegetables, eggs and cod liver oil that is essential for good vision

retraining *noun* the process of becoming fit again after detraining due to a period of inactivity, e.g. after recovering from injury

retrieve *verb* (*in a game such as tennis or badminton*) to return a difficult shot

retroactive inhibition *noun* the tendency of recently gained knowledge or skills to degenerate when new learning in a similar area is acquired

return *verb* **1.** to come back or to go back to an earlier position or place, or cause something to do so **2.** in sports such as tennis, to hit a ball, especially a service, back to an opponent ■ *noun* an instance of hitting or playing the ball back to an opponent in a sport such as tennis

reuptake *noun* the reabsorption of neurotransmitters by the nerve cells that produced them. Prozac™ and similar drugs work by inhibiting reuptake of the neurotransmitter serotonin so that circulating levels are high and depression is eased.

reverse crunch *noun* a crunch in which the legs are lifted rather than the shoulders

reverse lunge *noun* a lunge in which a leg is extended behind the body, rather than in front

rhabdomyoma *noun* a benign tumour that affects striated muscle tissue

rhabdomyosarcoma *noun* a malignant tumour of striated muscle tissue that occurs mostly in children

rheobase *noun* the minimum electrical nerve impulse necessary to cause a twitch in a muscle

rheumatism *noun* a painful condition of the joints or muscles in which neither infection nor injury is a contributing cause

rheumatoid arthritis *noun* a general painful disabling collagen disease affecting any joint, but especially the hands, feet and hips, making them swollen and inflamed. ◊ **osteoarthritis**

rheumatology *noun* the branch of medicine dealing with the study and treatment of rheumatic diseases

rhizotomy *noun* a surgical operation to cut or divide the roots of a nerve to relieve severe pain

rhomboid major *noun* the larger of the two rhomboid muscles

rhomboid minor *noun* the smaller of the two rhomboid muscles

rhomboid muscles *plural noun* muscles in the upper back that connect the spine to the shoulder blades

RHR *abbreviation* resting heart rate

rhythm *noun* a regular movement or beat

rhythmic *adjective* regular, with a repeated rhythm

rhythmic gymnastics *noun* a sport in which athletes combine gymnastic dance movements with the use of apparatus such as ribbons and hoops

rhythm training *noun* exercises that teach a sportsperson to be agile

rib *noun* any of a set of bones that form a protective cage across the chest

rib belt *noun* a support garment worn after a rib injury to aid healing

ribbon *noun* a long thin flat piece of material

riboflavin *noun* vitamin B2, the yellow component of the B complex group, an important coenzyme in many biochemical processes, found in foods such as spinach, eggs, milk and liver

RICE *abbreviation* rest, ice, compression, elevation

ridge *noun* a long raised part on the surface of a bone or organ

right-footed *adjective* **1.** having a natural tendency to lead with or use the right foot, especially in playing sports such as football **2.** performed using the right foot

right-footer *noun* a right-footed sportsperson

right-handed *adjective* **1.** having a natural tendency to use the right hand, especially in playing sports such as tennis **2.** performed using the right hand

right-hander *noun* **1.** a right-handed sportsperson **2.** a blow delivered with the right hand

right wing *noun* (*in some team games*) the space or position on the right-hand side of a playing area when facing an opponent, or a player who plays in this area

rigor *noun* stiffness and lack of response to stimuli in body organs or tissues

ring *noun* **1.** a raised square roped platform on which a boxing or wrestling match takes place **2.** a circle of tissue, or tissue or muscle shaped like a circle

ringo *noun* a sport, similar to volleyball, played using a small rubber ring, popular in Poland

rings *plural noun* a pair of metal rings that are suspended from a ceiling and used to perform gymnastic routines

ringworm *noun* any of various infections of the skin by a fungus, in which the infection spreads out in a circle from a central point. Also called **tinea**

rink *noun* a smooth, enclosed and often artificially prepared ice surface used for ice-skating, ice hockey or curling

ripped *adjective* with strong muscle definition and low body fat achieved through exercise

risk *noun* **1.** the danger that injury, damage or loss will occur **2.** something likely to cause injury, damage or loss

risk assessment *noun* a process used for determining the risk from a substance, technology or activity

RMR *abbreviation* resting metabolic rate

rock climbing *noun* the activity of scaling rock faces, usually using ropes and other specialised equipment and often in a team

roid rage *noun* an outburst of violent or aggressive behaviour supposedly caused by taking too many anabolic steroids to improve athletic performance (*slang*)

rolfing *noun* a form of soft tissue manipulation that is supposed to realign the body and control the formation of scar tissue

Rollerblades a trade name for a type of roller skate on which the wheels are arranged in one straight line

rollerblading *noun* the sport of travelling or racing on Rollerblades

roller hockey *noun* hockey played on a roller-skating rink or other hard surface by players wearing roller skates

ROM *abbreviation* range of motion

roster *noun* a list of personnel, especially employees, athletes, or members of the armed forces, often detailing their duties and the times when they are to be carried out

rotate *verb* to move in a circle, or make something move in a circle

rotation *noun* movement of a ball-and-socket joint so that the limb turns inwards or outwards

rotator cuff *noun* the group of muscles and tendons at the shoulder joint

Rothbart's foot structure *noun* same as **fallen arches**

roughage *noun* same as **dietary fibre**

round-arm *adjective* (*in cricket*) bowled with the bowler's arm coming over the shoulder at an angle that is away from the vertical, which can be outlawed if regarded as excessive

rounders *noun* a ball game in which batters score a point, or rounder, if they run round all four marked fielding positions or bases after a single hit of the ball

round-robin *noun* a tournament in which each player or team plays against every other player or team in turn

routine *noun* **1.** a regular pattern of activity **2.** a rehearsed set of movements or actions that make up a performance, such as a gymnast's sequence of exercises

rowing *noun* the propelling of a small boat through the water using oars, especially the sport of racing in specially designed lightweight boats

rowing machine *noun* a fitness machine that imitates the action of rowing a boat

RPE *abbreviation* rate of perceived exertion

RSI *noun* a condition in which a group of muscles, tendons and nerves becomes weak and painful from prolonged overuse. Full form **repetitive strain injury**

rub *noun* a massaging of part of the body ■ *verb* to move something, especially the hands, backwards and forwards over a surface

rub down *verb* to massage someone or part of the body vigorously

rubor *noun* the redness of inflamed tissue, usually accompanied by the other signs of inflammation such as pain, heat and swelling, owing to increased blood circulation to the affected area

ruck *noun* (*in rugby*) a loose scrum formed around the ball when it is on the ground ■ *verb* (*in rugby*) to form a loose scrum around the ball on the ground

rugby *noun* a team sport in which players run with an oval ball, pass it laterally from hand to hand, and kick it

rugby league *noun* a form of rugby that has teams of 13 players

rugby union *noun* a form of rugby that has teams of 15 players

rulebook *noun* **1.** a book or pamphlet containing the official rules of a game or sport **2.** the strictly correct or orthodox way of doing something

run *verb* to move rapidly on foot so that both feet are momentarily off the ground in each step ■ *noun* **1.** a rapid pace faster than a walk or jog **2.** a race in which the competitors run **3.** a point scored in cricket, usually when one or both batsmen run between the wickets **4.** a score in baseball made by travelling round all the bases to home plate

runner *noun* **1.** an athlete or horse in a race **2.** the blade of an ice skate

runner's knee *noun* same as **chondromalacia patellae**

runner-up *noun* a contestant or competitor who comes near the winner in an event or race and often receives a small prize

running *noun* **1.** rapid movement on foot, with long strides and both feet momentarily off the ground **2.** the sport or exercise of running

running commentary *noun* same as **commentary**

run out *verb* (*in cricket*) to dismiss a player who is trying to complete a run by breaking the wicket with the ball before he or she has reached the crease

rupture *noun* **1.** the breaking or tearing of an organ such as the appendix **2.** same as **hernia** ■ *verb* to break or tear something

ruptured disc *noun* same as **displaced intervertebral disc**

ruptured eardrum *noun* same as **perforated eardrum**

ryu *noun* a style or method of practising a Japanese martial art

S

sacral nerves *plural noun* the nerves that branch from the spinal cord in the sacrum and govern the legs, the arms and the genital area

sacral plexus *noun* a group of nerves inside the pelvis near the sacrum that lead to nerves in the buttocks, back of the thigh and lower leg and foot

sacral vertebrae *plural noun* the five vertebrae in the lower part of the spine that are fused together to form the sacrum

sacrococcygeal *adjective* referring to the sacrum and the coccyx

sacroiliac joint *noun* a joint where the sacrum joins the ilium

sacrum *noun* a flat triangular bone, formed of five sacral vertebrae fused together, that is located between the lumbar vertebrae and the coccyx and articulates with the coccyx and the hip bones (NOTE: The plural is **sacra**.)

safety key *noun* a device that is attached to the emergency stop switch on a treadmill and to the runner's belt, which activates the switch if the runner slips or falls

sagittal plane *noun* the division of the body along the midline, at right angles to the coronal plane, dividing the body into right and left parts. Also called **median plane**

sailboard *noun* a large surfboard with a keel, a mast and a sail mounted on it that is operated by one person standing up

sailboarding *noun* same as **windsurfing**

sailing *noun* **1.** the sport or leisure activity of travelling in a boat propelled by sails **2.** the art or a method of controlling a boat or ship, especially one with sails

salbutamol *noun* a beta-agonist drug used as a short-term treatment for asthma

salinometer *noun* an instrument that measures the salinity of a solution

salmeterol *noun* a beta-agonist drug used as a long-term treatment for asthma and some pulmonary diseases

salt *noun* **1.** a substance consisting of small white tangy-tasting crystals, consisting mainly of sodium chloride, used for flavouring and preserving food **2.** any crystalline compound formed from the neutralisation of an acid by a base containing a metal

salt depletion *noun* the dangerous loss of salt from the body by excessive sweating, causing muscular weakness and cramps

sambo *noun* a modern martial art originating in the former Soviet Union, with forms similar to wrestling and aikido and a form based on self-defence

sample *noun* a small quantity of something used for testing

sample collection form *noun* a form that is filled in at a doping control station

SAM splint *noun* a splint that is worn to immobilise fractured limbs and can be worn during an x-ray examination without disrupting the results. Full form **structural aluminium malleable splint**

sand board *noun* a board similar to a surfboard or snowboard used for riding down sand dunes or performing stunts on a course covered in sand

sarcolactic acid *noun* a form of lactic acid produced by muscle tissue during anaerobic activity

sarcolemma *noun* a membrane surrounding a muscle fibre

sarcomere *noun* a filament in myofibril

sarcoplasmic reticulum *noun* a network in the cytoplasm of striated muscle fibres

sarcous *adjective* consisting of or relating to flesh or muscle tissue

sartorius *noun* a very long muscle, the longest muscle in the body, that runs from the anterior iliac spine across the thigh down to the tibia

saturated fat *noun* a type of fat that is typical of animal-derived fats, is not essential in the diet and is thought to increase blood cholesterol. Compare **unsaturated fat**, **polyunsaturated fat**

saturated fatty acids *plural noun* fatty acids that are non-essential in the diet and are thought to increase blood cholesterol, typical of animal-derived fats

saturation diving *noun* a method of diving in which the diver's bloodstream is saturated with an inert gas so that the time required for decompression is unaffected by the duration of the dive

sauna *noun* **1.** a bath involving a spell in a hot steamy room followed by a plunge into cold water or a light brushing with birch or cedar boughs **2.** a room designed or prepared for having a sauna

scab *noun* a hard crust of dried blood, serum or pus that forms over a wound during healing

scalene muscles *plural noun* three pairs of muscles involved in rotating and tilting the neck

scales *plural noun* a device on which a person can be weighed

scaphoid fracture *noun* same as **carponavicular fracture**

scapula *noun* either of two large flat bones covering the top part of the back. Also called **shoulderblade** (NOTE: The plural is **scapulae**.)

Scarsdale diet *noun* a dietary plan that drastically reduces calorie intake for a period of between 7 and 14 days

scar tissue *noun* dense fibrous tissue that forms the scar over a healed wound

SCAT *noun* a set of questions and observations that a healthcare professional should use to diagnose concussion, typically an AVPU assessment, Maddocks questions, pupillary response and a cognitive assessment. Full form **sports concussion assessment tool**

Schwann cells *plural noun* the cells which form the myelin sheath around a nerve fibre

sciatic *adjective* **1.** relating to the hip **2.** relating to the sciatic nerve

sciatica *noun* pain along the sciatic nerve, usually at the back of the thighs and legs

sciatic nerve *noun* one of two main nerves that run from the sacral plexus into each of the thighs, dividing into a series of nerves in the lower legs and feet. They are the largest nerves in the body.

scintigram *noun* a two-dimensional image of the distribution of a radioactive tracer in a body organ such as the brain or a kidney, obtained using a special scanner

scintigraphy *noun* a method of detecting injuries in which a radioactive tracer is injected into the injury site and a reading taken, allowing a 2-dimensional image to be built up

scintiscanner *noun* an apparatus used in diagnosing some diseases that produces an image, called a scintigram, of the distribution in the body of a radioactive tracer that has been administered to the patient

scissors *noun* **1.** (*in gymnastics*) a movement of the legs that resembles the opening and closing of scissors **2.** (*in the high jump*) a simple technique of clearing the bar sideways on with a leading leg and then the other in a fast separating and closing movement, now rarely used **3.** (*in rugby*) a tactic in which a player passes the ball to another player running diagonally to his or her line of advance, thus changing the direction of an attack

scissors kick *noun* **1.** (*in swimming*) a kicking motion that resembles the opening and closing of scissors, used especially when doing the sidestroke **2.** (*in soccer*) a mid-air kick of the ball with the legs moving in a way that resembles the movement of scissor blades

sclerosis *noun* the hardening and thickening of body tissue as a result of unwarranted growth, degeneration of nerve fibres or deposition of minerals, especially calcium

scoliosis *noun* a condition in which the spine curves sideways

scoop stretcher *noun* a stretcher for transporting an injured person with a suspected spinal injury, assembled under the patient so that he or she need not be moved

score *noun* **1.** the total number of points gained by a player or team at the end of or during a match or game **2.** a record of the number of points gained by a player or team in a match or game **3.** an action that leads to the gaining of a point or points in a match or game ■ *verb* to gain a point or goal

scoreboard *noun* a board at a sporting venue on which the score of a game, match, or other competition in progress is displayed

score draw *noun* a result in a match, especially a football match, in which both sides have scored the same number of goals

scoreline *noun* same as **score**

score sheet *noun* a record of who has scored a point or goal in a game or match, especially in football or rugby

scout *noun* same as **talent scout** ■ *verb* to look for talented players for a sports team

scrambler *noun* a motorcycle designed for racing across rough terrain

scratch *noun* a person or team withdrawn from a race or competition

scrum *noun* a formalised contest for possession of the ball during a rugby match between the two sets of forwards who each assemble in a tight-knit formation with bodies bent and arms clasped around each other and push forwards together against their opponents

scrum half *noun* (*in rugby*) the halfback who places the ball in the scrum, or the position of this player

scuba diver *noun* a diver who takes part in scuba diving

scuba diving *noun* the sport of diving, using an apparatus for breathing underwater consisting of a portable canister of compressed air and a mouthpiece

sculpt *verb* to change the shape or contours of something by natural processes such as erosion. Also called **sculpture**

sculpted *adjective* with an athletic physique that is aesthetically pleasing

season *noun* the performance of a player or team during a sporting season in relation to others

seasonal training *noun* training that is intense when preparing for competition and lessens or stops in the periods in between, leading to detraining and retraining patterns

season ticket *noun* a ticket valid for a specific period of time for travel on public transport, use of leisure facilities, or attendance at sporting or cultural events

seated exercise *noun* any exercise that is performed sitting down, e.g. a leg extension

secondary curve *noun* (*in scoliosis*) a compensatory curve of the spine that realigns the shoulders and head so that they are still level

secondary protein energy malnutrition *noun* malnutrition caused by the body's inability to absorb protein and energy from dietary sources, caused by serious illness such as cancer

second wind *noun* a renewal of energy following a period of effort and exertion

secretagogue *noun* an agent that stimulates the pituitary gland to release more growth hormone, used by athletes

secrete *verb* to produce a substance such as a hormone, oil or enzyme

seed *noun* a competitor who is graded according to the perceived likelihood of his or her winning a specific tournament ■ *verb* to rank a player according to the perceived likelihood of his or her winning a specific tournament

segment training *noun* training for each muscle group in turn, with the aim of identifying weaknesses

seitan *noun* a foodstuff that consists of wheat gluten obtained by washing the starch out of flour dough, processed in various ways and often used as a vegetarian alternative to meat

seizure *noun* a sudden attack of an illness or condition, especially of the kind experienced by people with epilepsy

selection *noun* the process by which an athlete is chosen for a team of competition

selenium *noun* a non-metallic trace element (NOTE: The chemical symbol is **Se**.)

self-defence *noun* fighting techniques used for defending oneself against physical attack, especially unarmed combat techniques such as those used in many of the martial arts

self-discipline *noun* the ability to do what is necessary or sensible without needing to be urged by someone else

self-efficacy *noun* confidence and efficient stress-management techniques that positively affect an athlete's performance

self-fulfilling *adjective* used for describing an event, e.g. a failure in competition, that is brought about or proved true because of having been expected or predicted

self-image *noun* the opinion that a person has about how worthwhile, attractive or intelligent he or she is

self-modelling *noun* the memories of your own accomplishments, used during self-talk as a method of achieving a positive mindset

self-paced *adjective* used for describing an exercise regime or a race that is controlled by the athlete and not by external stimuli

self-regulation *noun* an athlete's ability to follow a training regime and adapt it according to current needs, e.g. to resist training while injured, without supervision

self-respect *noun* belief in your own worth and dignity

self-talk *noun* the things that an individual says mentally to himself or herself, often to instil a positive attitude before a competition

self-test *noun* a diagnostic test that you give yourself to determine your health, e.g. a blood-pressure test

self-treatment *noun* an individual's treatment of his or her own illnesses or injuries, as distinct from treatment provided by a doctor or other medical professional

semi-curved last *noun* same as **standard last**

semi-final *noun* either of two matches or games, the winners of which will play each other in the final round of a competition

semi-finalist *noun* a player or team that is playing in a semi-final

semi-lunar cartilage *noun* one of two pads of cartilage, the lateral meniscus and medial meniscus, between the femur and the tibia in the knee

semi-lunar valve *noun* either of two valves in the heart, the pulmonary valve and the aortic valve, through which blood flows out of the ventricles

semi-professional *adjective* **1.** participating in a sport for pay but not as a full-time professional **2.** played in or contested by semi-professional sportspeople **3.** displaying some aspects of a professional

semitendinosus *noun* a muscle extending from the hip joint to just below the mid-thigh

send off *verb* to dismiss a player from a game or competition for breaking the rules, e.g. in football, rugby or hockey

sensei *noun* an instructor in karate, aikido and various other Japanese martial arts

sense organ *noun* any organ in which there are various sensory nerves that can detect environmental stimuli such as scent, heat or pain and transmit information about them to the central nervous system, e.g. the nose or the skin

sensitise *verb* to produce in someone an unusual sensitivity to a substance such as a food ingredient or drug so that subsequent exposure to the substance triggers an allergic reaction

sensitive *adjective* having an unexpected reaction to an allergen or to a drug, caused by the presence of antibodies which were created when the person was exposed to the drug or allergen in the past

sensitivity *noun* **1.** the fact of being able to detect and respond to an outside stimulus **2.** the rate of positive responses in a test from persons with a specific disease. A high rate of sensitivity means a low rate of people being incorrectly classed as negative. Compare **specificity**

sensorium *noun* **1.** the sensory components of the brain and nervous system that deal with the receiving and interpreting of external stimuli **2.** all the sensory functions in the body, considered as a single unit

sensory input *noun* stimulation provided by the senses

sensory nerve *noun* a nerve which registers a sensation such as heat, taste or smell and carries impulses to the brain and spinal cord. Also called **afferent nerve**

sensory receptor *noun* a cell which senses a change in the surrounding environment, e.g. cold or pressure, and reacts to it by sending out an impulse through the nervous system. Also called **nerve ending**

sensory science *noun* the application of scientific principles to the evaluation of the human senses and interpretation of the signals that they pick up

septum *noun* a wall between two parts of an organ, e.g. between two parts of the heart or between the two nostrils in the nose (NOTE: The plural is **septa**.)

sequela *noun* a condition that is a consequence of an earlier disease or injury, e.g. chronic pain or reduced mobility

sequestrum *noun* a fragment of dead tissue, usually bone, that separates from surrounding living tissue

serial skill *noun* a series of discrete skills performed in sequence, e.g. the run, jump and landing required for the triple jump

series *noun* in some sports such as cricket and baseball, a set of matches between the same teams

serine *noun* an amino acid produced in the hydrolysis of protein

serotonergic *adjective* describes neurons or nerves that are capable of releasing serotonin as a neurotransmitter at their endings

serotonin *noun* a compound that is a neurotransmitter and exists mainly in blood platelets, released after tissue is injured

serratus anterior *noun* a muscle that connects the ribs to the scapula at the sides of the torso

serve *verb* (*in racket sports*) to begin a point by launching the ball or shuttlecock towards an opponent ■ *noun* (*in racket sports*) an act of serving the ball or shuttlecock

sesamin *noun* a supplement that improves liver function, releasing thermogenic enzymes, used as a sports supplement

sesamoid *noun* a small, roughly spherical bone lying within a tendon to assist in its mechanical action or to bear pressure

sesamoiditis *noun* pain in the balls of the feet caused by repeated stress on that area

set *noun* 1. a number of repetitions of an exercise 2. a part of a tennis match that is won when one player or couple wins a minimum of six games

set piece *noun* a planned manoeuvre used by a team in a game, e.g. the way a football team takes a corner or free kick

set point *noun* 1. the body weight at which a person's metabolism is naturally constant and balanced 2. a situation in a tennis match in which a player has only to win the next point to win the set, or the point he or she has to win

severe *adjective* used for describing an injury that is very bad or painful

Sever's disease *noun* same as **calcaneal apophysitis**

shadow boxing *noun* a form of training for boxing in which there is no opponent, with the boxer's own shadow on the wall used for reference

shaft *noun* same as **diaphysis**

shamateur *noun* an athlete who is officially an amateur but who is secretly paid

shape *noun* the condition of someone's health or fitness

shiatsu *noun* a form of healing massage in which the hands are used for applying pressure at acupuncture points on the body in order to stimulate and redistribute energy. Originating in Japan, it is used for treating various conditions, including back pain, migraine, insomnia, depression and digestive problems.

shin *noun* the front part of the lower leg

shinbone *noun* same as **tibia**

shinny *noun* (*in the United States and Canada*) an informal game similar to hockey, played with a small hard ball and curved wooden sticks

shin splints *plural noun* extremely sharp pains in the front of the lower leg, felt by athletes

shintaido *noun* a form of exercise based on the movements used in Japanese martial arts, performed by a group

shinty *noun* a game loosely resembling hockey traditionally played in the Highlands of Scotland, in which players are allowed to hit the ball in the air

shock *noun* a state of physiological collapse, marked by a weak pulse, coldness, sweating and irregular breathing, and resulting from a situation such as blood loss, heart failure, allergic reaction or emotional trauma

shock absorber *noun* a device designed to absorb jarring or jolting

shock-absorbing *adjective* minimising the damage caused to the body by an impact

shoe supports *plural noun* same as **orthotics**

shoot *verb* **1.** (*of pain*) to seem to move suddenly through the body with a piercing feeling **2.** in a sport such as football or basketball, to kick, hit or throw a ball in an attempt to score a goal or point

short leg *noun* a condition in which one leg is shorter than the other, either because of a difference in bone length (anatomical short leg), or because of pelvic misalignment or other postural problems (functional short leg)

short-term goal *noun* something that a person wants to achieve in the near future, which they are working towards

short-term memory *noun* the part of the mind used for retaining temporary information over a short period

shot *noun* **1.** an attempt to score points by throwing, hitting, kicking or shooting something **2.** in golf, tennis etc, an act of hitting the ball **3.** same as **shot put 2**

shot consistency *noun* (*in racket sports*) the skill of making each shot played consistent with the others

shot put *noun* **1.** an athletics event in which contestants compete to throw a heavy metal ball as far as possible **2.** a heavy metal ball used in the shot put

shot selection *noun* the process by which someone decides which type of shot to play next, e.g. in tennis by taking into account their own position on the court and that of their opponent (NOTE: Shot selection is also an important part of other ball games such as cricket and golf.)

shoulderblade *noun* same as **scapula**

shoulder girdle *noun* same as **pectoral girdle**

shoulder press *noun* an exercise in which the arms are pushed upwards from the shoulders against some resistance, e.g. a dumbbell lift, while seated upright

shoulder separation *noun* an injury in which the ligaments connecting the collarbone to the shoulder are torn, common in contact sports

shoulder shrug *noun* an exercise in which weights are held with the arms loosely hanging at the front of the body and the shoulders are slowly raised and lowered

shoulder support *noun* a supportive wrap used for protecting the shoulder from injury during exercise

showing *noun* the way a player or team performs

sick *adjective* (*in snowboarding*) used for describing a move that is performed so skilfully as to cause envy

sida cordifolia *noun* a supplement for athletes containing ephedrine, extracted from an Indian plant

sideslip *verb* (*in skiing*) to slide at an angle down a slope

sidespin *noun* a rotary motion put on a ball that causes it to spin horizontally

sidestroke *noun* a swimming stroke performed on the side by thrusting the arms alternately forwards and downwards while doing a scissors kick

sight *noun* a device on an archer's bow, on a pistol, on a rifle and on similar weapons that allows the user to take aim at the target

silly *adjective* (*in cricket*) used for describing a fielder or fielding position very close to the batsman, closer than a similar position described as 'short'

silver medal *noun* an award for taking second place in a race or other competition, usually in the form of a silver disc on a ribbon

simple carbohydrates *plural noun* carbohydrates with simple molecules containing few linked glucose units, broken down very quickly by the body

simple fracture *noun* a fractured bone in which there is one break and no fragments or other cracks

simvastatin *noun* a drug that lowers lipid levels in the blood

sin bin *noun* an area with a bench beside an ice hockey rink or a rugby pitch where penalised players must stay during the period that they have to serve as a time penalty for an offence

single-blind testing *noun* a form of blind testing in which the researchers are aware from the beginning which subjects are receiving the supplement and which are receiving a placebo. Compare **double-blind testing**

singles *noun* a game of tennis, badminton or table tennis between two players. Compare **doubles**

sinoatrial node *noun* a node in the heart which regulates the heartbeat

sinus tarsi syndrome *noun* pain in the soft area of the foot above the heel bone on either side, caused by sprain or overpronation

site injection *noun* the act of injecting a steroid directly into a specific muscle

sitology *noun* the scientific study of food, diet and nutrition as they relate to health

sitotherapy *noun* the use of food as a therapeutic treatment

sit-up *noun* an exercise in which you lie flat on your back with your legs bent and then raise the upper part of your body to a sitting position without using your hands

Six Nations *noun* an international rugby championship between teams representing England, France, Ireland, Italy, Scotland and Wales, held annually since 2000

six-pack *noun* a well-developed block of abdominal muscles (*informal*)

skateboard *noun* a short narrow board to which a set of small wheels is fitted on the underside, used to move rapidly or to perform jumps and stunts

skateboarding *noun* the sport or pastime of riding a skateboard

skating *noun* the pastime or sport of sliding on ice skates or rolling on roller skates

skeet *noun* a form of clay-pigeon shooting in which targets are thrown from two traps, the targets being either singles or in pairs

skeletal muscle *noun* a muscle that is attached to a bone and makes a limb move

skeleton *noun* **1.** the set of bones that make up the framework of the body **2.** a small sled used for high-speed racing, on which the driver lies head first

ski *noun* either of a pair of long thin boards made of wood, metal, or other material that curve up at the front and are used to slide across snow ■ *verb* to glide over the surface of snow or water wearing skis, as a means of travel or as a leisure pursuit or sport

skier's thumb *noun* same as **ulnar collateral ligament sprain**

skiing *noun* the activity, sport, or pastime of travelling on skis

skijumping *noun* a sport in which a person skis down a slope that has an upturned curve at the end, allowing them to perform a jump into the air

skill *noun* an ability to do perform an action well, acquired by training

skill acquisition *noun* the process of learning a skill, either by being taught or by observation

skillless *adjective* **1.** used for describing a person who has not mastered any skills **2.** of a sport or activity, not requiring any skills

skill retention *noun* the fact of remembering learned skills

skill transfer *noun* the act of learning a new skill using aspects of other skills that have already been mastered

ski machine *noun* an exercise machine that recreates the motion of skiing

skinfold *noun* a test for subcutaneous fat deposits that measures how much skin and tissue can be 'pinched' at various sites on the body

skinny *adjective* thin, especially in an unappealing or unhealthy way

skin-tight *adjective* fitting tightly to the body

skipper *noun* a team captain (*informal*)

skipping rope *noun* a piece of rope, often with handles at either end, for skipping over

slalom *noun* a downhill ski race in which competitors follow a winding course and zigzag through flags on poles or other obstacles

slashing *noun* the illegal striking or swinging of a stick at an opposing player in hockey or lacrosse

sledging *noun* (*in cricket*) the attempt by a fielder or bowler to undermine a batsman's confidence by verbal abuse

slice *noun* a stroke in which a ball is hit off-centre on the side nearest the player, so that it follows a curving path away from the player ■ *verb* to hit a ball off-centre so that it follows a curving path, whether intentionally or as a result of a bad swing or stroke

sliding filament theory *noun* a theory of muscle contraction in which the myosin filaments form a bond with the actin filament, drawing them closer and contracting the muscle

slim *adjective* attractively thin

slimline *adjective* designed to help with a weight-reducing diet

slimming *noun* the use of a special diet or special food that is low in calories and is supposed to help a person lose weight

slimming pill *noun* a pill that supposedly helps to reduce weight, whether by increasing the metabolism, suppressing hunger or blocking the absorption of fats

slimming product *noun* a food product that is low-calorie and designed especially for people on a weight-reducing diet

sling *noun* a wide bandage suspended from someone's neck to support an injured arm or hand

sliotar *noun* the ball used in the sport of hurling

slip *verb* to dislocate or displace a bone, especially in the spine ■ *noun* (*in cricket*) the position of a fielder behind and near the wicketkeeper, especially on the off side, or the fielder who takes up this position

slip-lasted *adjective* used for describing a training shoe constructed without a rigid last to give greater flexibility

slipped disc *noun* same as **displaced intervertebral disc**

sloth *noun* a dislike of work or any kind of physical exertion

slow *adjective* used for describing a surface that tends to reduce the speed or ability to travel of a ball, runner or other competitor

slow twitch fibre, slow fibre *noun* a type of muscle fibre that is not able to contract swiftly

smooth muscle *noun* a muscle found in the viscera that functions by slow contraction and is not under voluntary control. Compare **skeletal muscle**

SMT *abbreviation* stress management training

snapping hip syndrome *noun* a condition in which the muscles connecting the thighbone to the pelvis are too tight to comfortably move over the hipbone during activities such as running

snatch *noun* a lift in weightlifting in which the bar is lifted from the floor to above the head in a single movement. Also called **clean and snatch**

snooker *noun* a game played on a table in which a white ball struck with a cue is used to hit fifteen red balls and six balls of different colours into holes called pockets at the edges of the table

snorkel *noun* a curved tube that projects above the water and enables someone to breathe while swimming face down near the surface

snorkelling *noun* the activity or pastime of swimming with a snorkel

snowboard *noun* a board with bindings for the feet that somebody stands on to slide down snow slopes

snowboarding *noun* the sport or pastime of riding a snowboard, also an extreme sport with acrobatic tricks and moves

soccer *noun US* same as **football**

social approval *noun* respect from other people for your achievements, a motivating factor for many sportspeople

social learning theory *noun* a theory that people learn ways of coping with stress and managing aggression by observing others who are calm and controlled

social loafing *noun* a tendency to work less hard when sharing the responsibility with others, as can occur with members of sports teams

sodium *noun* a chemical element that is the basic substance in salt (NOTE: The chemical symbol is **Na**.)

softball *noun* **1.** baseball played with a larger softer ball on a smaller field, between two teams of ten people **2.** the ball used for playing softball

soft tissue *noun* the soft parts of the body such as muscles and skin, as distinct from than bone or cartilage

solar plexus *noun* a nerve network situated at the back of the abdomen between the adrenal glands

soleus *noun* a flat muscle that goes down the calf of the leg (NOTE: The plural is **solei**.)

soluble fibre *noun* a type of fibre in vegetables, fruit, pulses and porridge oats that is partly digested in the intestine and reduces the absorption of fats and sugar into the body, so lowering the level of cholesterol

somatic anxiety *noun* anxious arousal that comes from high levels of adrenaline in the body, causing jittery, restless feelings

somatic nervous system *noun* the part of the nervous system that serves the sense organs and muscles of the body wall and limbs, and brings about activity in the voluntary muscles

somatology *noun* the study of both the physiology and anatomy of the body

somatomedin *noun* a hormone produced in the liver that stimulates the growth of bone and muscle

somatotrophin *noun* a hormone secreted by the pituitary gland that controls bone and tissue development

sore *adjective* **1.** rough and inflamed **2.** painful

South Asian Games *plural noun* a multi-sport event for athletes from the South Asian area, including India, Pakistan and Nepal, held every two years

Southeast Asian Games *plural noun* a multi-sport event for athletes from Southeast Asia, held every two years

South Pacific Games *plural noun* a multi-sport event for athletes from South Pacific islands, including Fiji, Guam, Samoa and Tahiti, held every four years

soya protein *noun* protein found in soya beans, which is low in fat and cholesterol

SPARC *abbreviation* Sport Performance Assessment and Rehabilitation Centre

spare *adjective* with a muscular physique and no excess fat

spasm *noun* a sudden, usually painful, involuntary contraction of a muscle, as in cramp

spastic *adjective* with spasms or sudden contractions of muscles

spasticity *noun* a condition in which a limb resists passive movement

special dietary requirements *plural noun* the requirements of someone who has a restricted diet, e.g. who is vegetarian, vegan, eats only kosher or halal food, is pregnant or breastfeeding or has wheat, gluten or nut allergies

Special Olympics *noun* an international athletic competition for athletes with mental disabilities

specific exercise *noun* an exercise that is targeted at a particular muscle or group of muscles, rather than for general fitness

specific gravity *noun* the ratio of the density of a substance to the density of water at the same temperature. Abbreviation **SG**. Also called **relative density**

specificity *noun* the rate of negative responses in a test from persons free from a disease, with a high specificity indicating a low rate of false positives. Compare **sensitivity**

spectator sport *noun* a sport that attracts spectators in large numbers

speedball *noun* **1.** a training aid for boxing that is like a light punchbag fixed at both ends, not hanging freely **2.** a fast-paced game that combines elements of football and handball

speed development *noun* improving physical and mental reaction times

speed drill *noun* same as **speed training**

speed reverse board *noun* a rubber mat fixed to the wall in a sports hall to protect it

speed skate *noun* an ice skate designed for racing, with a blade that is much longer than on a standard skate

speed skating *noun* the sport of racing competitively on speed skates, in which two or more skaters race against each other on a wide oval track divided into two lanes

speed training *noun* training that uses exercises designed to improve reaction times

sphygmomanometer *noun* a device for measuring blood pressure

spike *noun* **1.** a pointed metal stud, part of a set attached to the sole of an athlete's shoe to give better grip **2.** a hard smash of a volleyball, hit close to the net and straight down into the opponent's court ■ *verb* **1.** to injure another player or competitor with the spikes of an athletic shoe **2.** to leap high close to the net and hit a volleyball straight down into an opponent's court

spikes *plural noun* a pair of athletic shoes with soles equipped with pointed studs to give better grip

spina bifida *noun* a congenital condition in which part of the spinal cord or meninges protrudes through a cleft in the spinal column, resulting in loss of voluntary movement in the lower body

spinal *adjective* relating to the spine

spinal anaesthesia *noun* the loss of sensation in part of the body caused by injury to the spinal column

spinal board *noun* a rigid plastic board used for transporting casualties with suspected spinal injuries

spinal canal *noun* a passage that runs through the opening in the middle of each vertebra of the spinal column and contains the spinal cord, the meninges, nerve roots and blood vessels

spinal column *noun* same as **spine**

spinal cord *noun* the part of the central nervous system that runs from the brain down the spine to the lower back, protected by the vertebral canal

spinal fusion *noun* surgery to fuse together two or more vertebrae, used to treat scoliosis or long-term problems caused by a herniated disc

spinal instrumentation *noun* the use of rods or screws to stabilise the spine to correct long-term problems such as scoliosis

spinal nerves *plural noun* the thirty-one paired nerves arising from the spinal cord and emerging on either side of the spinal column to supply the rest of the body

spine *noun* the series of bones, the vertebrae, linked together to form a flexible supporting column running from the pelvis to the skull

spinning *noun* a fitness class in which the participants work on exercise bikes, led by an instructor

spirometer *noun* a device used for measuring oxygen consumption

spirometry *noun* the act of measuring the capacity of the lungs

splanchnic *adjective* used for referring to the internal organs (*technical*)

spleen *noun* a ductless vascular organ in the left upper abdomen that helps to destroy old red blood cells, form lymphocytes and store blood

splenic rupture *noun* a swelling and potentially fatal tearing of the spleen, the risk of which is raised by returning to sports too early after a mononucleosis infection

splenius *noun* either of two muscles on each side of the neck that reach from the base of the skull to the upper back and rotate and extend the head and neck (NOTE: The plural is **splenii**.)

splint *noun* a support for an injured body part that holds it rigid while the tissues heal

split decision *noun* (*in boxing and similar sports*) a win awarded by a majority of judges, rather than by a unanimous decision

splits *plural noun* a gymnastic action in which the legs are fully extended in opposite directions until the body is sitting on or very close to the floor

spondylitis *noun* inflammation of the vertebrae and the attached discs and ligaments

spondylolisthesis *noun* a fracture in a single vertebra of the lower back that allows it to slip forwards, commonly suffered by gymnasts and dancers

spondylolysis *noun* a fracture in a single vertebra of the lower back, caused by repeated extension of the spine and commonly suffered by gymnasts and dancers

sport climbing *noun* a sport in which competitors ascend walls, often artificial ones, on difficult routes that have bolts in place

sportglasses *plural noun* sunglasses designed for wear while taking part in sports

sportive *adjective* regularly taking part in sport

Sport Performance Assessment and Rehabilitation Centre *noun* a service that provides sports science consultancy for professional athletes, based at Roehampton University, London. Abbreviation **SPARC**

sports acrobatics *noun* acrobatics performed as a competitive sport

sports bottle *noun* a drinking bottle with a specially-designed cap that does not spill, for use while exercising

sports bra *noun* a bra designed to offer additional comfort, support and protection during physical activity such as jogging or sports

sports concussion assessment tool *noun* full form of **SCAT**

sports counselling *noun* a professional who gives emotional guidance to an athlete and helps them to cope with issues such as injury or retirement

sports drink *noun* a soft drink that is intended to quench thirst faster than water and replenish the sugar and minerals lost from the body during physical exercise

sports fatigue syndrome *noun* same as **unexplained underperformance syndrome**

sports gel *noun* a concentrated carbohydrate gel that is easy to metabolise during exercise

sports ground *noun* a place where sports are performed

sports hernia *noun* same as **athletic pubalgia**

sports injury *noun* any injury incurred as a result of taking part in sports, e.g. a sprain, shin splints or tendinitis

sportsman *noun* **1.** a man who participates in sport **2.** someone who behaves fairly, observing rules, respecting others and accepting defeat graciously

sportsmanlike *adjective* used for describing conduct considered fitting for a sportsperson, including observance of the rules of fair play, respect for others and graciousness in losing

sportsmanship *noun* **1.** conduct considered fitting for a sportsperson, including observance of the rules of fair play, respect for others and graciousness in losing **2.** participation in sport

sports massage *noun* massage for professional sportspeople, aimed at relaxing overused muscles and preventing or healing injury

sports medicine *noun* the study of the treatment of sports injuries

sports nutrition *noun* specialised nutrition for a professional sportsperson, designed to provide enough energy to sustain a very active lifestyle as well as providing nutrients that support tissue growth and repair

sports nutritionist *noun* a professional who looks after the specialised dietary needs of athletes

sportsperson *noun* **1.** someone who participates in sport **2.** someone who behaves fairly, observing rules, respecting others, and accepting defeat graciously

sports psychology *noun* the scientific study of the mental state of sportspeople, looking at issues such as motivation, concentration, stress and self-confidence

sports shoes *plural noun* same as **trainers**

sports supplement *noun* a dietary supplement used by athletes to enhance performance

sports towel *noun* a highly-absorbent small towel that dries quickly

sports watch *noun* a durable watch designed to be worn during sports, often with extra features such as a stopwatch

sporty *adjective* **1.** designed or appropriate for sport or leisure activities **2.** enthusiastic about sport or outdoor activities and regularly taking part in them

spot *verb* **1.** to watch someone performing an exercise **2.** to identify someone, especially a performer, as having a promising talent worthy of being developed to a high, often professional standard

spot reduction *noun* the notion that the amount of fat in a particular area of the body can be reduced by working the muscles in that area, disputed by some experts

spotter *noun* a partner who watches a person performing an exercise to check that they are performing it safely and with proper technique

sprain *noun* a condition in which the ligaments in a joint are stretched or torn because of a sudden movement

springboard *noun* **1.** a flexible board secured to a base at one end and projecting over the water at the other, used for diving **2.** a flexible board on which gymnasts bounce in order to gain height for vaulting

sprint *noun* **1.** a short race run or cycled at a very high speed **2.** a burst of fast running or cycling during the last part of a longer race **3.** a sudden burst of activity or speed ■ *verb* to run, swim or cycle as rapidly as possible

sprinter *noun* an athlete or cyclist who takes part in a short race run or cycled at a very high speed

sputum *noun* mucus that is formed in an inflamed nose, throat or lungs and is coughed up. Also called **phlegm**

squad *noun* **1.** a small group of people engaged in the same activity **2.** a number of players from which a team is selected **3.** *US* an athletics or sports team

squamosal *noun* a thin plate-shaped bone of the vertebrate skull that forms the forward and upper part of the temporal bone in humans

square *verb* to level the scores in a ball game

squash *noun* a game for two or four participants played in an enclosed court with long-handled rackets and a small ball that may be hit off any of the walls

squat *noun* an exercise in weightlifting in which the lifter raises a barbell while rising from a crouching position

squat thrust *noun* an exercise performed on the hands and knees in which the feet are brought forwards and backwards in a jumping motion

S-R connection *noun* (*in psychology*) the relationship between a stimulus and a response

stabilise *verb* (*in immediate care*) to make sure that a casualty has a healthy breathing pattern and pulse and that he or she is in a comfortable position while awaiting medical attention

stabilisers *plural noun* any muscles that provide stability while performing a movement

stability control *noun* a feature of running shoes designed to reduce overpronation

stability last *noun* same as **straight last**

stadium *noun* a place where people watch sports or other activities, usually a large enclosed flat area surrounded by tiers of seats for spectators

stamina *noun* enduring physical or mental energy and strength that allows somebody to do something for a long time

stamina training *noun* training that is designed to build stamina for competition

stance *noun* the position in which a player holds the body in attempting to hit a ball, e.g. in cricket or golf

standard last *noun* a last with an average curve, suitable for all runners. Compare **straight last**, **performance last**

standing jump *noun* a jump performed from a static standing position, with no momentum gained from a run-up

stand-off half *noun* same as **fly-half**

starch *noun* the usual form in which carbohydrates exist in food, especially in bread, rice and potatoes

starchy *adjective* containing a lot of starch

star jump *noun* an exercise in which a person jumps in the air with legs apart and arms extended out from the shoulder in a comparable direction

starter *noun* someone who gives the signal for a race to start

starting blocks *plural noun* either of a pair of objects that runners brace their feet against at the start of a sprint race. The blocks are made up of a base that can be firmly fixed to the track and angled supports for the runners' feet.

starting drill *noun* a drill performed at the start of a training session, as a warm-up or to check skill levels before training

starting grid *noun* a pattern of lines marked on a motor racing track, with numbered starting positions. The cars that record the fastest times in practice or qualifying occupy the front positions.

starting gun *noun* a gun fired as the signal for a race to start

starting line *noun* a line marked across a racetrack to show runners where to start

starting line-up *noun* an official list of the players who will begin a game or the competitors who will begin a race

stasis *noun* a condition in which body fluids such as blood are prevented from flowing normally through their channels

state registered podiatrist *noun* a healthcare provider who specialises in disorders of the feet and lower legs

static active stretch *noun* same as **active stretch**

static conditioning *noun* conditioning of muscles through a series of controlled movements, as in a gym

static contraction *noun* the practice of contracting a muscle against resistance and then holding the contraction for a set length of time

static passive stretch *noun* same as **passive stretch**

static strength *noun* force exerted by a muscle while it is neither extending nor contracting

static stretching *noun* stretching in which a position that stretches a muscle is assumed and then held

stationary bike *noun* same as **exercise bike**

staunch *verb* to stop the flow of a liquid, particularly blood

steady *adjective* constant and unchanging

steatosis *noun* the accumulation of fat in an internal organ such as the liver, caused by diseases and exposure to toxins

steeplechase *noun* **1.** a horse race run over a course that has constructed obstacles, e.g. hedges, ditches and water jumps, that the horses must jump over **2.** an athletics event in which runners must jump over very high hurdles and a water jump

step aerobics *noun* a form of aerobic exercise in which the participants step up and down to music, using a low platform

step block *noun* a solid block used for step aerobics

step machine *noun* a type of exercise machine with two large pedals that are depressed alternately to imitate the action of stepping

steristrip *noun* an adhesive piece of tape used for closing an open wound

sternum *noun* same as **breastbone**

steroid, steroid hormone *noun* any of a large group of natural or synthetic fatty substances containing four carbon rings, including the sex hormones. ◊ **anabolic steroid**

stick *noun* the implement with which the ball is struck in some sports, e.g. hockey and lacrosse

stick-handle *verb* (*in ice hockey and lacrosse*) to control and manoeuvre a ball or puck using a stick

sticking point *noun* the most difficult part of a movement

stick tackle *noun* (*in hockey*) an illegal challenge in which a player hits another player's stick instead of the ball

sticky wicket *noun* (*in cricket*) a pitch that has been made wet by rain and is in the process of being dried by sun, providing a surface on which the ball bounces awkwardly when it pitches

stiff *adjective* not able to be bent or moved easily

stiffness *noun* the fact of being stiff

stimulant *noun* something such as a drug that produces a temporary increase in the activity of a body organ or part

stimulant drink *noun* a drink that contains stimulants, typically caffeine

stimulate *verb* to make a person or organ react, respond or function

stimulation *noun* the action of stimulating something

stimulus *noun* something that has an effect on a person or a part of the body and makes them react (NOTE: The plural is **stimuli**.)

stinger *noun* same as **brachial plexus neurapraxia**

stitch *noun* **1.** same as **suture 2.** cramp in the side of the abdomen caused e.g. by exercising

stock car *noun* a standard passenger car that has been modified for professional racing

Stokes-Adams syndrome *noun* episodes of temporary dizziness or fainting caused by disruption or extreme slowing of the heartbeat and consequent brief stoppage of blood flow

stomach crunch *noun* an exercise in which you lie flat on your back with your legs bent and then raise the upper part of your body a few centimetres off the ground without using your hands

stone *noun* the shaped and polished mass of granite or iron that is slid along the ice in the game of curling

stoppage *noun* a time during which the play in a game, especially football or rugby, is briefly halted, because of an injury to a player or other situation

stoppage time *noun* especially in football or rugby, extra time played at the end of a game to make up for time lost in dealing with injured players or through other interruptions

stopwatch *noun* a special watch that can be started and stopped instantly and is used to measure the amount of time somebody or something takes, e.g. a runner in a race

storming *noun* the second stage of team development according to the Tuckman model, in which individual preferences are raised and the conflicts resolved

straight last *noun* a last which is slightly less inwardly curved than average, suitable for runners with flat feet. Compare **standard last**, **performance last**

straight sets *plural noun* sets of exercises with only a short rest interval between them

strain *verb* to damage a part of the body through using it too hard or too much ■ *noun* **1.** a condition in which a muscle has been stretched or torn by a strong or sudden movement **2.** nervous tension and stress

strategy *noun* a carefully devised plan of action to achieve a goal, or the art of developing or carrying out such a plan

strength *noun* the fact of being strong

strength training *noun* training that aims to build muscle strength, usually resistance training

strenuous *adjective* used for describing exercise that involves using a lot of force

stress *noun* **1.** physical pressure on an object or part of the body **2.** a factor or combination of factors in a person's life that make him or her feel tired and anxious **3.** a condition in which an outside influence such as overwork or a mental or emotional state such as anxiety changes the working of the body and can affect the hormone balance

stress fracture *noun* a fracture of a bone caused by excessive force. Also called **fatigue fracture**

stress management training *noun* professional counselling that explores the reasons for which an athlete suffers from stress and suggests coping mechanisms to reduce this. Abbreviation **SMT**

stress test *noun* an athletic test that determines a person's training zone by pushing them to the point of exhaustion

stretch *verb* to pull something out, or make something longer ■ *noun* **1.** the straightening and extending of a part of the body, e.g. as an exercise **2.** the straight part of a racecourse, especially the final section approaching the finishing line

stretchband *noun* a piece of equipment like a soft extensor, used for stretching out muscles

stretcher *noun* a device consisting of a sheet of material such as canvas stretched over a frame, used to carry someone in a lying position who is sick, injured or dead

stretch marks *plural noun* lines on the skin caused by losing or gaining weight rapidly

stretch reflex *noun* a reflex reaction of a muscle that contracts after being stretched

stria *noun* a pale line on skin that is stretched, as is sometimes observed in obese people (NOTE: The plural is **striae**.)

striated muscle *noun* a type of muscle found in skeletal muscles whose movements are controlled by the central nervous system. Also called **striped muscle**

striations *noun* deep ridges in muscles tissue visible through the skin

stridor *noun* a wheezing sound when breathing, made by the passage of air through narrowed airways

striker *noun* an attacking player in a football team whose main role is to score goals

strike shield *noun* a large pad used for target practice by boxers and martial artists

stringer *noun* a member of a team who is ranked according to excellence or skill

stringy *adjective* unattractively thin, with bones or muscles showing beneath the skin

strip *noun* same as **football strip**

striped muscle *noun* same as **striated muscle**

stroke *noun* **1.** (*in racket games or golf*) the hitting of a ball or the way in which this is done **2.** a style of swimming, using the arms and legs in a specific way **3.** a single complete movement of the arms and legs when swimming **4.** (*in rowing*) a single movement of the oars through the water **5.** a rower in a racing boat who sets the pace for the crew **6.** a sudden blockage or breaking of a blood vessel in the brain that can result in loss of consciousness, partial loss of movement or loss of speech ■ *verb* **1.** to hit or kick a ball smoothly **2.** to be the rower who sets the pace for the crew **3.** to row at a particular speed or rate of the oars

stroke volume *noun* the amount of blood pumped out of the ventricle at each heart-beat

structural aluminium malleable splint *noun* full form of **SAM splint**

structural exercise *noun* an exercise that works more than one large muscle or muscles groups

studs *plural noun* small protuberances on the sole of a sports shoe, designed to give better grip

stump *noun* (*in cricket*) each of the three upright posts that form part of the wicket

styptic *adjective* slowing down the rate of bleeding or stopping bleeding altogether, whether by causing the blood vessels to contract or by accelerating clotting

subaqua *adjective* relating to or providing facilities for underwater sports such as scuba diving

subcutaneous *adjective* under the skin. Abbreviation **s.c.**

subdural haematoma *noun* a blood clot over the brain caused by a head injury, usually fatal if left untreated

subluxation *noun* same as **dislocation**

submaximal *adjective* not at maximum intensity or effort

submaximal testing *noun* testing performed on a person exercising at below the maximum intensity

submaximal workload *noun* a workout performed at below maximum intensity

subperiosteal *adjective* immediately beneath the connective tissue around bones

subskill *noun* a specialised skill within a broader, more general skill

substance abuse *noun* the excessive consumption or misuse of a substance, especially drugs or alcohol, for the sake of its non-therapeutic effects on the mind or body

substance P *noun* a peptide found in body tissues, especially nervous tissue, that is involved in the transmission of pain and in inflammation

substantive injury *noun* a sports injury that needs medical attention, resulting in lost game time for the player

substitute *noun* a player brought onto the field during a team game to replace a player who has left the field through injury

substitution *noun* the replacement of someone or something with another, especially one team member with another on the field

success *noun* **1.** the fact of doing something well, or doing what you set out to achieve **2.** something that goes well

successful *adjective* working well or achieving a desired goal

success-orientated *adjective* used for describing a competing athlete who is keen to win in order to have the joy of succeeding, rather than to avoid the disappointment of failing

sucrose *noun* a sugar, formed of glucose and fructose, found in plants, especially in sugar cane, beet and maple syrup

sudden cardiac death *noun* unexpected heart failure in an otherwise healthy athlete, caused by a heavy blow to the chest

sudden death *noun* the continuation of play in a tied sports contest until one team or player scores, that team or player being declared the winner

sugar *noun* any of several sweet carbohydrate substances that occur naturally

sugar-free *adjective* not containing sugar

Summer Olympics *noun* the Olympic event that takes place during the summer of an Olympic year. Compare **Winter Olympics**

sumo wrestling *noun* traditional Japanese wrestling in which each contestant tries to force the other outside a circle or force him to touch the ground other than with the soles of his feet

superfood *noun* a nutritionally rich food that is eaten for health

super heavyweight *noun* (*in amateur boxing*) the heaviest weight category, for competitors whose weight is over 91 kg

superior *adjective* used for describing a body part that is situated in the upper half of the body

superleague *noun* an international rugby league competition that was introduced alongside or superseded various national rugby league competitions

supinate *verb* to fail to roll the foot inwards slightly while running

supination *noun* ineffective rolling inward of the foot while running, with the result that the foot is inadequately cushioned

supine *adjective* **1.** lying on the back. Opposite **prone 2.** used for describing the position of the arm with the palm facing upwards

supplement *noun* **1.** a substance with a specific nutritional value taken to make up for a real or supposed deficiency in diet **2.** a substance added to improve the nutritional content of a diet or foodstuff

supplementation *noun* the act of enriching a diet or a foodstuff with nutritional supplements

supplement stacking *noun* the practice of taking multiple bodybuilding supplements at the same time

support bandage *noun* an elastic wrap used for protecting parts of the body from injury during sports or support it during recovery

surface *noun* the type of ground that a sport is played on

surfboard *noun* a long narrow board, with a rounded or pointed front end, on which a surfer stands while riding waves

surfing *noun* to ride waves on a surfboard for sport or recreation

surgical emphysema *noun* trapped air present in bodily tissues as a result of a open wound or surgical procedure

suspensory *noun* **1.** a ligament or muscle from which a structure or part is suspended **2.** something that holds part of the body in position while it heals, e.g. a bandage or a sling

suture *noun* **1.** a fixed joint where two bones are fused together, especially the bones in the skull **2.** a procedure for attaching the sides of an incision or wound with thread, so that healing can take place. Also called **stitch 3.** a thread used for attaching the sides of a wound so that they can heal

svelte *adjective* graceful and slender

sweat *noun* **1.** a salty liquid produced by the sweat glands to cool the body as the liquid evaporates from the skin. Also called **perspiration 2.** a run that a horse has before a race, as exercise

sweatband *noun* a strip of terry towelling worn around the head or wrists to stop sweat running into the eyes or onto the hands while playing sport

sweat suit *noun* a semi-permeable or impermeable suit worn during exercise to acclimatise the wearer to hot temperatures

Swedish massage *noun* a system of massage employing both active and passive exercising of the muscles and joints

sweep *verb* (*in cricket*) to hit a ball from a half-kneeling position by bringing the bat, held almost horizontally, across the body with a long smooth stroke

sweet spot *noun* the most effective place to hit the ball on a racket, bat, club or other piece of sports equipment

swell *verb* to become larger, or cause something to become larger

swelling *noun* a condition in which fluid accumulates in tissue, making the tissue become large

swim *verb* to move or propel yourself unsupported through water ■ *noun* a period of time spent swimming, usually for pleasure or exercise

swimmer *noun* a person who swims for pleasure or sport

swimmer's ear *noun* same as **otitis externa**

swimming *noun* the action or activity of making progress unsupported through water using the arms and legs, whether for pleasure, exercise or sport

swimming pool *noun* a water-filled structure in which people can swim, usually set into the ground outdoors or the floor indoors, or a building that houses such a structure

swimsuit *noun* a piece of clothing worn for swimming, especially a one-piece garment worn by women

swingball *noun* a game for two players who use their hands to hit in opposite directions a ball that is on a length of rope attached to the top of a pole

Swiss ball *noun* same as **exercise ball**

switch *adjective* (*in skateboarding and similar sports*) used for describing a stance in which the foot that the rider usually puts nearer the front is nearer the back

swollen *adjective* **1.** increased in size **2.** containing more water than usual

sympathetic *adjective* **1.** feeling or showing shared feelings, pity or compassion **2.** relating to or belonging to the sympathetic nervous system, or to one of its parts

sympathetic nervous system *noun* one of two complementary parts of the nervous system that affects involuntary functions. Compare **autonomic nervous system** (NOTE: It is activated by danger or stress and causes responses such as dilated pupils and a rapid heart rate.)

sympatholytic *adjective* describes a drug that opposes or blocks the effects of the sympathetic nervous system

sympathomimetic *adjective* used for describing a drug such as dopamine hydrochloride that stimulates the activity of the sympathetic nervous system and is used in cardiac shock following myocardial infarction and in cardiac surgery

symphysis *noun* **1.** the point at which two bones are joined by cartilage that makes the joint rigid **2.** a condition in which two or more separate bones or parts of the body have merged

synapse *noun* a point in the nervous system where the axons of neurons are in contact with the dendrites of other neurons

synaptic *adjective* relating to a synapse

synaptic cleft *noun* the small space between neurons through which neurotransmitters travel

synarthrosis *noun* a joint between tissues, typically bone, that is fixed and does not allow movement

synbiotic *noun* a supplement consisting of both a probiotic and a prebiotic

synchondrosis *noun* a joint, as in children, where the bones are linked by cartilage, before the cartilage has changed to bone

synchronised swimming *noun* a sport in which swimmers perform coordinated movements in time to music in the manner of a dance

syncope *noun* a loss of consciousness due to lack of oxygen to the brain

syndesmosis *noun* a joint in which the bones are tightly linked by ligaments

synergist *noun* same as **antagonist**

synergistic effect *noun* a reaction that needs two or more substances in combination to take place

synergy *noun* a situation where two or more things are acting together in such a way that both are more effective

synovial fluid *noun* a fluid secreted by a synovial membrane to lubricate a joint

synovial joint *noun* a joint where the two bones are separated by a space filled with synovial fluid which nourishes and lubricates the surfaces of the bones

synovial membrane *noun* a smooth membrane that forms the inner lining of the capsule covering a joint and secretes the fluid that lubricates the joint

synovitis *noun* inflammation of the synovial membrane

synovium *noun* the lining of the joints, which can become inflamed

synthesis *noun* the formation of compounds through chemical reactions involving simpler compounds or elements

synthesise *verb* to produce a substance or material by chemical or biological synthesis

synthetic *adjective* artificial, not natural

syssarcosis *noun* the joining of bones by muscle

systematic desensitisation *noun* a therapy for phobias and other anxiety disorders in which patients are gradually given longer and longer exposures to the object of their fears

systemic circulation *noun* the circulation of blood around the whole body, except the lungs, starting with the aorta and returning through the venae cavae

systole *noun* a phase in the beating of the heart when it contracts as it pumps blood out. Opposite **diastole**

systolic *adjective* relating to the systole

systolic blood pressure *noun* the pressure of blood in a person's artery when the heart rests between beats, shown written under the diastolic blood pressure reading. Compare **diastolic blood pressure**

T

table tennis *noun* a game that resembles tennis and is played with small bats and a light hollow ball on a table divided by a low net

tachycardia *noun* a rapid heartbeat, sometimes linked to anaemia and vitamin B1 deficiency

tachypnoea *noun* rapid breathing of the kind that takes place after physical exertion, distinct from hyperventilation in that it is not excessive

tackle *noun* **1.** in football, hockey and some other games, a physical challenge against an opposing player who has the ball, puck, or other object of possession **2.** the equipment used for a specialised activity such as angling or rock climbing **3.** (*in American football*) a lineman positioned between a guard and an end, or the position of such a player ∎ *verb* (*in football, hockey and some other games*) to make a physical challenge against an opposing player who has possession of the ball, puck or other object of play

tactics *plural noun* the art of finding and implementing means to achieve immediate or short-term aims

tae bo *noun* a fitness regime based on exercising to music, involving movements that derive from martial arts such as taekwondo

taekwondo *noun* a Korean martial art that resembles karate but also employs a wide range of acrobatic kicking moves

taenia *noun* **1.** a long ribbon-like part of the body **2.** a large tapeworm

tag team *noun* a team of two or more wrestlers, only one of whom may wrestle at a time. Wrestlers can change places only after touching hands.

tai chi *noun* a Chinese form of physical exercise characterised by a series of very slow and deliberate balletic body movements

TAIS *abbreviation* Test of Attentional and Interpersonal Style

talent scout *noun* somebody whose job is to search for people who have exceptional abilities and recruit them for professional work. Also called **scout**

talk test *noun* a test of aerobic capacity in which the athlete must try to maintain a conversation while exercising

talus *noun* the top bone in the tarsus which articulates with the tibia and fibula in the leg, and with the calcaneus in the heel. Also called **anklebone** (NOTE: The plural is **tali**.)

tandem *noun* a bicycle with two saddles and two sets of handlebars and pedals, one behind the other, so that it can be ridden by two people at the same time ∎ *adjective* describes sports activities undertaken by two people together, usually positioned one behind the other, especially when one person is a novice

tapering *noun* a reduction in training intensity shortly before a major competition to give the mind and body time to relax and prepare

taping *noun* the practice of wrapping supportive tape around areas of the body during sport to protect them from injury or aid recovery from a previous injury

tapotement *noun* a type of massage in which the therapist taps the person with his or her hands

target heart rate *noun* the heart rate at which a person should aim to exercise in order to maximise the effects of the exercise

target training zone, target zone *noun* same as **training zone**

tarsal *adjective* relating to the ankle

tarsal tunnel syndrome *noun* compression of a nerve in the foot, causing pain, tingling and a burning sensation

tarsus *noun* **1.** the seven small bones of the ankle **2.** a connective tissue that supports an eyelid (NOTE: The plural is **tarsi**.)

task *noun* a single piece of work that someone has to do

task-specific *adjective* used for describing a skill that is applicable only to particular task and rarely replicated elsewhere, e.g. the skill of swinging a golf club or throwing a javelin

taurine *noun* an amino acid that forms bile salts

taxis *noun* the manipulating of a displaced body part to return it to its normal position, carried out, e.g., in a case of hernia

TE *abbreviation* Trolox equivalent

team *noun* a group of people who work together

team-building *noun* the process of bringing individuals together into a cohesive and effective team

team dynamic *noun* the interpersonal relationships within a team

teammate *noun* a player on the same team as someone else

team spirit *noun* an enthusiastic attitude towards working productively with a team or work group

team sport *noun* any sport that is played between two or more teams, e.g. football, tennis or hockey

teamwork *noun* cooperative effort by the members of a team

tear *verb* to make a hole or a split in a tissue by pulling or stretching it too much

technical foul *noun* in basketball, a foul against a player or coach for unsporting behaviour or language rather than for physical contact with an opponent

technical knockout *noun* (*in boxing*) a decision that ends a match because one of the participants is too badly injured to continue fighting

technique *noun* a way of performing an action

technique analysis *noun* same as **biomechanical analysis**

telemark skiing *noun* same as **freeheel skiing**

telemetry *noun* a method of measuring a person's heart rate continuously using wires attached to the chest

tempo manipulation *noun* control of the speed at which reps of an exercise are performed

tender *adjective* hurting or unusually sensitive when touched or pressed

tendinitis *noun* an inflammation of a tendon, especially after playing sport, and often associated with tenosynovitis

tendinopathy *noun* any pain felt in a tendon

tendinous *adjective* relating to, consisting of or resembling a tendon

tendon *noun* a sinew or strand of strong connective tissue that attaches a muscle to bone

tendo-osseus junction *noun* same as **enthesis**

tennis *noun* a game played on a rectangular court by two players or two pairs of players, who use rackets to hit a ball back and forth over a net stretched across a marked-out court

tennis ball *noun* a white or yellow fuzzy cloth-covered hollow rubber ball about 7.5 cm/3 in in diameter, used in tennis. In lawn tennis the ball is pressurized.

tennis elbow *noun* same as **lateral epicondylitis**

tenosynovitis *noun* a painful inflammation of the tendon sheath and the tendon inside. Also called **peritendinitis**

tenotomy *noun* the surgical cutting of a tendon

ten-pin bowling *noun* an indoor game in which players try to knock down ten skittles at the far end of a special bowling alley by rolling a heavy ball at them

TENS *noun* pain treatment that works by interrupting normal pain signals sent by the nerve to the brain, which may also promote healing and muscle strength. Full form of **transcutaneous electrical nerve stimulation**

tense *verb* to become tense, or make something such as a muscle or part of the body become tense

tension *noun* the act of stretching or the state of being stretched

tension pneumothorax *noun* a collapse of the lung caused by seepage of air into the space around the lung

tensor *noun* a muscle that makes a joint stretch out. Compare **extensor, flexor**

tent *noun* a cone-shaped expandable plug of soft material such as gauze used to keep a wound or orifice open

terbutaline *noun* a beta-agonist used for treating lung disorders such as emphysema and asthma by dilating the airways

terrain board *noun* same as **mountain board**

testicle shrinkage *noun* a reduction in the size of the testicles, a common side-effect of steroid abuse that interferes with natural testosterone production

test match *noun* any of a series of cricket or rugby matches between two international teams

Test of Attentional and Interpersonal Style *noun* a test that measures how athletes perform in different situations according to their personality types. Abbreviation **TAIS**

testosterone *noun* a male steroid hormone produced in the testicles and responsible for the development of secondary sex characteristics

tetanus *noun* an acute infectious disease, usually contracted through a penetrating wound, that causes severe muscular spasms and contractions, especially around the neck and jaw

tetherball *noun* same as **swingball**

tetracosactide *noun* a synthetic hormone that acts on the adrenal glands to stimulate the production of steroid hormones

tetrahydrogestrinone *noun* full form of **THG**

textured vegetable protein *noun* a substance made from processed soya beans or other vegetables, used as a substitute for meat. Abbreviation **TVP**

TFCC *abbreviation* triangular fibrocartilage complex

Thai pad *noun* a heavy-duty pad used for training in kickboxing

thalamus *noun* either of a pair of egg-shaped masses of grey matter lying beneath each cerebral hemisphere in the brain that relay sensory information to the cerebral cortex

therapeutic *adjective* used in the treatment of disease or disorders

therapeutic food *noun* an enriched food product that is used as a nutritional supplement for elderly people or people who are ill

therapeutics *noun* the branch of medicine that deals with methods of treatment and healing, especially the use of drugs to treat diseases

therapeutic use exemption *noun* official permission for an athlete to use a banned substance, on the grounds that it is needed to treat a medical condition

thermal effect of food *noun* same as **diet-induced thermogenesis**

thermogenesis *noun* the process in which food or fat deposits in the body are burned to produce heat

thermogenic *adjective* used for describing a food supplement that raises the metabolic rate and causing thermogenesis

thermoreceptor *noun* a sensory nerve which registers heat

thermoregulation *noun* the control of body temperature by processes such as sweating and shivering

thermotherapy *noun* treatment using heat, e.g. from hot water or infrared lamps, to treat conditions such as arthritis and bad circulation. Also called **heat therapy**

THG *noun* a banned anabolic steroid that has been implicated in several scandals involving top athletes. Full form **tetrahydrogestrinone**

thiamin *noun* ♦ vitamin B1

thiazide *noun* a compound that inhibits the reabsorption of sodium, promoting greater water excretion, used for the treatment of high blood pressure

thigh *noun* the top part of the leg from the knee to the groin

thigh bone *noun* same as **femur**

thigh support *noun* an elastic wrap used for supporting the thigh and prevent injury or aid rehabilitation

thirst *noun* a feeling of wanting to drink

thirsty *adjective* wanting to drink

thoracic *adjective* relating to the upper back

thoracic cavity *noun* the chest cavity, containing the diaphragm, heart and lungs

thoracic outlet syndrome *noun* compression of the nerves and blood vessels running between the neck and armpit, which can be caused by muscle overdevelopment in the area

thorax *noun* same as **chest**

thrash *verb* to defeat a person or team decisively (*informal*)

threonine *noun* an essential amino acid

threshold *noun* **1.** the point at which something starts, e.g. where something can be perceived by the body or where a drug starts to have an effect **2.** the point at which a sensation is strong enough to be sensed by the sensory nerves

thrombin *noun* a blood protein that activates blood clotting

thrombocyte *noun* same as **platelet**

throw *verb* to lose a fight, race or contest deliberately, e.g. by not trying or by committing a foul (*informal*)

throw-in *noun* **1.** an act of returning a football to play from the sideline by propelling it from behind the head with both hands **2.** an act of returning a basketball to play by passing it onto the court

thyrocalcitonin *noun* same as **calcitonin**

thyroid gland *noun* an endocrine gland in the neck that secretes a hormone that regulates the body's metabolism

thyroid hormone *noun* a hormone produced by the thyroid gland

thyrotoxicosis *noun* same as **hyperthyroidism**

tibia *noun* the larger of the two long bones in the lower leg between the knee and the ankle. Also called **shinbone**

tic *noun* a sudden involuntary spasmodic muscular contraction, especially of facial, neck or shoulder muscles, which may become more pronounced when someone is stressed

tidal air, tidal volume *noun* the volume of air that passes in and out of the body during normal breathing

tie *noun* a single game in a competition

Tietzes syndrome *noun* same as **costochondritis**

tights *noun* a one-piece close-fitting garment covering the body from the neck or waist to the feet, worn especially by men and women dancers and acrobats

timekeeper *noun* a recorder of the time elapsed during a sporting event

time trial *noun* a race in which competitors compete individually for the fastest time

time-wasting *noun* the employment of negative tactics to prevent an opponent from scoring towards the end of a match, for which a player may be penalised in some situations

tinea *noun* same as **ringworm**

tinea cruris *noun* a fungal infection of the groin, sometimes caused by spending extended periods of time in wet sports clothing

tinea pedis *noun* same as **athlete's foot**

tissue *noun* a type of substance that the body is made up of, e.g. skin, muscle or nerves

tissue adhesive *noun* a substance in place of sutures used for closing and sealing open wounds

tissue repair *noun* the rebuilding of damaged body tissues using dietary nutrients to synthesise new tissue

titin *noun* an elastic connective protein found in muscle fibres

title *noun* the status of champion in a sport or competition

title fight *noun* a battle for the status of champion in a sport or competition

TOBEC *noun* a way of measuring the amount of fat in the body using the difference in electrical conductivity between fat and lean tissue. Full form **total body electrical conductivity**

toboggan *noun* a long narrow sledge without runners, made of strips of wood running lengthways and curled up at the front, used for coasting downhill on snow

tolerance *noun* the loss of or reduction in the usual response to a drug or other agent as a result of use or exposure over a prolonged period

tone *noun* the slightly tense state of a healthy muscle when it is not fully relaxed. Also called **tonicity**, **tonus** ■ *verb* to make muscles firmer and stronger

tone up *verb* to make muscles, or the body in general, firmer and stronger

tonic *adjective* relating to or affecting muscular tone or contraction

tonicity *noun* same as **tone**

tonus *noun* same as **tone**

topspin *noun* forward spin given to a ball by hitting it on its upper half, making it arc more sharply in the air or bounce higher on impact

torque *noun* the force that an object such as a lever exerts on something to cause it to rotate

torsion *noun* **1.** the twisting of something, or a twisted state **2.** the stress placed on an object that has been twisted

torso *noun* the main part of the body, not including the arms, legs and head

torticollis *noun* a stiffness and deformation of the neck caused by swelling around the muscle

total body electrical conductivity *noun* full form of **TOBEC**

total body workout *noun* a workout that does not concentrate on one particular area of the body

total energy expenditure *noun* the number of calories needed to maintain the body's normal function during all normal activities over the course of a day

total football *noun* a style of football in which players' positions are interchangeable as part of a general method of attack. This playing style was developed by the Dutch national team of the 1970s.

touch *noun* in some team sports, the area beyond the touchlines in which the ball is out of play

touchdown *noun* **1.** in American football, a scoring of six points achieved by being in possession of the ball behind an opponent's goal line **2.** in rugby, a touching of the ball on the ground that scores a try

touch football *noun* an informal noncompetitive version of American football in which touching replaces tackling

touch judge *noun* (*in rugby*) either of the two assistant referees whose main task is to decide when and where the ball has gone into touch

touchline *noun* especially in rugby or football, either of the lines that mark the side boundaries of a playing area

tour *noun* a series of games or tournaments played by the same sports team in different locations

tour de force *noun* something done with supreme skill or brilliance

trabecula *noun* a thin strip of stiff tissue that divides an organ or bone tissue into sections (NOTE: The plural is **trabeculae**.)

trabecular *adjective* same as **cancellous**

trace element *noun* a substance that is essential to the human body but only in very small quantities, e.g. iron, copper and iodine

trachea *noun* the main air passage that runs from the larynx to the lungs, where it divides into the two main bronchi. Also called **windpipe**

track *noun* a surface on which athletes run, usually a prepared surface with long straight sides and rounded ends, divided into lanes ■ *verb* to follow the progress of something such as an athlete's physical development

track-and-field *noun* same as **athletics**

track cycling *noun* competition cycling indoors around a steeply banked oval track with a surface of wooden strips

track event *noun* a sports competition that takes place on a running track

track record *noun* a record set at a specific sports arena, as opposed to a national or international record

traction *noun* a procedure that consists of using a pulling force to straighten a broken or deformed limb

train *verb* to prepare for a sporting competition, or prepare someone for a sporting competition, usually with a planned programme of appropriate physical exercises

trainer *noun* same as **personal trainer**

trainers *plural noun* shoes designed to be worn during athletic activities or exercising, but worn with casual clothing for any activity

training *noun* the process of improving physical fitness by exercise and diet

training arena *noun* the place in which an athlete trains, which may differ in important ways from the contest arena

training cycle *noun* for a professional athlete, a phase of training which is repeated at regular intervals, such as weekly

training effect *noun* an increase in muscle strength or size caused by training

training manual *noun* a book that gives practical advice on exercise and training

training programme *noun* a coordinated programme of exercise designed to make an athlete fit for competition

training response *noun* an increase in aerobic capacity, strength, flexibility or body shape caused by exercise

training routine *noun* the usual exercises that an athlete performs each time he or she trains

training session *noun* a period of time during which an athlete trains, either alone, with a trainer or with their team

training shoes *plural noun* same as **trainers**

training straps *plural noun* any of various types of strap designed for isolating or supporting an area of the body, especially in weightlifting or bodybuilding

training to failure *noun* the practice of performing an exercise until it is physically impossible to do another rep

training zone *noun* the heart rate range within which a person should aim to exercise for maximum effect

trampette *noun* a small trampoline used as a home exercise tool

trampoline *noun* a strong sheet, usually of canvas, that is stretched tightly on a horizontal frame to which it is connected by springs

trampolining *noun* the activity of performing acrobatics on a trampoline

transcutaneous electrical nerve stimulation *noun* full form of **TENS**

transdermal *adjective* used for describing nutrients that are able to be absorbed through the skin

trans fatty acids *plural noun* unsaturated fats formed during the hydrogenation of vegetable oils to produce margarine, viewed as a health risk because they raise cholesterol levels

transfer *verb* **1.** to pass from one place to another, or cause someone or something to pass from one place to another **2.** especially in professional football, to sign for a different sports club, or sign someone for a different sports club ■ *noun* the act moving of someone or something from one place to another

transferable skill *noun* a skill that is not limited to a specific area of knowledge or task and is useful in many situations

transfer fee *noun* a fee that is paid for a professional footballer or rugby player who is transferred from one club to another before his or her contract has expired

transfer list *noun* a list of professional footballers or rugby players who are available to be transferred

transfusion *noun* the procedure of transferring blood or saline fluids from a container into someone's bloodstream

transgenic *adjective* **1.** used for describing an organism into which genetic material from a different species has been transferred using the techniques of genetic modification **2.** used for describing the techniques of transferring genetic material from one organism to another

transient ischaemic attack *noun* a temporary blockage of blood circulation in some part of the brain, causing short-term stroke symptoms such as dizziness, inability to speak or move, or loss of senses

transverse chest width *noun* an anthropometric measure of chest breadth

transverse plane *noun* a plane at right angles to the sagittal plane, running horizontally across the body

trapeze *noun* a horizontal bar attached to the ends of two ropes hanging parallel to each other, used for gymnastics or for acrobatics, especially in a circus

trapezium *noun* one of the eight small carpal bones in the wrist, below the thumb (NOTE: The plural is **trapeziums** or **trapezia**.)

trapezius *noun* a triangular muscle in the upper part of the back and the neck that moves the shoulder blade and pulls the head back

trapezoid *noun* a small bone in the wrist near the metatarsal bone that connects with the index finger

traps *abbreviation* trapezius

trauma *noun* **1.** a wound or injury **2.** a very frightening or distressing experience that gives a person a severe emotional shock

traumatise *verb* to cause physical injury to someone or something

traumatology *noun* the branch of medicine that deals with serious injuries and wounds and their long-term consequences

tread *noun* a series of patterns moulded into the surface of a tyre to provide grip

treadmill *noun* a machine with an endless belt on which someone can walk, jog or run, used for exercise and stress testing

treadmill test *noun* a test of oxygen consumption in which a treadmill is used

triage *noun* the process of prioritising sick or injured people for treatment according to the seriousness of the condition or injury

trial *noun* a sports competition or preliminary test to select candidates for a later competition

trialist, triallist *noun* a sports player or competitor who is given a chance to prove worthy of being included in a team for a major competition

triamcinolone *noun* a synthetic corticosteroid drug used in the treatment of skin, mouth and joint inflammations

triangular fibrocartilage complex *noun* a set of ligaments and cartilage joining the hand to the wrist below the little finger, vulnerable to twists and sprains during sporting activities. Abbreviation **TFCC**

triathlete *noun* an athlete who competes in triathlons

triathlon *noun* an athletics competition in which the contestants compete in three different events and are awarded points for each to find the best all-round athlete. The events are usually swimming, cycling and running.

tribunal *noun* a panel that makes a ruling following drug testing

triceps *noun* a muscle formed of three parts joined to form one tendon, especially the **triceps brachii** at the back of the upper arm

triceps brachii *noun* a muscle in the back part of the upper arm which makes the forearm stretch out

triceps pushdown *noun* an exercise in which the forearms are held horizontally out in front at waist height and are pushed down against resistance to a vertical position

triceps tendonitis *noun* strain of the tendon connecting the triceps muscles to the elbow, usually caused by repetitive throwing motions

tricuspid valve *noun* an inlet valve with three cusps between the right atrium and the right ventricle in the heart

trigeminal nerve *noun* the fifth cranial nerve, formed of the ophthalmic nerve, the maxillary nerve and the mandibular nerve, which controls the sensory nerves in the forehead, face and chin, and the muscles in the jaw

trigger point *noun* a small area of muscle that has been subjected to repeated stresses and is painful and hypersensitive

trimming down *noun* same as **cutting up**

Tri Nations *adjective* used for describing a rugby union competition between the national sides of Australia, New Zealand and South Africa

triple crown *noun* **1.** victory in all three of a set of major events in some sports **2.** (*in rugby*) victory in the home championships contested between England, Ireland, Scotland and Wales by one team over the other three in the same season **3.** the accomplishment of leading a baseball league in batting average, runs batted in, and home runs in a single season

triple jump *noun* an athletics event in which contestants perform a short run and three consecutive jumps, landing first on one foot, then the opposite foot, and finally both feet, in continuous motion

trochanter *noun* two bony lumps on either side of the top end of the femur where muscles are attached

trochanteric bursitis *noun* bursitis at the top of the thighbone

trochlea *noun* an anatomical part or structure with a grooved surface that resembles a pulley, especially the surface of a bone over which a tendon passes

trochlear nerve *noun* the fourth cranial nerve which controls the muscles of the eyeball

Trolox *noun* a derivative of vitamin E that functions as an antioxidant

Trolox equivalent *noun* vitamin E derivatives with the same antioxidant properties as Trolox, measured in oxygen radical absorbance capacity tests. Abbreviation **TE**

trophic *adjective* relating to nutrition, digestion and growth

trophic hormone *noun* a hormone that stimulates an endocrine gland

trophology *noun* the study of dietary requirements in humans and animals

trophonosis *noun* any disease or disorder caused by nutritional deficiencies

trophotherapy *noun* treatment of a condition using appropriate foodstuffs

trophy *noun* a cup, shield, plaque, medal or other award given in acknowledgment of a victory or achievement in a sporting contest

tropomyosin *noun* a protein in muscle that interacts with other proteins to regulate contraction

troponin *noun* a protein complex that plays a role in muscle contraction

true rib *noun* one of the top seven pairs of ribs that are attached to the breastbone. Compare **false rib**

trunk *noun* same as **torso**

try *noun* (*in rugby*) a score achieved by touching the ball on the ground behind the line of the opposing team's posts (NOTE: Five points are scored for a try in rugby union, and four points in rugby league.)

trypsin *noun* a protein-digesting enzyme secreted by the pancreas

trypsin inhibitor *noun* a substance found in some beans that inhibits the action of trypsins

tube bandage *noun* an elastic bandage in the shape of a tube that fits tightly over a limb to support it

tuberosity *noun* a large lump on a bone

tuck *noun* a compact body position, adopted in sports such as diving, with the knees drawn up to the chest, the hands round the shins, and the chin held on the chest

Tuckman model *noun* a four-stage model of team development, with the four stages labelled 'forming', 'storming', 'norming' and 'performing'. ◊ **forming, storming, norming, performing**

tug of war *noun* an athletic contest in which two teams pull at opposite ends of a rope, the winner being the one who drags the other across a fixed line

tumble *verb* to perform athletic or gymnastic leaps, rolls or somersaults ■ *noun* an athletic or gymnastic leap, roll or somersault

turf toe *noun* pain in the big toe caused by repetitive pressure on it, e.g. during running or jumping

turgescent *adjective* swollen or becoming swollen, usually as a result of an accumulation of blood or other fluids

Turkish bath *noun* a bath in which the bather sweats freely in hot air or steam, followed by a shower and often a massage

turnout *noun* **1.** the number of people who attend or take part in an event **2.** the outward rotating movement from the hip sockets of a classical ballet dancer's legs

twintip *noun* a ski of the type worn in the sport of freeskiing, broader and softer than a downhill ski and with turned-up points front and back, designed so that the wearer can move forwards and backwards on a slope and execute the complex moves performed in freeskiing

twist *verb* to hurt a joint by turning or bending it too much or the wrong way ■ *noun* **1.** a painful wrench or pull in a wrist, ankle or another body part **2.** a complete turn of the body around a vertical axis, e.g. in gymnastics or diving

twitch *noun* a small movement of a muscle in the face or hands, usually an involuntary movement

tyrosine *noun* an amino acid in protein that is a component of thyroxine and is a precursor to the catecholamines dopamine, noradrenaline and adrenaline

U

U&Es *plural noun* blood tests of the body's chemistry used for determining the general health of a patient and, specifically, kidney and lung function, effects of medications and state of hydration. Full form **urea and electrolytes**

ulcer *noun* an open sore in the skin or in a mucous membrane that is inflamed and difficult to heal

ulna *noun* the longer and inner of the two bones in the forearm between the elbow and the wrist

ulnar collateral ligament sprain *noun* pain and restricted motion in the thumb caused by accidentally bending it back too far

ulnar nerve *noun* a nerve that runs from the neck to the elbow and controls the muscles in the forearm and some of the fingers

ulnar neuropathy *noun* tingling and numbness in the wrist and hand caused by repeated stress on the wrist, often suffered by cyclists

Ultimate Frisbee *noun* a team sport played with a Frisbee that combines some of the rules of football, netball and rugby

ultrasound treatment *noun* treatment for injured muscles and soft tissues that sends sound waves into the body, generating heat

umpire *noun* an official who supervises play and enforces the rules of the game in some sports, e.g. cricket and baseball

unchallenging *adjective* demanding little or no physical or psychological effort of a stimulating kind

unconscious *adjective* unable to see, hear or otherwise sense what is going on, usually temporarily and often as a result of an accident or injury

undamaged *adjective* not harmed physically or psychologically

underarm *adjective* carried out with the arm kept below shoulder height and usually close to the body

undereat *verb* to eat an insufficient amount of food

undernourished *adjective* having too little food

undernutrition *noun* the fact of not receiving enough nutrients in the diet

underperformance *noun* ♦ unexplained underperformance syndrome

undertrained *adjective* used for describing an athlete who has not trained hard enough to be fit for competition

underwater hockey *noun* same as **octopush**

underweight *adjective* used for describing someone whose body weight is less than is medically advisable

unexplained underperformance syndrome *noun* a situation in which an athlete fails to perform to his or her full potential, caused by a change in their emotional state or physical or mental burnout. Abbreviation **UPS**

unipennate *adjective* used for describing a muscle with fibres that run along one side of a single lateral tendon

universal machine *noun* an exercise machine that allows the athlete to exercise many different parts of their body

unperfused *adjective* used for describing a muscle or tissue that is inadequately supplied with blood

unsaturated fat *noun* a type of fat that does not contain a large amount of hydrogen and so can be broken down more easily. Compare **saturated fat**, **polyunsaturated fat**

unseasoned *adjective* lacking the skills or knowledge that experience provides

unseeded *adjective* not assigned a position in a draw arranged so that the best players or teams can, in theory, avoid meeting until the later rounds

unsegregated *adjective* not segregated according to race or sex

unsigned *adjective* not having signed a contract to join a sports team as a player

unsound *adjective* not in a healthy physical or psychological state

unsporting *adjective* acting contrary to the rules and spirit of a sport

unsportsmanlike *adjective* being or acting contrary to fair play or the rules and spirit of a sport or of sport in general

upper abs *plural noun* the abdominal muscles that are above the navel

upright rowing *noun* an exercise that replicates the in-and-out movement of a rowing machine but is performed standing up using dumbbells or a barbell

upset *noun* an unexpected result in a sports contest ■ *verb* to defeat an opponent unexpectedly

urea *noun* a substance produced in the liver from excess amino acids, and excreted by the kidneys into the urine

urea and electrolytes *plural noun* full form of **U&Es**

uric acid *noun* a chemical compound that is formed from nitrogen in waste products from the body and that also forms crystals in the joints of people who have gout

urine sample *noun* a small volume of urine provided by an athlete for drugs testing or to allow a diagnosis of a medical condition, e.g. diabetes

urine substitution *noun* the act of passing off a 'clean' urine sample from another person as your own, in order to pass a drugs test

urine test *noun* a test performed on the urine sample of an athlete that detects the markers or metabolites of banned substances

urokinase *noun* an enzyme formed in the kidneys that begins the process of breaking down blood clots

urticarial rash *noun* an itchy rash that can be symptomatic of exercise-induced anaphylaxis

utility player *noun* a player who can play in several positions in a team

V

vaccination *noun* the use of a vaccine to provide immunity against a disease

vaccine *noun* a preparation containing weakened or dead microbes of the kind that cause a disease, administered to stimulate the immune system to produce antibodies against that disease

vacuum mattress *noun* a firm inflated mattress used for transporting casualties with suspected spinal injuries

vagus nerve *noun* a nerve that carries sensory and motor neurons serving the heart, lungs, stomach, intestines and various other organs

valgus *noun* the position or state in which a bone or body part is bent or twisted outwards away from the midline of the body

valine *noun* an essential amino acid

vanadium *noun* an essential mineral that activates enzymes in the body

variable resistance *noun* same as **accommodating resistance**

varied diet *noun* a diet that includes a range of different foods

vascular *adjective* relating to blood vessels

vascularisation *noun* the development of vessels, especially blood vessels, in an organism or tissue

vascularity *noun* prominence of veins, desirable in bodybuilding

vasculature *noun* the arrangement of blood vessels in the body or in an organ or tissue

vasoactive *adjective* same as **vasomotor**

vasoconstriction *noun* the narrowing of blood vessels, which allows less blood to flow through

vasoconstrictive *adjective* causing vasoconstriction

vasoconstrictor *noun* a chemical substance that makes blood vessels become narrower, causing blood pressure to rise, e.g. ephedrine hydrochloride

vasodilation *noun* the widening of blood vessels, which allows more blood to flow through

vasodilator *noun* a chemical substance that makes blood vessels become wider, causing blood to flow more easily and blood pressure to fall

vasodilatory *adjective* causing vasodilation

vasoinhibitor *noun* a chemical substance that reduces or stops the activity of the nerves that control the widening or narrowing of the blood vessels

vasomotor *adjective* causing or influencing changes in the diameter of blood vessels

vasomotor nerve *noun* a nerve in the wall of a blood vessel which affects the diameter of the vessel

vasospasm *noun* sustained contraction of the muscular walls of the blood vessels with a resultant reduction in blood flow

vasovagal syndrome *noun* an irregular or slowed heartbeat caused by stimulation of the vagus nerve

vastus intermedius *noun* one of the four muscles that form the quadriceps

vastus lateralis *noun* one of the four muscles that form the quadriceps

vastus medialis *noun* one of the four muscles that form the quadriceps

vaulting horse *noun* a piece of gymnastic equipment with four legs and a solid leather-covered oblong body, used for exercises and especially for vaulting over

vegan *adjective* involving a diet of only vegetables and fruit, with no dairy products

veganism *noun* the state of eating a vegan diet

vegetarian *adjective* involving a diet without meat

vegetarianism *noun* the state of eating a vegetarian diet

vegetative nervous system *noun* the part of the body's nervous system that controls involuntary functions such as the beating of the heart

vein *noun* a blood vessel that takes deoxygenated blood containing waste carbon dioxide from the tissues back to the heart

velocity *noun* the rate of change of position in a given direction, composed of both speed and direction

vena cava *noun* one of two large veins which take deoxygenated blood from all the other veins into the right atrium of the heart (NOTE: The plural is **venae cavae**.)

venous return *noun* the return of blood to the heart via the veins

ventilation *noun* the fact that air enters and leaves the lungs

ventilator a machine that keeps air moving in and out of the lungs of a patient who cannot breathe unaided

ventilatory threshold *noun* the point during exercise at which a person can no longer comfortably speak, as measured by a talk test

ventral *adjective* **1.** referring to the abdomen **2.** referring to the front of the body. Opposite **dorsal**

ventricle *noun* **1.** a cavity in an organ, especially in the heart or brain **2.** either of the two lower chambers of the heart that receive blood from the atria and pump it into the arteries by contraction of their thick muscular walls

ventricular *adjective* referring to the ventricles

ventricular hypertrophy *noun* an enlargement of the ventricles, typically the left ventricle, caused by high blood pressure or excessive exercise

venule *noun* a small vein or vessel leading from tissue to a larger vein

verbal persuasion *noun* same as **pep talk**

verruca *noun* a wart that grows on the foot, usually on the sole

vertebra *noun* a bone of the spinal column, typically consisting of a thick body, a bony arch enclosing a hole for the spinal cord, and stubby projections that connect with adjacent bones (NOTE: The plural form is **vertebrae**.)

vertebral disc *noun* same as **disc**

vertebral foramen *noun* a hole in the centre of a vertebra which links with others to form the vertebral canal through which the spinal cord passes

vestibulocochlear nerve *noun* the eighth cranial nerve which governs hearing and balance. Also called **acoustic nerve**, **auditory nerve**

victory *noun* success in a competition against an opponent

vinculum *noun* a band of tissue, especially a ligament

violent *adjective* very strong or very severe

viosterol *noun* same as **vitamin D2**

viscera *plural noun* the internal organs, e.g. the heart, lungs, stomach and intestines

visceral fat *noun* same as **abdominal fat**

vision-impaired *adjective* (*in disabled sport events such as the Paralympics*) a category for athletes with visual problems

visual acuity *noun* the sharpness of someone's vision, especially as it relates to skills such as hand-eye coordination

visual defect *noun* a condition that makes a person unable to see clearly, or at all

visualisation *noun* the act of vividly imagining a desired solution to a problem in order to build happiness and self-confidence

vitafoods *plural noun* food products that are designed for health-conscious consumers

vital signs *plural noun* the signs that indicate life, e.g. pulse, body temperature, breathing and blood pressure

vitamin *noun* any of various substances that are not synthesised in the body but are found in most foods, essential for good health

vitamin A2 *noun* a form of vitamin A obtained from fish liver

vitamin B1 *noun* a water-soluble vitamin that maintains normal carbohydrate metabolism and nervous system function and is found in high concentration in yeast, in the outer layers and germ of cereals, in beef, in pork and in pulses. Also called **aneurin**, **thiamin**

vitamin B2 *noun* a water-soluble vitamin that is essential for metabolic processes and for cell maintenance and repair, present in all leafy vegetables, in eggs, milk and the flesh of warm blooded animals. Also called **riboflavin**

vitamin B3 *noun* a water-soluble vitamin that occurs in the form of niacin, nicotinic acid and nicotinamide and is widely distributed in foodstuffs, with meat, fish, wholemeal flour and peanuts being major sources

vitamin B6 *noun* a water-soluble vitamin that consists of the compounds pyridoxal, pyridoxol and pyridoxamine, found in low concentration in all animal and plant tissues, especially in fish, eggs and wholemeal flour

vitamin B12 *noun* a cobalt-containing water-soluble vitamin that, together with folic acid, has a vital role in metabolic processes and in the formation of red blood cells and is responsible for the general feeling of well-being in healthy individuals (NOTE: It is normally found only in animal products, particularly ox kidney and liver and oily fish.)

vitamin B15 *noun* same as **orotic acid**

vitamin B complex *noun* a group of vitamins such as folic acid, riboflavine and thiamine

vitamin C *noun* a vitamin that is soluble in water and is found in fresh fruit, especially oranges and lemons, raw vegetables and liver. Also called **ascorbic acid** (NOTE: Lack of vitamin C can cause anaemia and scurvy.)

vitamin D *noun* a vitamin which is soluble in fat, and is found in butter, eggs and fish (NOTE: It is also produced by the skin when exposed to sunlight. Vitamin D helps in the formation of bones, and lack of it causes rickets in children.)

vitamin D1 *noun* a form of vitamin D obtained through ultraviolet irradiation of a type of alcohol called ergosterol

vitamin D2 *noun* a precursor of vitamin D. Also called **viosterol**

vitamin D3 *noun* a precursor of vitamin D. Also called **cholecalciferol**

vitamin E *noun* a vitamin found in vegetables, vegetable oils, eggs and wholemeal bread

vitamin H *noun* ♦ biotin

vitamin K *noun* a vitamin, found in green vegetables such as spinach and cabbage, that helps the clotting of blood and is needed to activate prothrombin

vitamin P *noun* same as **bioflavonoid**

vitamin pill, vitamin supplement *noun* a pill containing one or several vitamins or minerals, taken as a food supplement

vitamin-rich *adjective* containing high levels of vitamins

vitellin *noun* the protein found in egg yolk

VO2 *abbreviation* Volume of Oxygen

VO2Max *noun* the maximum possible intake of oxygen for aerobic metabolism during exercise

voice box *noun* same as **larynx**

Volkmann's contracture *noun* same as **compartment syndrome**

volley *noun* (*in tennis, football and other ball sports*) a hit of a ball before it touches the ground ■ *verb* to hit or kick a ball before it touches the ground

volleyball *noun* **1.** a sport in which two teams hit a large ball over a high net using their hands, played on a rectangular court **2.** a large, usually white inflated ball used for playing volleyball

Volume of Oxygen *noun* the amount of oxygen in millilitres that can be inspired by a person in a single breath. Abbreviation **VO2**

voluntary muscle *noun* a muscle that is consciously controlled, usually made up of striated fibres

Vorlage *noun* a skiing position in which a skier leans forward from the ankle but keeps his or her heels on the skis

v-taper *noun* a term that describes the body shape of a person with well-developed shoulders and a comparatively small waist

W

WADA *abbreviation* World Anti-Doping Agency

waist-to-hip ratio *noun* a way of describing the distribution of adipose tissue in the body

wakeboarding *noun* a water sport in which someone riding a single board is pulled behind a motor boat and performs jumps while crisscrossing the wake of the boat

walkover *noun* an easy victory or one that is obtained without a contest, e.g. because the opposing side did not turn up (*informal*)

wallbars *plural noun* a series of horizontal bars attached to a wall and used for exercise

warm *adjective* used for describing muscles that are prepared and loosened by stretching and ready to undertake heavier exercise

warm down *verb* same as **cool down**

warm-down *noun* same as **cool-down**

warm up *verb* to prepare the body for exercise by stretching muscles and loosening joints

warm-up *noun* an exercise or a period spent exercising before a contest or event

washboard *adjective* describes a stomach that is flat with well-defined muscles

water balance *noun* a state in which the water lost by the body, e.g. in urine or sweat, is made up by water absorbed from food and drink

water filter *noun* an appliance or fitting for removing unwanted matter from water, especially bacteria or harmful chemicals from drinking water

water on the knee *noun* the accumulation of watery fluid in or around the knee indicating disease or injury of the knee joint

water polo *noun* a game played in a swimming pool by two teams of seven players, in which the object is to score by sending a large ball into the opposing team's goal

water retention *noun* the build-up of fluid in bodily tissues, causing swelling

waterskiing *noun* the sport of skiing on water, on one or two skis, while being pulled by a motorboat and holding a rope

water-soluble vitamins *plural noun* vitamins B and C, which can form a solution in water

water sports *plural noun* sports carried out on or in water

WBC *abbreviation* white blood cell

weak *adjective* not strong

weakness *noun* **1.** the fact of lacking strength **2.** a feature of someone's character regarded as unfavourable and can therefore be exploited by an opponent

weigh in *verb* to be weighed before or after a boxing match, horse race or similar contest

weigh-in *noun* an official occasion on which athletes in particular sports such as boxing are weighed, so that they can be placed into categories for competition

weight *noun* **1.** how heavy someone or something is **2.** something that is heavy, especially an object lifted, pushed or pulled in order to develop muscle tone or strength

weight bearing activity *noun* resistance exercises that strengthen the bones and prevent osteoporosis

weight control, weight management *noun* the act of keeping your weight within healthy limits with a sensible diet and exercise plan

weighted vest *noun* a vest top with weights attached, worn to provide added resistance during exercise

weight-for-age *noun* an index of a child's weight against the average weight for a child of that age, showing whether they are being adequately nourished for growth

weight-for-height *noun* an index of a child's weight against the average weight for a child of that height, showing whether they are being adequately nourished for growth

weight gain *noun* the fact of becoming fatter or heavier

weight gain formula *noun* any high-calorie sports supplement taken to promote muscle growth. Abbreviation **WGF**

weightlifter *noun* a person who takes part in weightlifting

weightlifting *noun* the sport of lifting heavy weights, either for exercise or in competition

weight loss *noun* the fact of losing weight or of becoming thinner

weight-loss plan *noun* a scheme to reduce body weight, usually by reducing calorie intake, increasing physical activity or a combination of both

weight reduction *noun* same as **weight loss**

weights *plural noun* heavy objects that a person lifts in order to build muscular strength or as a sport

weights bench *noun* a sturdy bench that a person can lie on while lifting weights

weight training *noun* physical training using weights to strengthen the muscles

weight training belt *noun* a thick belt worn during exercise to support the lower back

wellness *noun* physical wellbeing, especially when maintained or achieved through good diet and regular exercise

wellness foods *plural noun* nutritionally rich foods eaten for health

well-taken *adjective* performed or executed skilfully or effectively

welterweight *noun* **1.** (*in boxing*) a weight category for competitors who weigh between 63.5 kg and 66.7 kg **2.** a professional or amateur boxer who competes at welterweight **3.** a sports contestant ranked by body weight between a lightweight and a middleweight

West Asian Games *plural noun* a multi-sport event in which athletes from West and Central Asia are invited to participate, taking place every two years

wet pack *noun* a piece or pieces of material dampened with hot or cold water and wrapped around a patient's body for therapeutic purposes

WGF *abbreviation* weight gain formula

wheat protein *noun* same as **seitan**

wheelchair *noun* (*in disabled sport events such as the Paralympics*) a category for athletes confined to a wheelchair

wheelchair marathon *noun* a marathon that is open to athletes in wheelchairs only

wheelchair rugby *noun* same as **quad rugby**

wheeze *verb* to breathe with an audible whistling sound and with difficulty, usually because of a respiratory disorder such as asthma

whey protein concentrate *noun* a high-protein supplement used by bodybuilders, containing bioavailable milk proteins. Abbreviation **WPC**

whey protein isolate *noun* a sports supplement that is more purified than whey protein concentrate. Abbreviation **WPI**

whiplash *noun* an injury to the muscles, ligaments, vertebrae or nerves of the neck caused when the head is suddenly thrown forward and then sharply back. Also called **whiplash injury**

whirlpool bath *noun* a bath or outdoor pool with powerful underwater jets that keep the water constantly moving or swirling around the body. It is sometimes used in physical therapy.

white adipose tissue *noun* fat stored in the body that is not metabolically active and is hard to burn. Compare **brown adipose tissue**

white blood cell *noun* a colourless blood cell which contains a nucleus but has no haemoglobin, is formed in bone marrow and creates antibodies. Abbreviation **WBC**

white fat *noun* same as **white adipose tissue**

whites *plural noun* white or off-white sports clothing, especially as worn by tennis players or cricketers

whitewash *noun* a resounding defeat, especially one in which the losing player or team does not score (*informal*)

wholefoods *plural noun* foods that have been grown without the use of artificial fertilisers and have not been processed, thought to be healthier

wholegrain *adjective* describes food containing whole unprocessed grains of something

wholemeal *adjective* containing wheat germ and bran

wholesome *adjective* having a fit healthy appearance that suggests clean living

wholewheat *adjective* used for describing flour that contains a large proportion of the original wheat seed, including the bran, or for describing bread and other products made from it

wicket *noun* **1.** (*in cricket*) either of two sets of three upright sticks (**stumps**) on which are balanced two shorter sticks (**bails**) and in front of which the batsman stands **2.** the part of a cricket pitch between the two sets of stumps, which are placed 20 m/22 yd apart **3.** (*in cricket*) a batsman's turn of batting, or that of a pair of batsmen **4.** (*in cricket*) the ending of somebody's turn of batting, effected, e.g. by knocking down the stumps or catching the ball

wicket-keeper *noun* (*in cricket*) the player positioned behind the wicket to catch the ball or knock the bails off the stumps

wicking *adjective* of sports clothing, designed to draw perspiration away from the skin so that the wearer stays dry and comfortable

wind *noun* the power to breathe, especially when making an effort such as running ■ *verb* to make someone temporarily unable to breathe properly, e.g. because of too much exertion or by a blow to the abdomen

windpipe *noun* same as **trachea**

wind sprint *noun* a form of training exercise in which an athlete runs very fast for a short period of time, designed to build up endurance

Windsurfer a trade name for a type of sailboard

windsurfing *noun* the sport of riding and steering a sailboard

wing *noun* **1.** either of the longer sides of the field of play, at right angles to the sides where the goals are **2.** in some team sports such as football and hockey, an attacking player who plays down one side of the field **3.** in some sports, the position played by a wing

winger *noun* same as **wing 3**

Winter Olympics *noun* a multi-sport event held every four years during the winter months, in which winter sports such as ice hockey, skiing, skating and bobsleighing are performed

winter sports *plural noun* sports performed on snow and ice, e.g. skiing and ice skating

wipeout *noun* a fall from a surfboard, or a fall or crash in other sports such as skiing and cycling

withdrawal *noun* a period during which a person who has been addicted to a drug stops taking it and experiences unpleasant symptoms

wobbleboard *noun* an exercise device consisting of a small unstable board on which the exerciser must balance, used for injury rehabilitation and developing core stability

work *verb* **1.** to exert physical or mental effort in order to do, make or accomplish something, or make someone do this **2.** to move or exercise a muscle or part of the body, or be moved or exercised

working memory *noun* the contents of someone's consciousness at the present moment, containing only the information needed to perform the current task

work out *verb* to do a workout

workout *noun* a session of strenuous physical exercise or of practising physical skills as a way of keeping fit or as practice for a sport

workout class *noun* same as **fitness class**

World Anti-Doping Agency *noun* an independent professional body that campaigns against doping in sport and develops the World Anti-Doping Code each year. Abbreviation **WADA**

World Anti-Doping Code *noun* a set of anti-doping rules and measures from the World Anti-Doping Agency aimed at preventing drug abuse in sports, adopted in 2003 by most major international sporting organisations

World Cup *noun* a sports tournament, especially in football, contested by the national teams of qualifying countries, held every four years in a different country of a different continent

World Games *plural noun* an international multi-sport event held every four years featuring sports not included in the Olympic Games, including, e.g., orienteering, powerlifting and squash

World Health Assembly *noun* an annual meeting of delegates from all member states of the WHO, at which major policy decisions are made

World Health Day *noun* an annual event organised by the World Health Organisation, drawing global attention to a particular health issue

World Health Organisation *noun* the United Nation's agency for health, promoting global health education and provision of healthcare facilities. Abbreviation **WHO**

wound-up *adjective* extremely tense, nervous and agitated (*informal*)

WPC *abbreviation* whey protein concentrate

WPI *abbreviation* whey protein isolate

wrench *verb* to injure part of the body by twisting it suddenly and forcibly

wrestling *noun* a sport in which two contestants fight by gripping each other using special holds, each trying to force the other's shoulders onto a mat

wrist *noun* a joint between the hand and forearm

wrist drop *noun* paralysis of the wrist muscles that causes the hand to hang limp, caused by damage to the radial nerve in the upper arm

wrist guards *plural noun* protective gloves that cover the wrists, leaving the fingers exposed, used for protection by cyclists and skateboarders

wrist tendonitis *noun* strain to the tendons that connect the fingers to the forearm muscle, caused by repetitive hand movements

wristy *adjective* using a lot of wrist movement when hitting a ball

wrong-foot *verb* to cause an opponent to anticipate wrongly the direction in which you are going to move or hit, kick or pass a ball

wushu *noun* Chinese martial arts considered collectively

XYZ

xanthelasma *noun* yellow deposits on the eyelids caused by high levels of cholesterol in the blood

xenobiotic *adjective* used for describing a substance found in the body that is not normally expected to be there

xerosis *noun* abnormal dryness of an organ or tissue

X Games *plural noun* an annual multi-sports event that features mainly extreme sports

x-ray *noun* an image produced on photographic film by x-rays passing through objects or parts of the body, often used in medicine and science as a diagnostic tool

yacht *noun* a sailing boat, often one that has living quarters and is used for cruising or racing

yeast infection *noun* an overgrowth of a fungus in the vagina, intestines, skin or mouth, causing irritation and swelling

yellow card *noun* (*in some team sports*) a card shown by the referee to a player guilty of serious or persistent foul play as an indication that the player has been cautioned. ◊ **green card**, **red card** (NOTE: The punishment a player receives when they are shown a yellow card varies according to which sport they are playing. In football, if a player receives two yellow cards, they are sent off and can play no further part in the game. In rugby, on the other hand, if a player receives a yellow card they are immediately suspended from the game for 10 minutes.)

yellow fibre *noun* same as **elastic fibre**

yips *plural noun* nervousness that impairs the performance of a sportsman or sportswoman, especially a golfer

yoga *noun* **1.** a Hindu discipline which promotes spiritual unity with a Supreme Being through a system of postures and rituals **2.** any one of dozens of systems of exercise derived from or based on Hindu yoga, most of which include breathing exercises and postures designed to improve flexibility and induce wellbeing

yoga mat *noun* a soft mat used for performing yoga exercises on the floor

yohimbe *noun* a stimulant sports supplement that reduces fatigue

york *verb* (*in cricket*) to get a batsman out, or attempt to get a batsman out, by bowling a yorker

yorker *noun* (*in cricket*) a ball bowled so that it pitches on the ground immediately under the bat

yo-yo dieting *noun* a situation in which a person repeatedly loses weight through dieting and then regains the weight that he or she has lost

zen macrobiotics *noun* a very strict form of macrobiotic diet that avoids, e.g., eating foods that are out of season or foods that have been transported a long distance

zeranol *noun* a non-steroid oestrogenic growth agent

zero-sum competition *noun* a competition in which there is a single winner and the losing players do not win or achieve anything

zinc *noun* a white metallic trace element (NOTE: The chemical symbol is **Zn**.)

zinc deficiency *noun* a condition that can cause tissue wasting and delayed puberty in boys

zinc monomethionine aspartate and magnesium aspartate *noun* full form of **ZMA**

zinc oxide *noun* a thick cream made with zinc that is used as a sunblock on the face

Z-line *noun* a narrow dark line across striated muscle fibres that marks the boundaries between adjacent segments

ZMA *noun* a supplement for athletes containing zinc and magnesium, reputed to increase testosterone. Full form **zinc monomethionine aspartate and magnesium aspartate**

zone *noun* an area of the body

Zone diet *noun* a dietary plan in which 40% of daily calories should come from carbohydrates, 30% from proteins and 30% from fats

zurkhaneh *noun* a traditional Iranian gymnasium in which athletics and wrestling are practised along with meditative teaching

zygomatic *adjective* relating to the cheekbone

zygomatic fracture *noun* a fracture of the cheekbone, caused by a heavy blow such as during a contact sport or in a motor accident

zymoprotein *noun* a protein that also functions as an enzyme

SUPPLEMENTS

Body Mass Index Calculator
Measurement Conversion Table
Anatomical Figures: *Planes and Movements*
Lungs and Heart
Neuron and Brain
Foot and Hand
Joints and Bone Structure
British and International Sport Federations
Resources on the web

Body Mass Index Calculator

Height (cm)	Body Weight (kg)																
150cm	43	45	47	49	52	54	56	58	60	63	65	67	69	72	74	76	78
152cm	44	46	49	51	54	56	58	60	63	65	67	69	72	74	76	79	81
155cm	45	48	50	53	55	57	60	63	65	67	69	72	74	77	79	82	84
157cm	47	49	52	54	57	59	62	64	67	69	72	74	77	79	82	84	87
160cm	49	51	54	56	59	61	64	66	69	72	74	77	79	82	84	87	89
163cm	50	53	55	58	61	64	66	68	71	74	77	79	82	84	87	89	93
165cm	52	54	57	60	63	65	68	71	73	76	79	82	84	87	90	93	95
168cm	54	56	59	62	64	67	70	73	76	78	81	84	87	90	93	95	98
170cm	55	57	61	64	66	69	72	75	78	81	84	87	90	93	96	98	101
172cm	57	59	63	65	68	72	74	78	80	83	86	89	92	95	98	101	104
175cm	58	61	64	68	70	73	77	80	83	86	89	92	95	98	101	104	107
178cm	60	63	66	69	73	76	79	82	85	88	92	95	98	104	104	107	110
180cm	62	65	68	71	75	78	81	84	88	91	94	98	101	104	107	110	113
183cm	64	67	70	73	77	80	83	87	90	93	97	100	103	107	110	113	117
185cm	65	68	72	75	79	83	86	89	93	96	99	103	107	110	113	117	120
188cm	67	70	74	78	81	84	88	92	95	99	102	106	110	113	116	120	123
191cm	69	73	76	80	83	87	91	94	98	102	105	109	113	116	120	123	127
BMI	19	20	21	22	23	24	25	26	27	28	29	30	31	32	33	34	35

Find your height in the left-hand column, then move along the row to find your weight. The number at the bottom of that column is your BMI.

Less than 20 = underweight. 20-25 = desirable weight. 25-30 = overweight. More than 30 = obese.

Measurement Conversion Table

Conversions for some common metric units to imperial or US customary units are given below.

Metric	Imperial
length	
micrometre	= 0.00003937 inches
millimetre	= 0.03937 inches
centimetre	= 0.3937 inches
metre	= 39.37 inches
metre	= 1.094 yards
kilometre	≈ 0.621 miles
area	
square millimetre	≈ 0.00155 square inches
square centimetre	≈ 0.155 square inches
square metre	≈ 1.196 square yards
square metre	≈ 10.76 square feet
hectare	≈ 2.471 acres
square kilometre	≈ 0.386 square miles
volume or capacity	
cubic millimetre	≈ 0.000061 cubic inches
cubic centimetre	≈ 0.0610 cubic inches
cubic centimetre	≈ 0.0352 imperial fluid ounces
cubic centimetre	≈ 0.0338 US fluid. ounces
millilitre	≈ 0.0610 cubic inches
millilitre	≈ 0.0352 imperial fluid ounces
millilitre	≈ 0.0338 US fluid ounces
cubic decilitre	≈ 61.0 cubic inches
cubic decilitre	≈ 0.880 imperial quarts
cubic decilitre	≈ 1.057 US liquid quarts
cubic decilitre	≈ 0.908 US dry quarts
litre	≈ 61.0 cubic inches
litre	≈ 0.880 imperial quarts
litre	≈ 1.057 US liquid quarts
litre	≈ 0.908 US dry quarts
mass	
gram	≈ 0.0353 ounces avoirdupois
gram	≈ 0.0322 ounces troy
kilogram	≈ 2.205 pounds avoirdupois
tonne	≈ 2205 pounds avoirdupois
temperature	
degree Celsius	$(°C \times 1.8) + 32$ = degrees Fahrenheit

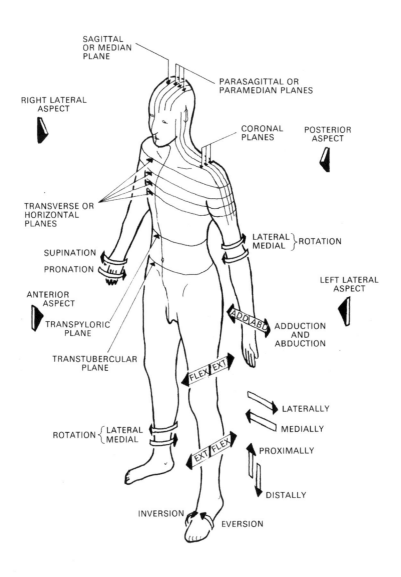

Anatomical terms

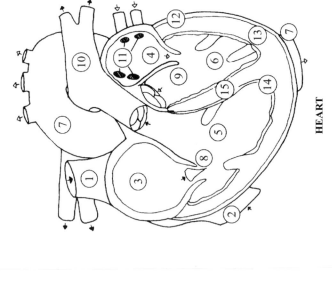

HEART

1. superior vena cava
2. inferior vena cava
3. right atrium
4. left atrium
5. right ventricle
6. left ventricle
7. aorta
8. tricuspid valve
9. bicuspid valve
10. pulmonary artery
11. pulmonary veins
12. epicardium
13. myocardium
14. endocardium
15. septum

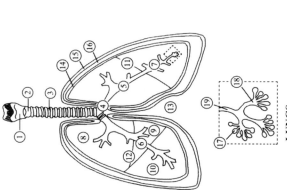

LUNGS

1. thyroid cartilage
2. cricoid cartilage
3. trachea
4. main bronchus
5. superior lobe bronchus
6. middle lobe bronchus
7. inferior lobe bronchus
8. superior lobe
9. middle lobe
10. inferior lobe
11. oblique fissure
12. horizontal fissure
13. cardiac notch
14. visceral pleura
15. parietal pleura
16. pleural cavity
17. alveolus
18. alveolar duct
19. bronchiole

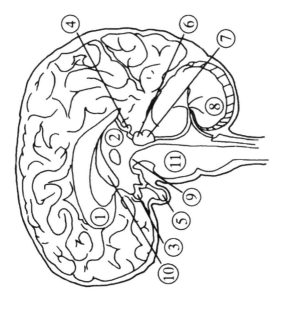

NEURON

(a) multipolar
1. nucleus
2. Nissl granules
3. neurofibrilla
4. dendrite

(b) bipolar
5. axon
6. myelin sheath
7. Schwann cell nucleus

(c) unipolar
8. node of Ranvier
9. neurilemma
10. terminal branch

BRAIN

1. corpus callosum
2. thalamus
3. hypothalamus
4. pineal body

5. pituitary gland
6. superior colliculi
7. inferior colliculi
8. cerebellum

9. cerebral peduncle
10. fornix cerebri
11. pons

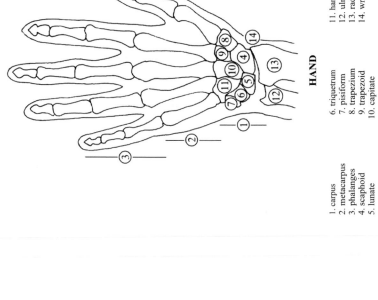

FOOT

1. tarsus
2. metatarsus
3. phalanges

4. cuneiforms
5. navicular
6. cuboid

7. calcaneus
8. talus

HAND

1. carpus
2. metacarpus
3. phalanges
4. scaphoid
5. lunate

6. triquetrum
7. pisiform
8. trapezium
9. trapezoid
10. capitate

11. hamate
12. ulna
13. radius
14. wrist

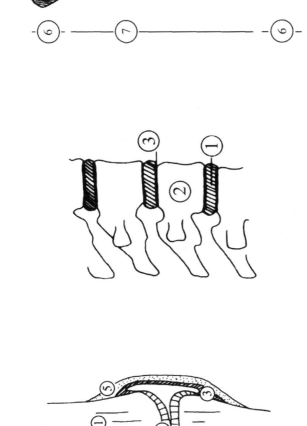

SYNOVIAL JOINT

1. bone
2. articular cartilage
3. synovial membrane
4. synovial cavity and fluid
5. joint capsule (ligament)

CARTILAGINOUS JOINT

1. intervertebral disc
2. vertebra
3. hyaline cartilage

BONE STRUCTURE

1. periosteum
2. compact bone
3. cancellous (spongy) bone (red marrow)
4. medullary cavity (yellow marrow)
5. articular cartilage
6. epiphysis
7. diaphysis

British and International Federations

Summer Olympic Sports:

Aquatics

Amateur Swimming Association
Derby Square
Loughborough
Leicestershire
LE11 5AL
www.britishswimming.com

International Swimming Federation
Avenue de l'Avant-Poste 4
1005 Lausanne
Switzerland
www.fina.org

Archery

Grand National Archery Society
Lilleshall National Sports Centre
nr Newport
Shropshire
TF10 9AT
www.gnas.org

International Archery Federation
Maison du Sport International
Avenue de Rhodanie 54
1007 Lausanne
Switzerland
www.archery.org

Athletics

UK Athletics
Athletics House
Blythe Valley Park
Solihull
West Midlands
B90 8AJ
www.ukathletics.com

International Association of
Athletics Federations
17 rue Princesse Florestine
BP 359
MC98007 Monaco
www.iaaf.org

Badminton

Badminton England
National Badminton Centre
Milton Keynes
MK8 9LA
www.badmintonengland.co.uk

International Badminton Federation
Batu 3 ½ Jalan Cheras
56000 Kuala Lumpur
Malaysia
www.internationalbadminton.org

Baseball

BaseballSoftballUK
Ariel House
74a Charlotte Street
London
W1T 4QJ
www.baseballsoftballuk.co.uk

International Baseball Federation
Avenue de Mon Repos 24
Case Postale 6099
1002 Lausanne
Switzerland
www.baseball.ch

Summer Olympic Sports *cont.*

Basketball

British Basketball Federation
PO Box 3971
Sheffield
South Yorkshire
S9 3TW
www.british-basketball.co.uk

International Basketball Federation
53 Avenue Louis-Casai
PO Box 110
1216 Cointrin
Switzerland
www.fiba.com

Boxing

British Boxing Board of Control
The Old Library
Trinity Street
Cardiff
CF10 1BH
www.bbbofc.com

International Boxing Association
Maison du Sport International
Avenue de Rhodanie 54
1007 Lausanne
Switzerland
www.aiba.net

Canoeing

British Canoe Union
John Dudderidge House
Adbolton Lane
Nottingham
East Midlands
NG2 5AS
www.bcu.org.uk

International Canoe Federation
Maison du Sport International
Avenue de Rhodanie 54
1007 Lausanne
Switzerland
www.canoeicf.com

Cycling

British Cycling Federation
National Cycling Centre
Stuart Street
Manchester
M11 4DQ
www.britishcycling.org.uk

International Cycling Union
CH 1860 Aigle
Switzerland
www.uci.ch

Equestrianism

British Equestrian Federation
Stoneleigh Park
Kenilworth
Warwickshire
CV8 2RH
www.bef.co.uk

International Federation for
Equestrian Sports
Avenue de Mon Repos 24
1002 Lausanne
Switzerland
www.horsesport.org

Summer Olympic Sports *cont.*

Fencing

British Fencing Association
1 Baron's Gate
33-35 Rothschild Road
London
W4 5HT
www.britishfencing.com

International Fencing Federation
Maison du Sport International
Avenue de Rhodanie 54
1007 Lausanne
Switzerland
www.fie.ch

Football

The Football Association
25 Soho Square
London
W1D 4FA
www.thefa.com

Federation Internationale de
Football Association
FIFA-Strasse 20
P.O. Box 8044
Zurich
Switzerland
www.fifa.com

Gymnastics

British Gymnastics
Lilleshall National Sports Centre
nr Newport
Shropshire
TF10 9AT
www.british-gymnastics.org

International Gymnastics Federation
Case Postale 359
Rue des Oeuches 10
2740 Moutier 1
Switzerland
www.fig-gymnastics.com

Handball

British Handball Association
40 Newchurch Road
Rawtenstall
Lancashire
BB4 7QX
www.britishhandball.com

International Handball Federation
Peter Merian-Strasse 23
P.O. Box
4002 Basle
Switzerland
www.ihf.info

Hockey

Great Britain Olympic Hockey Board
78 Gristhorpe Road
Birmingham
West Midlands
B29 7SW
(no website at present)

International Hockey Federation
Residence du Parc
Rue du Valentin 61
1004 Lausanne
Switzerland
www.worldhockey.com

Judo

British Judo Association
Suite B, Loughborough Tech Park
Epinal Way
Loughborough
LE11 3GE
www.britishjudo.org.uk

International Judo Federation
33rd FL Doosan Tower
18-12 Ulchi-Ro 6-Ka
Seoul
Republic of Korea 100-300
www.ijf.org

Modern Pentathlon

Modern Penthlon Association of
Great Britain
Norwood House
University of Bath
Claverton Down
BA2 7AY
www.mpagb.org.uk

Union Internationale de
Pentathlon Moderne
Avenue des Castellans
Stade Louis II
98000 Monaco
www.pentathlon.org

Rowing

Amateur Rowing Association
6 Lower Mall
Hammersmith
London
W6 9DJ
www.ara-rowing.org.uk

International Federation of
Rowing Associations
Avenue de Cour 135
Case Postale 18
1000 Lausanne 3
Switzerland
www.worldrowing.com

Sailing

Royal Yachting Association
Ensign Way
Hamble
Hampshire
SO31 4YA
www.rya.org.uk

International Sailing Federation
Ariadne House
Town Quay
Hampshire
SO14 2AQ
www.sailing.org

Shooting

GB Target Shooting Federation
1 The Cedars
Southend
Essex
SS3 0AQ
www.gbtsf.org.uk

International Shooting
Sport Federation
Bavariaring 21
D-80336 München
Germany
www.issf-shooting.org

Softball

BaseballSoftballUK
Ariel House
74a Charlotte Street
London
W1T 4QJ
www.baseballsoftballuk.co.uk

International Softball Federation
1900 S. Park Road
Plant City
FL 33563
USA
www.internationalsoftball.com

Table Tennis

British Olympic Table Tennis
Federation
90 Broadway
Letchworth
Hertfordshire
SG6 3PH
(no website at present)

International Table Tennis
Federation
Chemin de la Roche, 11
1020 Renens / Lausanne
Switzerland
www.ittf.com

Tae Kwon Do

British Tae Kwon Do Council
Yiewsley Leisure Centre
Otterfield Road
West Drayton
Middlesex
UB7 8PE
www.britishtaekwondocouncil.org

World Tae Kwon Do Federation
4F Joyang Building
Samseong-dong Gangnam-Gu
Seoul
Republic of Korea 135-090
www.wtf.org

Tennis

The Lawn Tennis Association
Palliser Road
West Kensington
London
W14 9EG
www.lta.org.uk

International Tennis Federation
Bank Lane
Roehampton
London
SW15 5XZ
www.itftennis.com

Triathlon

British Triathlon Association
PO Box 25
Loughborough
Leicestershire
LE11 3WX
www.britishtriathlon.org

International Triathlon Union
#221, 998 Harbourside Drive
North Vancouver
British Columbia
Canada
www.triathlon.org

Summer Olympic Sports *cont.*

Volleyball

British Volleyball Association
Suite B, Loughborough Tech Centre
Epinal Way
Loughborough
LE11 3GE
(no website at present)

International Volleyball Federation
Avenue de la Gare 12
1000 Lausanne 1
Switzerland
www.fivb.ch

Weightlifting

British Weight Lifting Association
Lilleshall National Sports Centre
nr Newport
Shropshire
TF10 9AT
www.bwla.org.uk

International Weightlifting Federation
H-1146 Budapest
Istvanmezei ut 1-3
Hungary
www.iwf.net

Wrestling

British Wrestling Association Ltd.
12 Westwood Lane
Chesterfield
Derbyshire
S43 1PA
www.britishwrestling.org

International Federation of
Associated Wrestling Styles
Rue de Chateau 6
1804 Corsier-sur-Vever
Switzerland
www.fila-wrestling.com

Winter Olympic Sports

Biathlon

British Biathlon Union
Old Road
Bwlch
Powys
LD3 7RS
www.britishbiathlon.com

International Biathlon Union
Peregrinstrasse 14
5020 Salzburg
Austria
www.biathlonworld.com

Bobsleigh

British Bobsleigh Association
4-10 Barttelot Road
Horsham
West Sussex
RH12 1DQ
www.bobteamgb.org

International Bobsleigh and
Tobogganing Federation
Via Piranesi 44/B
120137 Milan
Italy
www.bobsleigh.com

Winter Olympic Sports *cont.*

Curling

British Curling Association
Langhill
Lockerbie
Dumfriesshire
DG11 2QT
www.britishcurlingassociation.org.uk

World Curling Federation
74 Tay Street
Perth
PH2 8NN
Scotland
www.worldcurling.org

Ice Hockey

Ice Hockey UK
19 Heather Avenue
Rise Park
Romford
RM1 4SL
www.icehockeyuk.co.uk

International Ice Hockey Federation
Brandschenkestrasse 50
Postfach
8027 Zürich
Switzerland
www.iihf.com

Luge

Great Britain Luge Association
61 West Malvern Road
Malvern 8347
Worcestershire
WR14 4NF
www.gbla.org.uk

International Luge Federation
Rathausplatz 9
83471 Berchtesgaden
Germany
www.fil-luge.org

Skating

National Ice Skating Association
Lower Parliament Street
Nottingham 1007
NG1 1LA
www.iceskating.org.uk

International Skating Union
Chemin de Primerose 2
1007 Lausanne
Switzerland
www.isu.org

Skiing

Snowsport GB
Hillend
Biggar Road
Midlothian
EH10 7EF
www.snowsportgb.com

International Ski Federation
Blochstrasse 2
3653 Oberhofen/Thunersee
Switzerland
www.fis-ski.com

Sports and Exercise - Resources on the web

Athletic Coaches Association of the UK
A membership-only information resource for sports coaches.
www.acauk.co.uk

Athletic Insight
A US online journal of sports psychology.
www.athleticinsight.com

British Association of Sport and Exercise Medicine
A professional membership body for sports medicine students and
professionals.
www.basem.co.uk

British Association of Sports and Exercise Sciences
A professional body for those employed in the sports and exercise
professions.
www.bases.org.uk

British Olympic Association
The official website of the Olympics Games administration.
www.olympics.org.uk

British Paralympic Association
A registered charity which administrates the Paralympic Games.
www.paralympics.org.uk

British Universities Sports Association
A governing body which oversees university and inter-university sports.
www.busa.org.uk

Central Council of Physical Recreation
The governing body for national sports associations in the UK.
www.ccpr.org.uk

Commonwealth Games Federation
The official website of the Commonwealth Games administration.
www.commonwealthgames.com

Department for Culture, Media and Sport
The UK government department overseeing standards and practices in sport.
www.culture.gov.uk

Disability Sport Events
The events-organising arm of the English Federation of Disability Sport.
www.disabilitysport.org.uk

Division of Sports and Exercise Psychology
A membership body for sports psychologists, part of the British Psychological Society.
www.bps.org.uk/spex

English Federation of Disability Sport
A national body responsible for developing disabled sport facilities in England.
www.efds.net

English Institute of Sport
A national-Lottery funded sports organisation offering advice, support and medical services.
www.eis2win.co.uk

GCSE Bitesize –Physical Education
Revision aids for Sports Science at GCSE level.
www.bbc.co.uk/schools/gcsebitesize/pe

Human Kinetics
A US-based publisher of sports science resources.
www.humankinetics.com

Inclusive Fitness Initiative
An organisation which develops sport facilities for people with disabilities.
www.inclusivefitness.org

International Council of Sports Science and Physical Education
An organisation which disseminates sports science research worldwide.
www.icsspe.org

Journal of Sports Science and Medicine
A free online journal of sports medicine research.
www.jssm.org

Mencap Sport
An online resource for athletes with learning disabilities.
www.mencap.org.uk/html/mencap_sport

NHS Direct
A government health service offering advice on healthy exercise plans.
www.nhsdirect.nhs.uk

Osteopathic Sports Care Association
A membership body for osteopaths working in sports rehabilitation.
www.osca.org.uk

Peak Performance Online
A guide to physical training with suggested exercises and programmes.
www.pponline.com

Scottish Sports Association
A professional body which represents all sports associations in Scotland.
www.scottishsportsassociation.org.uk

Special Olympics
The official body which administers the event and also provides year-round training.
www.specialolympics.org

Sport England
A Government- and National Lottery-funded organisation which promotes sports development.
www.sportengland.org

SportsAid
An independent national organisation which gives grants to young British athletes.
www.sportsaid.org.uk

Sports Coach
A comprehensive online resource featuring articles on all aspects of sports science.
www.brianmac.demon.co.uk

Sports Coach UK
A charitable organisation which promotes high standards in sports coaching.
www.sportscoachuk.org

Sport Scotland
The national agency for sport in Scotland.
www.sportscotland.org.uk

Sports Council for Wales
A national organisation promoting sport in Wales.
www.sports-council-wales.co.uk

Sports Council Northern Ireland
A body providing sponsorship for talented young athletes in Northern Ireland.
www.sportni.net

Sports Injury Bulletin
An online medical resource for coaches, athletes and healthcare providers.
www.sportsinjurybulletin.com

Sports Massage Association
A membership body representing professional sports massage practitioners in the UK.
www.sportsmassageassociation.org

Sports Medicine
Publications and a list of specialised seminars run by the Royal Society of Medicine.
www.rsm.ac.uk/academ/secsport.htm

Talented Athlete Scholarship Scheme
A Government-funded programme which gives financial awards to young athletes in further education.
www.tass.co.uk

UK Sport
A government agency which works with local sports councils and distributes funds from the National Lottery.
www.uksport.gov.uk

Women's Sport Foundation
A charitable body campaigning for improved opportunities for women in sport.
www.wsf.org.uk

World Anti-Doping Agency
The organisation which develops and updates the official World Anti-Doping Code.
www.wada-ama.org

Youth Sport Trust
An organisation which develops sports programmes for schools and colleges.
www.youthsporttrust.org